The Consciousness' Drive

Charles Cole

The Consciousness' Drive

Information Need and the Search for Meaning

 Springer

Charles Cole
McGill University
Montreal, QC, Canada

ISBN 978-3-030-06434-1   ISBN 978-3-319-92457-1   (eBook)
https://doi.org/10.1007/978-3-319-92457-1

Cover illustration: The Creation of Adam by Michelangelo

This Springer imprint is published by the registered company Springer Nature Switzerland AG
The registered company address is: Gewerbestrasse 11, 6330 Cham, Switzerland

Preface

Needing information and searching for that information are things we do constantly every day of our waking and sleeping lives. We have always done this as a species: needing, finding, and using information to go about our business, to get through life relatively intact. With Google and mobile phone technology, this sort of low-level information search—the location of our next appointment, the weather forecast—has become more systematized. We have to clearly formulate our information need into a query, then select which source in the results list is the most relevant. But there is a difference with the advent of this systemization of information search. The information economy is, with the ubiquity of high-level information at our finger tips, transitioning into the artificial intelligence (AI) economy with the emphasis on new knowledge searching and production. Google now allows us to explore information when we need to produce new knowledge. We have to construct the new knowledge from the information but the effect of the search is the new knowledge production inside our heads.

These can be small knowledge production events like identifying a problem at the office. But these new knowledge production events can be important like discovering cancer drugs or solving a rocket problem so we can go to Mars.

The problem with using information search to produce new knowledge, both on a small, day-to-day basis, and for the much larger more important issues, is that we as humans don't know our real, deep-level information need in these situations, so we have to make do with a compromised-level of the need, where we have to guess at what we don't know but need to know.

I began to link information need levels and knowledge production in my previous book (Cole 2012). But that book had many references to previous research and was aimed at the scholar community.

In this book, I wanted to make the writing more conversational for a broader readership, keeping my references to research material to the bare minimum. I copied the structure of a detective novel, building my argument to a climax in Chap. 16. For our video game, video-on-demand times, I visualized the ideas that form the structure of the book's thesis or argument in over 90 original diagrams.

But above all, I set the link between information need and knowledge production in evolutionary psychology, a perspective people are reading and talking about. I step back from the minutiae of cognition to go as big-picture as humanly possible. In a way, it is a return to our sources: how we humans naturally think, and why we naturally search for new information because our consciousness drives us to need it.

There is another reason for my change in emphasis between the 2012 book and this one, an intervening factor: the rise of artificial intelligence (AI) as a topic of general discussion in the newspapers. *The New York Times* predicts that in a little over a decade from now up to a third of US jobs will be transformed by AI (Lohr 2017). AI-equipped devices or machines can now learn to respond to new stimuli they find in the environment, for which they haven't been programmed for in advance, by collecting large quantities of environmental data and ascertaining patterns from those data. We will soon be in the world of *2001: A Space Odyssey*, director Stanley Kubrick's prescient 1968 prediction of Hal, a super knowing AI-equipped computer, taking control of the spaceship.

What became evident to me is that the sciences involved in information search (computer science and information science, as well as cognitive science and psychology) must really look at how humans relate to the world, their consciousness, to distinguish human thinking from the computational thinking of the AI-equipped machines that will soon be living and working amongst us.

I asked myself: what is the uniquely human factor in finding and using new information to produce new knowledge. I'm thinking about big knowledge events underlying discovery, inventions and creativity. What is this exceptional human factor that can't be imitated by AI algorithms? Is there in fact an underlying aspect of our thinking that can't be imitated by these machines?

Humans actually ignore a great deal of data around them when they think. We know what information is generally relevant to our task, and ignore the rest. That is why we are so efficient, so able to make decisions, usually the correct one, quickly and without fuss. AI can certainly do this, and eventually it will make these calculations about what is relevant and what is not relevant faster and more efficiently than we can. I examine this in Part II of this book. But that is only half of our human exceptionality. What is the other half?

The other half of our consciousness' exceptionality is why we need new information, why we are constantly searching for it, not just to get by, but to produce new knowledge. We need information to perform tasks we have already done. Machines can do this. But we humans also seem to need information for things we don't have an immediate or even a potential use for. This is the more mysterious x-factor in our human species makeup that cannot be imitated by AI algorithms. It is something about our consciousness, its drive or intention in seeking out new information in the world around us that makes us an exceptional species. Somehow, the same world we've lived in for hundreds of thousands of years, changes. Not the world, but the way we see it. We see different information. We can not only recognize this new information, but we can bring it inside us where we use it to construct new knowledge.

Search engines must be designed in consequence in our new knowledge economy, shifting the searcher's search from what she already knows to what she doesn't yet know but needs to know. This is the true genesis of new knowledge production, not the pattern recognition learning of AI-equipped robots.

That is the perspective on information need, information search, and search engine design taken in this book.

*   *   *

The book is structured in three parts, with each part containing an Introduction and Conclusion that relates the theories and models of the book to the real conditions of a searcher conducting an information search using a search engine:

- Part I defines the exceptionality of human consciousness and its need for new information, how we frame our intersection with the world unlike any other species.
- Part II investigates the problem of finding our real Q1-level information need during information search: how we are blocked from finding it by our exceptional ability at framing our intersection with the world.
- Part III elaborates the book's solution to this framing problem and its operational implications for search engine design for searchers whose objective is the production of new knowledge.

There have been many influences in my 25-year career as an information scientist. I would like to acknowledge TD Wilson, Carol Kuhlthau, Brenda Dervin, Tefko Saracevic, Nicholas Belkin, Amanda Spink, and Marcia Bates. And there were professors during my McGill undergraduate days I would also like to acknowledge, as their teachings, which I didn't understand at the time, have unconsciously guided me in my research: Peter Hoffmann (German history) and Charles Taylor (philosophy).

Montreal, QC, Canada   Charles Cole

Contents

Part III   The Framing Solution

Chapter 1
Introduction

We take the consciousness approach to information need and information search in this book. The opposite is the computational approach, which is artificial intelligence's (AI) view that it can imitate human thinking. The AI view asks and answers in the affirmative: How do humans think and can it be put into a machine that imitates human thinking?

AI research began in 1936 when Alan Turing (1936–1937) investigated the possibility of developing a machine that could imitate human intelligence, "a thinking machine," later called the universal Turing machine. Turing envisaged that one day computers would in fact be able to perfectly imitate human thinking. In fact, he even developed a test that would establish this eventuality, called the Turing (1950) test, which he described in his famous article written for the journal *Mind*.

The Turing test places a human questioner in an isolated room; in a second room are a human and a Turing-type machine. Can the questioner tell whether it is the machine or the human that has answered her questions? If she cannot, the machine passes the Turing test. The machine so perfectly imitates how humans think that it can be said to think the same way as a human. The physicist-mathematician Roger Penrose (1997) asked: Are we humans just computational thinkers similar to a Turing-type machine or is human thinking something else?

We diagram a computational-thinking approach to human thinking in Fig. 1.1. The machine/human is programmed with instruction tables to recognize all possible expected stimuli from the outside world, and the machine must compute the most appropriate response, probably the most efficient response, which is controlled by a complete set of rules of conduct or behavior for each predicted stimulus. In Fig. 1.1, we use the example of a traffic accident. So for the stimulus:

If Event C—"traffic accident,"

the machine computes the response:

Then Response C—"traffic accident: most efficient response behavior."

© Springer International Publishing AG, part of Springer Nature 2018
C. Cole, *The Consciousness' Drive*, https://doi.org/10.1007/978-3-319-92457-1_1

From the world: all possible
predictable events that could happen.

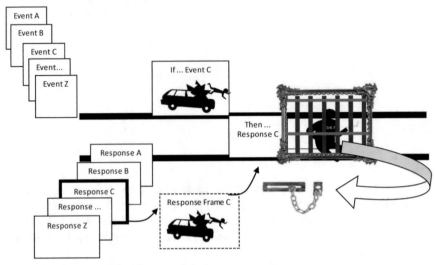

From the computational approach to the
human mind: all possible predicted responses.

Fig. 1.1 A computational approach to human thinking, which depicts human "thinking" as an "If ... Then ..." stimulus–response set of instructions that can be fed or programmed into a computation machine

In order to act fast, automatically, and at the same time be able to capture the complexity of each specific instance of a traffic accident, the machine's response is based on a prototype traffic accident with the features of a prototype traffic accident turned on their most probable default setting. The machine is now in a specific mind state—how the machine "frames" the stimulus–response situation—ready for action. Each feature of the prototype of the car accident "frame," however, must have quick, automatic access to alternative feature assignments to give the overall frame maximum flexibility. The speed of the car, the type of human, what the human was doing at the time of the accident. This sort of thing. In this way, the machine can custom-tailor its response to the specific set of facts of each possible traffic accident stimulus input.

As shown in Fig. 1.1, here is the problem or weakness of this computational approach to thinking:

Computational thinking imprisons the machine/human in the set of instructions written into the response framework. It/he-she can only see in the accident according to the programming instructions, creating a closed information loop between the outside world of stimuli and the machine/human's response frameworks.

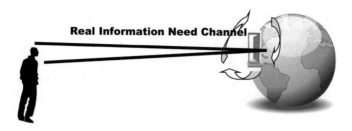

Fig. 1.2 Real information need opens a channel door from inside the individual to the outside information world, such as what we really see when witnessing a car accident

At the moment, AI machines can learn on their own, going beyond their instructions, but only in limited realms with controlled databases (Watson playing chess or the game *Jeopardy*). They can "learn" by detecting new patterns in the outside data environment, and categorizing the patterns into concepts, which would constitute a new response framework beyond what their original programmers' envisaged.

But this is not how humans produce new knowledge. Learning new concept categories is one step, and not the most important step in new knowledge production.

We humans have another, deeper way of thinking about the world than simply detecting, categorizing, and conceptualizing patterns in the data we find around us in the outside world. New knowledge production is started by something else, something more deeply rooted in our consciousness. It is started in our connection, our relationship to the world, and our place in the world.

At that "a-ha" moment of new knowledge recognition, do we not feel that we have, somehow, achieved a deeper connection to the world? Don't we feel that we have achieved when we identify a problem or solution, or discover an answer to a long-held question, that we have a sudden, deeper connection to the world and our place in the world?

This is what we investigate in this book by dividing information need into levels. The deepest level of our information need, our real Q1-level information need, is this connection or fit with our place in the world.

In Fig. 1.2, we show real Q1-level information need as the linking channel between what is inside our mind—how and what we think about, our consciousness—and the outside world of new information. When we find our real information need, it opens the channel door to new information in the outside world, suddenly letting it inside us.

This is the broad consciousness-approach to human thinking we take in this book.

The book is structured into three parts, with each part containing an Introduction and Conclusion that relates the theories and models of our consciousness approach to information need and information search, to the real conditions of a searcher conducting an information search when she is using a search engine:

- Part I defines the exceptionality of human consciousness and its need for new information, how we frame our intersection with the world unlike any other species.

- Part II investigates the problem of finding our real Q1-level information need during information search: how we are blocked from finding it by our exceptional ability at framing our intersection with the world.
- Part III elaborates the book's solution to this framing problem and its operational implications for search engine design for searchers whose objective is the production of new knowledge.

Part I: The Exceptional Human Species

Part I examines the exceptionality of human consciousness—how and what humans think about the world and our place in the world. What makes human consciousness exceptional compared to other species? For the answer, we follow humans into the caves, shown in Fig. 1.3. What they were searching for in the caves evolved over evolutionary time. But they left archeological artefacts, which also evolved over evolutionary time, primarily in caves, but also elsewhere in burials sites and tool-making locations. Based on this evidence, Merlin Donald (1991), in his book *Origins of the Modern Mind*, divides the evolution of human consciousness into four phases. Each phase remains a layer in our present-day consciousness. In Part I, we start with the first layer, the Episodic Mind. We directly experience and remember our intersection with the world in the unit of the episode. Other species also categorize this first layer intersection in like fashion. Edelman labels this a primary

Fig. 1.3 We follow a human entering a cave in a quest for meaning

consciousness. But humans also have a secondary or higher-order consciousness (Edelman 1989). What is the difference? How do we, directed by our consciousness, experience the world differently than other species?

Chapter 2 describes the mirror test. Different animal species are placed in front of a mirror to see if they are able to identify themselves in the mirror. If they can, their consciousness gives them self-awareness as individuals separate and distinct from the world. There are approximately nine species that have this advanced form of consciousness. That is a start. But what is the difference between these other "intelligent" animal species and human consciousness? Humans seem to be able to experience their relationship with the world more deeply.

In Chap. 3, Vermeer utilized a camera obscura to freeze frame an episode from his experience of observing a little street, purportedly across the canal from his child-hood bedroom. As Fig. 1.4 shows, Vermeer's framing of this episode included a detached quality of what he experienced in the episode, giving the framed episode a timeless quality that hits us hard 350 years later. Why do we humans do this, travel back in time via our episodic memory, to mentally reexperience our own episodes in life?

In Chap. 4, this uniquely human quality is something about how we store our experiences in memory. We go back to one of the species that passed the mirror test, the clever scrub jays. They too can remember past episodes from their experience in the world. Researchers have tested them to see what is it that they remember in these episodes that is different from humans. We use Endel Tulving's (1972) experiments to compare the scrub jay's memory of past episodes to an amnesiac who has no episodic memory.

In Chap. 5, Endel Tulving theorizes that, as shown in Fig. 1.5, humans alone can mentally time-travel back to a past episode of their experience, and forward in time to plan or rehearse a future experience. In fact, we humans go further than this: we use our past episode frames to guide us through real-time experience (Minsky 1975). Our episode frames allow us to see-as-understanding an episode we are just about to experience, before we experience it.

In Chaps. 6, 7, and 8, we add three further evolutionary layers to the base Episodic Mind layer of human consciousness. Each layer represents an evolutionary phase of human cognitive development. In Chap. 6, we describe the evolutionary transition to the Mimetic Mind—the ability to reproduce episodes of experience both to ourselves and to others in the group. In Chap. 7, we describe the pivotal transition to the Mythic Mind 40,000–60,000 years ago, when physically modern humans transitioned to become cognitively modern humans. And in Chap. 8, we describe the last evolutionary transition to our present-day Theoretic Mind—a scientific consciousness with a scientific way of framing and thinking about the world. The scientific perspective dominates the way we think today, but all three preceding evolutionary layers are actively present in the exceptional human consciousness we have today.

Fig. 1.4 Vermeer's *The Little Street*, c. 1658. Rijksmuseum, Amsterdam (© 2015. Txllxt TxllxT. Creative Commons Attribution-Share Alike 4.0 International license)

Part II: The Problem

But there is a problem of our exceptional human ability at framing our experience in the world. Because we are so adept at framing our experiences in memory, the frames become guidance interfaces for our subsequent experiences. We view the world through the interface frame of previous experience, through the frame of what we already know.

In Chap. 9, Minsky's (1975) frame theory describes how our memory frames direct, even control, our real-time episodes of experience in the world. Take a man "viewing" the episode of a real-life traffic accident in Fig. 1.6. He recalls his "traffic accident" frame from memory. It guides what he sees in the real-time accident. The

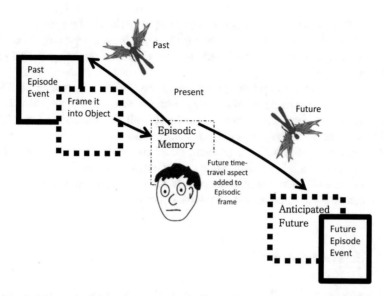

Fig. 1.5 Human episodic memory: via episodes of experience stored in and recalled from episodic memory, humans are constantly time-traveling back to the past and forward in time to an anticipated future

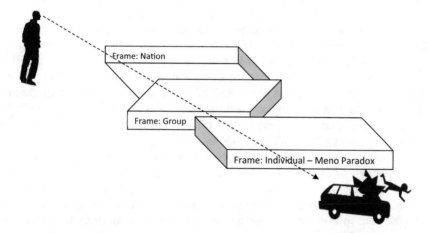

Fig. 1.6 Human framing levels: Nation, Group, and Individual frames leading to Meno's Paradox: we are imprisoned in our frames and prevented from picking up new information that is outside of these frames

problem is, our anticipatory guiding frames are so efficient we tend to default to what is already in the frame.

In Chap. 10, we humans can become prisoners of our frames. Information that contradicts the frame is avoided, or worse, not even recognized by the individual, which creates closed information loops between the frame and the outside world.

Plato's 2500-year-old Meno Paradox is the center of this book: If we recognize in the world only what we already know, contained in our frames, how can we come to know new things? And there is not only the individual frame: there are also group and nation frames.

In Chap. 11, we illustrate the group frame level with the example of Elfreda Chatman's (2000) examination of the small world of dirt-eaters in the USA. And in Chap. 12, we illustrate the nation frame level with the example of the Nazis' ideological hold over Germany's citizens during 1933–1945.

We conclude Part II with the problem posed by our levels of frames. When a searcher conducts an information search using Google or some other search engine, the frames close off the information loops between what we already know, inside our frames, and new information from the outside world.

Part III: The Solution

The Introduction to Part III shifts the framing problem for a searcher using Google to the solution. The searcher typically formulates his information need in a query based on his frames, i.e., what he already knows. The solution is to facilitate the searcher opening the information loop so that he can recognize new information in the results list. But how do we do this? Part III answers this question.

In Chap. 13, archeological evidence is described for a solution to the problem. The recent discovery of the first permanent construction from the Neolithic era, the 11,600-year-old ruins of a temple at Göbekli Tepe, Turkey. These ruins, which predate sedentary agriculture and permanent village-life, indicate that the human search for meaning, associated with the Mythic Mind layer of human consciousness, opened the information loop allowing the production of new knowledge in the fields of engineering, agricultural sciences, and village organization (Lewis-Williams and Pearce 2005; Mann 2011; Mithen 1996; and recently, Harari 2015).

In Chap. 14, from the archeological evidence at Göbekli Tepe, we develop the thesis that belief-begets-knowledge. The chapter argues that new knowledge production originates and is constructed inside our belief system not our knowledge system. The belief system is broader than religious belief; it is an existential belief that gives our species a mechanism for guessing at or believing something could be true. It opens the searcher's information loop to new information that has the potential to produce new knowledge.

Chapter 15 models the belief system-directed information search. The "spark" triggering the opening of the searcher's information loop to new information and new knowledge production occurs in a series of steps, and it begins inside the searcher's belief system. Somehow we must get the searcher out of his frames and what he already knows, into the guessing part of his frame located in his belief system. Figure 1.7 illustrates how this can be done. Here, we return to our previously mentioned traffic accident, dividing it into three parts. (a) It diagrams the unreliable witness to a car accident imprisoned inside his three levels of frames (the nation, the

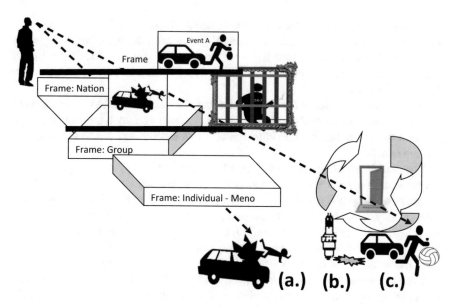

Fig. 1.7 (**a**) The searcher-witness views information in the outside world imprisoned in his nation, group, and individual frames. (**b**) A "spark" occurs (**c**) opening the door to new information being recognized and the production of new knowledge (the victim running after the basketball caused the accident)

group, and the individual frame levels); (b) the witness is "sparked" out of his frame imprisonment, (c) which opens the "door" of the information loop between the witness and new information in the accident scene. Let us briefly examine (b) the "spark" that opens the information loop.

The unreliable witness in Fig. 1.7 is a bicycle enthusiast who hates car drivers because he himself has been knocked over by cars. So he is guided by his group frame to only see the impact of the car against the pedestrian. He does not mean to misrepresent the accident to the police officer, but because he does not knowingly remember, to the point of awareness, the entire accident, he feeds in the missing information from his mental frame when he tells the police officer what he has witnessed. He attributes fault to the car driver. Later that afternoon, he is raking leaves and uncovers a basketball. Suddenly, he remembers that a man was running after a basketball just before the accident. He immediately changes his belief about the accident. And he puts the two together: accident + running-after-basketball. The victim in the car accident had actually run out into the street after a ball, making the victim responsible for the accident. The "spark" is seeing the basketball on his lawn + changing his belief about the accident, which allowed him to reconstruct what he thought he had seen into new knowledge.

In Chap. 16, we describe **The Consciousness' Drive Information Need-Search Model** with a detailed case study to illustrate how it works. We also describe **The Real Information Need Finding Device**, which facilitates the searcher shifting the search from her frames to her belief system. Again, we illustrate how the Device works with a detailed case study. The Device helps the searcher formulate her query to Google or some other search engine based on her real information need, accessed in her belief system, which switches what the searcher sees in the results list from what the searcher already knows in her frames, to what the searcher doesn't yet know but needs to know.

Finding the real information need is an experiential information event, causing new information to suddenly enter the searcher's belief system, a transfer of energy between the world and the individual searcher that the searcher can feel. It is an "a-ha" moment!

The book's final Conclusion (Chap. 17) returns to the very broad, species-level consciousness-approach to information need and the search for meaning. If we cannot solve the problem posed by Part II's Meno's Paradox, then human consciousness is only a product of stimulus-response operations of the brain, a form of neurological computing, which could be, conceivably, imitated in instructions to an AI computer like the universal Turing machine. But the intention underlying human consciousness to produce new knowledge is more than this.

Human consciousness as we describe it in this book cannot be imitated by an AI-equipped robot, even if it has perfect and complete frames for every possible stimulus. We discuss two arguments raised by Turing himself against the possibility of an AI-equipped machine truly imitating how humans think.

Part I
Human Exceptionality

Introduction to Part I

In Part I, we investigate the basis of our success as a species, our unique consciousness, as the reason for our exceptionality. Far more than any other animal, we have an obsessive need for information from the world around us, because we have an added layer of consciousness that other species don't have. This obsession is not only for information to ascertain our place in a hierarchy, a social or work group, or even in our intimate relations with others, but for the fundamental need to find out our relationship with the world. It is this fundamental type of information need we are talking about in this book because it is the basis of the link between information search and new knowledge production.

We cannot design intuitive search engines for information searches whose objective is new knowledge production until we begin to design for this fundamental level of information need. We begin to show how we can do this in the Conclusion to Part I. But Part I builds the argument slowly, starting from setting information need in its widest possible perspective: information need as a driving force of human consciousness, which includes its evolution. Over the hundreds of thousands of years of human evolution, driven by our information need faculty, humans have become more attuned to information in the world around us.

Our information-sensitive consciousness is the basis of our exceptionality.

The narrative device upon which we build our investigation of human consciousness is evolutionary psychologist Merlin Donald's (1991) groundbreaking book *Origins of the Modern Mind: Three Stages in the Evolution of Culture and Cognition*. Donald sets out a theory that divides the evolution of our consciousness into four phases and three transitions, illustrated in Fig. 1. We give a rough timeline for the phase transitions on the left-hand side of the figure. Each phase has a different type of cognitive architecture that defines human consciousness for that particular phase, which Donald calls the "Mind." What Donald means by "mind" is the way the outside world enters our brain, is stored there, and is constantly recalled and used by

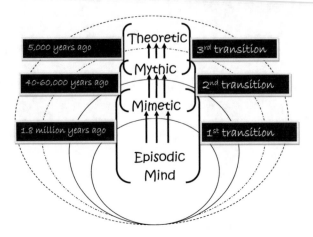

Fig. 1 Donald's four-phase, three-stage transition theory of the evolution of human cognition (with approximate timeline for each transition on the left), which remain as layers in our present-day consciousness

5,000 years ago

40-60,000 years ago

1.8 million years ago

Theoretic

Mythic

Mimetic

Episodic Mind

3rd transition

2nd transition

1st transition

us to shape and determine, not only how we think and what we think about, but also the way we interact with the world and each other.

Each new "Mind" phase engenders a new human lifestyle, a new way of living—a new "culture" to use Donald's term. This is because the "epigenetic influence" (the nongenetic influence on genetic expression) exploits the "latent cognitive potential" in a given culture phase (Donald 1998, p. 1), which drives the evolutionary transition to the next mind phase. We presently live in the Theoretic Culture, but the Episodic Mind phase of our brain's evolution is still present as the base-layer of our memory system and consciousness. In fact, it gives the name to our primary memory system concerned with how we experience the world: episodic memory. The episodes we experience and then store in episodic memory provide the vehicle or channel interface between the reality of the outside world into ourselves, what is inside us. That is, we remember and think about our intersection with the world in the unit of episodes of experience.

If you think about it, a lot of our culture, the way we do things, the way we relate to each other, and the way we experience and represent ourselves in the world to others, is based on the episode. It forms the basic structure for our literature, our TV, our movies. But the episode is also how we frame our experience of life to ourselves.

We get up from bed in the morning and the shower is ruined by the hot water heater breaking down. When we remember the episode, and recount it to someone else, there is a story-like quality with a beginning, middle (the climax), and an end—a cause-and-effect structure if you will. The same is true of a lovely moment the first day of school when our frightened child turned to us and held our hand, tight, before being taken away by the kindergarten teacher. You say to yourself: "I didn't want to let her hand go." Or you say: "I told her in my tight grip to be strong; she can do it." These reactions of ours to our experience, contained within the episode, codify how we feel about ourselves and who we are. We go over and over again in our mind our experienced episodes—Donald's second layer of consciousness, the Mimetic Mind—trying to understand them. But because the episode is the vehicle through which we connect ourselves to the outside world, by mimicking the episode in our mind over and over again, we are also trying to understand the world and our place in that world.

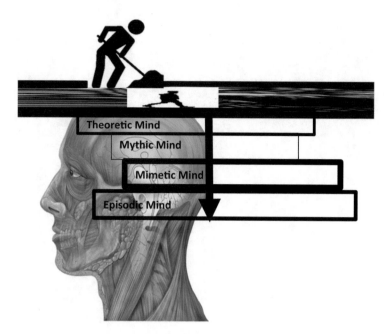

Fig. 2 The layers of human consciousness: Digging down to the fundamentals of human consciousness, to get to our first evolutionary self

The Mythic Mind, Donald's third layer of human consciousness, underlies a sort of parallel narrative in all our literature, movies, theater, and paintings. All our best movies—Ridley Scott's *The Blade Runner*, Lucas's *Star Wars* saga, Fellini's *La Dolce Vita*, Bertolucci's *The Conformist*, Coppola's *The Godfather*, or this year's *Dunkirk*—all these movies set the narrative of their characters' lives in some sort of spiritual or mythic dimension. To most people, this spiritual or mythic dimension of our lives is more relevant than the Theoretic Mind.

The Theoretic Mind, Donald's fourth and final layer of human consciousness, marks our present-day society as a culture that is constantly moving forward, progressing scientifically and technologically as we come to fully understand our world in terms of scientific laws, models, and theories.

As shown in Fig. 2, Part I is a digging operation through the four evolutionary layers to establish a definition of human consciousness as it is today. In this book, and in Part I in particular, we spend a lot more time and effort examining the Episodic Mind layer of human consciousness than Donald does. Donald's theory focuses on the third layer, the Mythic Mind layer. We spend a lot of time on this third layer as well. But it is the Episodic Mind layer of consciousness that forms the basis our examination of information need and information search.

The Fig. 1 diagram serves as a navigation guide for the following chapters in Part I.

Chapter 2
Human Exceptionality: How We See Ourselves in Relation to the World

To better examine the role of information need and information search in human life, we take a broad, species-level perspective in this book. How and what do humans think about in their relationship to the world and their place in the world? This is examining information need in the most fundamental way, as a function of human consciousness.

So what is human consciousness? The dictionary says it is

- The nature of our awareness of the human mind of itself and the world.
- The awareness of our identity.
- The awareness of our thoughts. (Oxford Dictionary of Current English 1985)

But we can do better than this here. In this book, we represent what consciousness is in terms of Donald's (1991) four-phase approach to the evolutionary development of consciousness in the human species. Each phase remains a layer of consciousness as it is today, so that by examining each layer we can build a complex, nuanced definition of consciousness as it relates specifically to information need and information search.

In Fig. 2.1, the four-phase structure is in light gray outline, with a human standing before it, his consciousness. He is thinking about the world as separate from himself. And he is able to think about himself as separate from the world. We usually think of ourselves as part of the fabric of the world, so it is difficult to imagine it as separate. There is an inside us, our physical form and the way we think, and an outside world around us; not only its physical presence, providing us with air to breath and water to drink, but also its existential dimension as something different from us.

Consciousness is the self-awareness of this separation of ourselves—our consciousness of our consciousness, if you like—as we are traveling through the world in time and space. It is like we are taking photographs of our experiencing of the world, and then constructing our place in the world by manipulating these photographs, putting them in order. But all of this is done in our own minds. In our age of taking selfies with our mobile phones, this operation of separating ourselves from our experience of the world, living in the representation of the experience rather than

© Springer International Publishing AG, part of Springer Nature 2018

C. Cole, *The Consciousness' Drive*, https://doi.org/10.1007/978-3-319-92457-1_2

Fig. 2.1 Human consciousness: the fundamentals of how and what we think about the world outside us and our place in that world

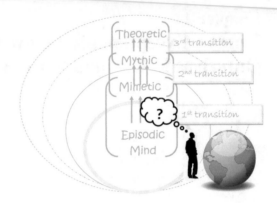

experiencing the experience, has become almost literal. Now that we have the technology to do it, is selfie-taking so frequent because it is second nature to us, something we have always done inside our heads as part of our exceptional consciousness? But is it really that exceptional? What do animals think?

What Do Animals Think?

In varying degrees, the trend in science, exemplified by the 2012 signing of the Cambridge Declaration on Consciousness (Harari 2016, p. 122), is to attribute to most mammal and bird species some sort of consciousness—meaning, most mammals and bird species have the ability to separate out themselves as autonomous entities from their real-time experience of the world. Being able to mentally step out of the world, however minimally, is essential for the survival of most animal species. To find food, they must remember where to find the best supply of food. They must remember how to protect offspring by climbing a tree or digging a hole. Knowing how to survive in a hostile and changing environment requires the animal to be aware of itself and to construct a narrative of its "best-practices" behavior that is separate from a passive experiencing of the world. Nobel Prize winner Gerald Edelman (1989) in his book *The Remembered Present: A Biological Theory of Consciousness* calls this animal consciousness a primary consciousness. Humans have it, animals have it, and extinct species like the Neanderthals had it as well. But modern humans also have a secondary or higher-order consciousness.

Armed with this higher-order consciousness, humans alone among all other species are able to take an experience they have experienced in the world out of the world as if it were an object like a movie or painting. They can then store it in memory, recall it from memory, manipulate it one way or the other; mentally do anything they want with it. In other words, when we experience the world in real time, the experiencing of it seems to leave an echo or image of itself in our memory which can be re-experienced by going over it again in our minds. So being able to separate ourselves and our experiences in the world from the world, is an essential component to our exceptional species consciousness.

Let's give our human form of consciousness compared to other species a mark or level on a scale of 0–5: Level 5. This leaves us with room to nuance consciousness in animals to focus in on the essential difference that marks humans as the exceptional species.

Dogs and cats obviously have an ability to learn a routine from the repetition of an episode of their experience. Dogs can catch a stick or fetch a Frisbee in repetition. They must somehow store the routine in memory. In this way, they can develop expertise in various skills by repetition. More fundamentally, a bear in the wild acquires food by going to a certain protected, fish-laden place in a stream to catch fish. If it is successful once, it then goes back there over and over again. Some animals like beavers even construct artificial water sources out of wood and leaves to artificially produce the most optimum conditions, based on their previous experience. But most animal species don't do complicated planning tasks very well. They seem to be more reactive than we are, living in the moment. Cats and squirrels cross a busy street, but they seem disconnected from learning from their memories of previous crossing-the-street episodes, particularly how cars behave and where they are in relation to cars, leading to a high incident of death or injury. Let's give the animal form of consciousness a lower mark, but not all animals are equal so the mark is variable: Level 1–Level 4.

Lower forms of animals have an awareness of their physical actions and the effects these actions have on others in their species as well as on other species that they hunt for food. They have a sort of map or mental representation of their position in relation to the animal they are hunting, for example. Without this, they couldn't hunt. What then is a criterion that differentiates the consciousness of the lower forms of animal species as being separate from the world during the hunt from the human form of consciousness?

It must be something to do with the degree of its awareness or recognition of its separation from the world.

The mirror test developed by Gordon Gallup (1970) sets out to prove if an animal has "the cognitive ability to recognize its separation from nature" (Shreeve 2015, p. 53). With few exceptions, even for animals we consider our closest relatives, most animal species fail the test. Monkeys, for example, fail the test. If the researchers paint a spot on the monkey's forehead and put it in front of a mirror, the monkey is not able to associate the mirror image's forehead spot with the spot on its own forehead. Orangutans, chimpanzees, bottlenose dolphins, elephants, orcas, bonobos, rhesus macaques, and various members of the corvid family (European magpies, scrub jays, etc.) can do this, but not monkeys or dogs (Fig. 2.2). So there are levels of self-awareness among the species in their faculty to understand and act according to their awareness of their position as separate vis-à-vis the outside world.

Based on the mirror test, we have levels of consciousness based on the awareness-of-separation from the world criterion, with monkeys, dogs and lower forms of animals who fail the mirror test in the first levels, then chimpanzees at a higher level

Fig. 2.2 Mirror test: chimpanzees pass, humans pass, but dogs and all but seven other animal species fail (© 2006 Georgia Pinaud. CC-BY-SA license)

of self-awareness who pass the mirror test, and finally humans at the highest level of self-awareness.

Human infants reach the fifth and highest level of self-consciousness only gradually (Fig. 2.3), but before the age of 5, according to Rochat's (2003) 0–5 scale:

Level 0: Confusion: Newborn babies skip this stage, because they show they know that the reflection in the mirror is something different than simply an extension of the world. Most other species, however, are in this stage with mirrors.

Level 1: Differentiation: Newborns only 24 hours old indicate they know something is different in their reflection in the mirror, different than an extension of the world that surrounds it.

Level 2: Situation: 6-week-old babies can map out their movements using a mirror, copying the direction of an adult sticking out her tongue.

Level 3: Identification: By 18 months, infants can identify themselves, who they are, in the mirror.

Level 4: Permanence: 3-year-olds recognize themselves in photos and movies indicating they model themselves going through time, identifying themselves in photos taken the week before, etc.

Level 5: Self-consciousness, or "meta" self-awareness—again humans reach this stage before 5 years. Children can recognize themselves as others see them; for instance, they can recognize they are reading or dreaming in photos.

Humans have the exceptional ability because of a qualitatively different factor than the eight other animals who passed the mirror test referred to above: To take ourselves out of the motion of the ongoing world, to think of ourselves as a sort of thought experiment, in a mental representation of our presence in the world as if we were an object. Malafouris (2009, p. 99) calls this "self-recognition through objectification." The other eight animals that passed the mirror test can also do this trick of extracting themselves mentally from the world. But there is of course a difference. Can we get at this essential difference between the consciousness of the intelligent animal species that pass the mirror test and the exceptional consciousness of our own species?

The starting position for this exceptionality, which we develop over the course of this book, is the way humans frame their experience in the world, objectifying it into something that is separate from the world, an object they remember and can return to. We frame, store, and use, by mentally revisiting it—our experience in the world—differently than other animal species, as illustrated in Fig. 2.4.

All of us build a frame around the episodes of our experience. The framing can be somewhat arbitrary, subjective. Someone else after listening to you explain it says: "What about this other thing that happened?" To which you answer: "Forget about

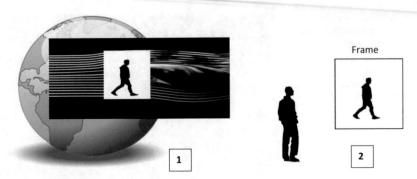

Fig. 2.4 Humans can (1) frame themselves and their experience in the ebb and flow of the ongoing world differently than other animal species, allowing us to store it in memory, which (2) we can mentally revisit

that. What is important is . . ." It is somehow ours, ours alone. In a way, we create a narrative of our life in the action of framing our experience into an object. We then revisit the episode in memory to think about it. For some episodes—the important ones to our sense of identity—we think about them, obsessively or intermittently, for the rest of our lives.

Chapter 3
Framing: Lessons from Vermeer

In the last chapter, we began to conceptualize human consciousness—how and what we think about the world and our relationship or place in the world. Humans have a different relationship with the world than any other species. We can separate our experience from the ebb and flow of the world by framing it in the unit of the episode, which takes it out of the world and puts it inside us into our memory. Then we return to the memory episode to think about it. The framed episode is our relationship vehicle with the world. And it also gives us, because it is our experience and our memory and no one else's, an exceptional vehicle for thinking about our personal place in the world.

In this chapter, we return to an overview of how we think and what we think about that constitutes our consciousness, by examining archeological evidence of this thinking in an artist's painting of an episode experience, shown in Fig. 3.1. We utilize the example of seventeenth-century Dutch painter Johannes Vermeer's painting of a memory episode that took place across the canal from his bedroom window.

Framing a Part of Our Experience with the World

Framing a part of reality, and thus objectifying it in memory or concretely as a work of art, is a uniquely human cognitive ability that defines our exceptionality as a species. Other animal species do not have this uniquely human consciousness that drives us to try to think about the world and our place in the world.

Let us start by looking at framing in a narrower sense than how we've referred to it thus far. Let us start with a picture frame. A picture frame outlines or delineates a portion of the world that the artist or photographer wishes to represent. Outside the frame is something else that is not relevant to the painter. Let us examine one famous painting inside a frame, the painting by the seventeenth-century Dutch painter Johannes Vermeer called *The Little Street*, shown in Fig. 3.2.

© Springer International Publishing AG, part of Springer Nature 2018

C. Cole, *The Consciousness' Drive*, https://doi.org/10.1007/978-3-319-92457-1_3

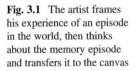

Fig. 3.1 The artist frames his experience of an episode in the world, then thinks about the memory episode and transfers it to the canvas

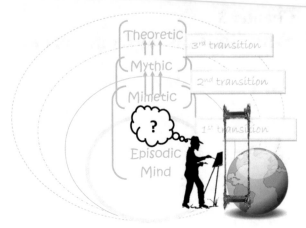

This painting, which only measures 1′9″ by 1′5″, is now located in Amsterdam's Rijksmuseum. To see it in person, a gallery-goer enters the Rijkmuseum itself and then makes her way to the large room or gallery where *The Little Street* hangs on a wall along with many other paintings. She then stands in front of the painting and looks at it. If she is serious, she lets go of her present-day concerns a bit, shifting her mind toward the world portrayed in the painting. This may be difficult. There are a dozen people around her looking at both *The Little Street* and other paintings in the gallery; perhaps there are other people standing right next to her, to her immediate right and to her left, craning their necks looking at this same painting. They breathe out unpleasant odors, make strange sounds. They are laughing and talking. Nevertheless, the viewer is able to let her mind enter the world that the artist is representing. In this case, seventeenth-century Delft, which is a small town in a small country at the northern edge of Europe undergoing its golden age—a time of wealth, culture, and religious conflicts. This was the time and the place of Rembrandt and Fabritius and many other artists that today we consider foundational works of Western civilization.

We actually know very little about Vermeer. Here, we rely on the main texts on Vermeer's life and art by Montias (1989), Steadman (2001, 2017), and Swillens (1950). Figure 3.3 frames the Vermeer world we do know, consisting of a few blocks in the middle of Delft, his hometown. Framed in this way, Vermeer's life appears to be a very small world. The enlarged map shown in Fig. 3.4 enables us to label the important reference points in our Vermeer-world frame immediately around the New Church of Delft. There is the town's market square just in front of this church, and then going out a few streets on either side of the market square, there are the various houses Vermeer lived in over the course of his 43-year-long life.

Within this geographical frame, we actually know or think we know something about where the house portrayed in the painting *The Little Street* was located. (For a discussion of alternative possible locations, see Steadman 2017.) Perhaps it was the Old Woman's and Old Man's Almshouse, torn down in 1661. Its presumed location was the street to the left of the New Church, the Number "3" on the Fig. 3.4 map. As

Fig. 3.2 Vermeer's *The Little Street*, c. 1658. Rijksmuseum, Amsterdam (© 2015. Txllxt TxllxT. Creative Commons Attribution-Share Alike 4.0 International license)

described in P.T.A. Swillen's (1950) classic account of the circumstances surrounding Vermeer's paintings, there is some belief that Vermeer's father's tavern, the Mechelen, may have backed onto this little street. It is possible that Vermeer painted this episodic scene from observations from an upstairs room in his father's house, perhaps his childhood bedroom.

What was the artist thinking when he painted the episode depicted in *The Little Street*, perhaps one that unfolded as he looked out of his bedroom window? Vermeer painted slowly, usually taking many months to a year to paint each one of his paintings. Only 35–37 of his paintings exist to this day, out of an estimated total 22-year long career production of 40. So the painting of the episodic scene depicted in *The Little Street* may not have been based on a single painted episode. In other words, the episode itself could have been manipulated by the artist himself.

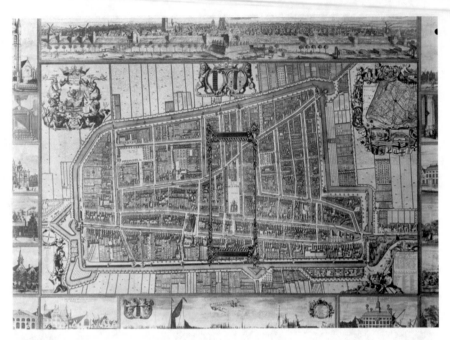

Fig. 3.3 We frame for closer observation the small physical space of seventeenth century Delft that constituted Vermeer's world. Enlarged in Fig. 3.4. *Kaart Figuratief* by Dirck van Bleyswijck, 1678. © 1966 A. J. van der Wal Creative Commons Attribution-Share Alike 4.0 International license

What is the small part of the world Vermeer frames in this famous painting *The Little Street*? Let's enlarge the painting so we can see it better in Fig. 3.5. Now we can see that Vermeer portrayed people as well as a house on a little street. They are dressed in period costumes. There are two women and two children, with the two children engaged in playing a game on the stoop. The Dutch are famous for washing their stoops so it is very clean there. With such thoughts, the modern-day viewer looks at this evocative painting and begins to go back in time to a small seventeenth-century street in Delft.

We will focus here on a universal quality of the human framing of life and experience that is illustrated by this marvelous painting. Let us assume that one day Vermeer himself was standing at his bedroom window looking out at exactly this scene depicted in *The Little Street* and decided to paint it. What did Vermeer see when he looked upon this house, the alley beside it, and the various people of seventeenth-century Delft engaged in everyday activities? Look at any streetscape yourself. Can you see that the framing plays a role in what you see? Because you just don't see one thing. You see a larger context of things around the thing you are focusing on. Likewise, an artist can determine what he paints depending upon the context he includes in his painting, and what he leaves out, which is dependent on the framing of the episode both in terms of time and its physical dimensions. The

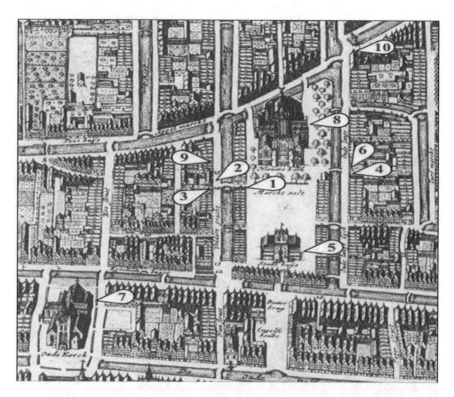

Fig. 3.4 Vermeer's world in Delft: (1) Mechelen, Vermeer's father's tavern. (3) Behind Mechelen, the assumed streetscape painted by Vermeer in his painting *The Little Street*. (4) Vermeer's mother-in-law, Maria Thin's house, where Vermeer lived with his wife and children for most of his adult life. A detail of Willem Blaeu's City Plan of Delft from Joh. Blaeu's Toonneel der Steden van de Vereenigde Nederlanden, 1649 (© 2001–2018 Jonathan Janson Reprinted with Permission)

painter includes and excludes items from inside the frame. We will label these: framing-in and framing-out.

If it is true that *The Little Street* was painted from Vermeer's upstairs bedroom at the back of his father's tavern, Vermeer framed-out the canal called the Voldersgracht that came between Mechelen and the episode he painted on the little street. We can see the canal right there in the map of Delft shown in Fig. 3.4. Instead, the painting starts at the bottom of the frame from a cobble-stoned street; and it then goes upward taking in everything all the way up to the sky.

The sky forms the top part of the painting at the frame on the painting's left-hand side (from the viewer's point of view) but not on the right-hand side. On the right-hand side, Vermeer chose to frame-out of the painting starting at the very top of the house, but frame-in the beginning part of the top of the house. For some reason, he framed-out the top inch or two of the house.

Again, on the right-hand side of the painting, Vermeer frames-in only three-quarters of the width of the house, the house that takes up most of the painting. And

Fig. 3.5 Enlargement of Vermeer's The Little Street, c. 1658. Rijksmuseum, Amsterdam (© 2015 Txllxt TxllxT. Creative Commons Attribution-Share Alike 4.0 International license)

on the left-hand side, he frames-out more than half of a smaller house in front of which is a tree. There are four people in the painting, but these people are very small. Vermeer framed-in so much of the cobble-stoned street in the foreground and so

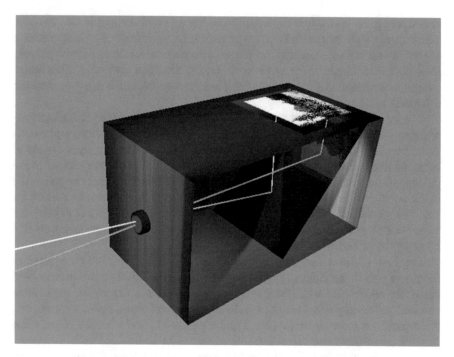

Fig. 3.6 Camera obscura (© 2005 en:User:Meggar. GNU Free Documentation License)

much of the house in the middle-ground, that the two children playing a game at the front of the house, and the two adult women—one sitting in the doorway, the other under an arch in a laneway bent over a wood basket—don't appear to be the primary subject of the painting. If these people had been the object of the painting, Vermeer certainly could have framed-out the top two floors of the 3-storey house to make the people larger, more individual.

Even though the people are heavily engaged in seemingly interesting activities, their smallness indicates Vermeer was after something larger than these individual people. The cloudy, dark sky, the carefully painted crumbling nature of the brick of the house and the archway may have been his objective. The house's decrepitude—again, if we have the right location for *The Little Street*, behind the Mechelen tavern—is reinforced by the fact that the dilapidated house was torn down soon after Vermeer painted it to make way for the St. Luke's Guildhall—a far grander building. The decrepit, old brick of the painted houses suggests the subject of the painting is the passing of time. If it is indeed Vermeer's theme, the passing of time is conveyed by what Vermeer chose to include inside the frame, and what he chose to leave outside the frame.

It is now thought, by Philip Steadman (2001) among others, that Vermeer used a device called the camera obscura, shown in Fig. 3.6, to help to freeze-frame the images he wished to paint. The camera obscura was made up of a box with amplifying glass lenses that captured the real image and brought it into the box, which then projected the desired image onto a blank canvas. By coincidence, a pivotal person in the development of the microscope lens, Anton van Leeuwenhoek, lived in Delft at the same time as Vermeer, and the two knew each other. The camera obscura was more than a copying device; it was, as Steadman calls it, a "composition machine."

If indeed Vermeer used a camera obscura to compose or construct his paintings— we cannot know this for sure—the camera obscura certainly performed a compositional function, allowing Vermeer to compose and recompose exactly, in terms of light and dimension and mood and theme, the objects he wished to portray in the painting. But its function was more than this. Once Vermeer selected the part of the world he wished to paint, the camera obscura froze the framing of the part of the world he wished to paint and transferred the frame to his canvas. We will divide what we mean by this machine-aided framing into the two unnatural phenomena created by using the camera obscura.

The first unnatural phenomenon achieved by the camera obscura was, as Steadman puts it, the flattening of three-dimensional space onto a two-dimensional plane. By eliminating what the eye normally sees in the real world, the camera obscura facilitated placing the objects, in compositional terms, inside a frame, i.e., the objects can more easily be placed and represented, vis-à-vis each other, when they are two-dimensional representations of three-dimensional objects.

The camera obscura objectifies in two dimensions the three-dimensional world that Vermeer the artist wished to put inside the frame, enabling the artist, as Steadman puts it, "to abruptly and arbitrarily" cut in half-objects like the house and tree in *The Little Street*. When painting a streetscape, or anything based on real objects from real life, the painter frames what he sees in the real world and transfers what's in the frame to the canvas. While most painters include whole objects in their frame, Vermeer, perhaps because of his use of the camera obscura, framed the objects he represented as they would be in the real world as if they were objectively represented by his eye in one gaze, not as they are subjectively represented to us inside our mind. In other words, we don't cut objects in half when we represent them in our mind's eye; we subjectively fill-in the added information based on our memory of the framed-out parts of the objects, which are of course stored in memory. So we normally fill-in, or subjectively frame-in what we don't actually objectively see in one gaze. The camera obscura fights this normal mental procedure, enabling objective-seeing, so to speak.

The second unnatural phenomenon achieved by the camera obscura was the feeling the viewer of the painting gets when looking at the people depicted in *The Little Street*. The transference of the real people to Vermeer's canvas was, again, objective and not as it would have been done subjectively if the artist's mind's eye had been in charge of the transference, unaided by a camera device. This objective transference of the people, in turn, influences the viewer's frame when she looks at a painting such as *The Little Street*. The act of looking at is influenced by the feelings evoked in the viewer by the act of observing the painting. Let us concentrate on a

Fig. 3.7 *Courtyard of a House in Delft* by Pieter de Hooch 1658 (© 1658 National Gallery, London. GNU Free Documentation License)

viewer looking at *The Little Street* with full intent, who really engages in the seventeenth-century episode Vermeer painted.

The streetscape portrayed in the painting *The Little Street* started at the bottom of the frame just beyond the canal that Vermeer framed-out of the painting. A canal not only imparts a different view to the viewer, but also a different feeling. By framing-out the canal, Vermeer leaves us with two adults and two children. The two adults are doing everyday tasks like sweeping while the two children are bent over playing a game of some sort. There are so many aspects we could focus on to convey what the viewer feels when she sees *The Little Street*, but here we will focus on just one. To do this, we need to look at another Dutch painting of children in a street, shown in Fig. 3.7.

The painting, *Courtyard of a House in Delft,* by Pieter de Hooch, was painted around the same time as Vermeer's *The Little Street*, and is also of a streetscape in

Delft. There is the same old-looking brickwork, and the same mixture of adults and children. There is the same cloudy sky, the kind of weather we typically associate with the Netherlands. The primary difference between the two paintings, however, is that the figures in the de Hooch painting look staged while the figures in the Vermeer painting do not look staged. To the viewer, it looks like Vermeer caught them in the act of living their everyday lives. Vermeer does this in a number of ways. If we compare *The Little Street* to *Courtyard of a House in Delft*, the figures appear to be highlighted in the latter; they are larger and they are more in the middle of the viewer's view of the seventeenth-century Dutch streetscape being portrayed. And the walls of the buildings are used to strengthen the frame. In other words, de Hooch is telling the viewer a story.

How does the fact that de Hooch draws the viewer into a story-like observation of the episode depicted in his painting while Vermeer does not affect the viewer's act of observation? Remember, we are talking about Vermeer's framing of an episode of his experience in the world, separating it out from the ongoing world, and finally objectifying it inside an actual frame with the aid of a camera obscura. He is aware that how we perceive the world is different from the objective world. By using the camera obscura, and evoking the two unnatural phenomena previously discussed, the viewer of the Vermeer painting is forced into uncertainty because Vermeer doesn't tell a story—he forces the viewer herself to categorize the painting's message.

The deliberately random-like, everyday-like composition of the Vermeer painting's elements, forces the viewer to reach for her own meaning. She is forced to fill in the blanks deliberately and carefully left by Vermeer by recalling episodes or fragments of episodes from her own life that connect her, if the search for meaning is successful, to the seventeenth-century episode depicted in the Vermeer painting. In this way, Vermeer succeeds in communicating something of the episode he saw and felt from his bedroom window across 350 years. No other species comes close to achieving this exceptional ability to frame and represent their experience.

Fig. 3.8 The artist's intersection with the world is explosive, like a piece of dynamite combusting. The artist takes out the framed intersection, mentally, in his mind, and objectifies the part of the world and his place in it, then transfers it to the canvas

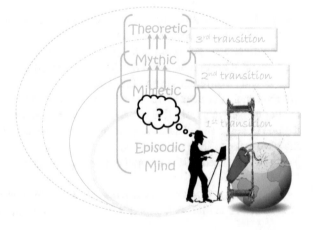

Fig. 3.9 A partial view of an episode of lions (on the right) hunting bison (on the left) painted on wall of Chauvet Cave 32,000 years ago (© 2016 Claude Valette. Creative Commons Attribution-Share Alike 4.0 International license)

The way human consciousness experiences the world is more than just observing and framing the experience in the unit of the episode. We experience our intersection with the world explosively, as if our consciousness comes attached to a piece of dynamite that we throw into the world as we experience it, shown in Fig. 3.8. (The intersection with the world is that intense!)

The First (Recorded) Human Episode

Let us very briefly go back even further in time to examine one of the first recorded episodes in the human timeline, a 32,000-year-old painting in the Chauvet Cave, France, of lions hunting a herd of bison, shown in Fig. 3.9. It is one of the oldest figurative cave paintings found so far (cave wall hand-stencil paintings are older, about 40,000 years old). We examine this painting much more extensively later on in Part I (Chaps. 6 and 7).

The Chauvet Cave painting depicts what at first glance looks like a pride of 16 lions hunting down a herd of 7 bison. There is a fevered quality to this cave painting. On closer inspection, the 4 lions on the bottom row running in a straight line seem to be, in fact, a single lion represented by the artist in various positions as it moved forward toward its prey.

Looking at it closely, it is very modern, like a photograph. In fact, it is far more sophisticated than much of human representational art over our recorded history. It

Fig. 3.10 The human species is (1) part of the ebb and flow of the world, but it is not just part of the ongoing ebb and flow of the world. (2) We separate our experience in the ebb and flow by framing our experience in the unit of the episode, store it in memory, and then afterward we recall the episode to (3a) dig into the outside world and (3b) dig into the frame via our layers of consciousness

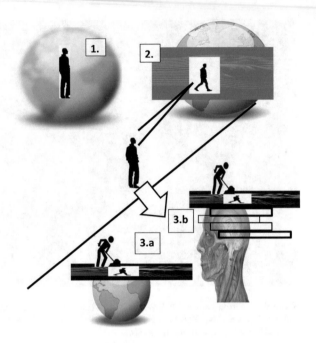

catches the movement aspects of film, of capturing the world speeding around us, in front of us in real time, especially the feeling of motion, the excitement of our real-time experiencing of the world.

Let's go back to what the Paleolithic artist or artists thought when they painted the lions and the bison. Their real-time experiencing of the hunting episode depicted in the Chauvet Cave painting moved fast in front of the artist(s). Everything moves fast in life, in the world around us. But the Chauvet Cave artists were able to freeze-frame the experience of the episode in memory, then recall the frame—complete with the impression or feeling of speed it left them with—when they painted it on a cave wall. It is a tour-de-force of the human endeavor to dig into the framed episode of human-kind's experience of the world, to define and represent its essence by accessing not only its visual impact, but also how it felt.

We divide up the digging into two categories in Fig. 3.10 (3.a and 3.b within artwork).

The Digging

Vermeer and the Paleolithic cave painters teach us several lessons about human consciousness. When humans intersect with the world, and this is contrary to the animal species that fail the mirror test, human consciousness frames the experience as separate from the ebb and flow of the world, and stores it as a unit in memory to think about later.

Let's divide the intersection more carefully, diagramming it in Fig. 3.10. To begin with,

1. Human consciousness experiences the ebb and flow of the world, but it is self-aware, meaning we are aware that we are experiencing the world.
2. This enables us to step back to look carefully at and frame what we are experiencing. We frame the experience (objectify the experience by labeling and conceptualizing it) in the unit of the episode, and store it in memory so that we can afterward recall the episode and think about it.
3. The thinking afterward is a digging process. There is an outward digging behavior and inward digging behavior:

   a. Our consciousness goes outward to the world to dig into the world, frequently with the aid of a technological device such as Vermeer's camera obscura, and
   b. Our consciousness goes inward into itself where it digs through its layers via the memory frame of the experience.

The digging into the mental frame of experience by Vermeer or the Chauvet Cave artist, or for that matter any individual digging into or interpreting his or her episode of experience, is the essence of human consciousness. It defines our place in the world. It constitutes **what we think about** and **how** we think about it. It defines who we are.

The rest of the chapters in Part I are devoted to defining in a more specific manner this digging activity we do inside our consciousness. And most importantly for the subject of this book: the role of information need and information search in this digging.

Chapter 4
Episodic Memory: Lessons from the Scrub Jays

We begin our description of human consciousness in its first evolutionary phase: the Episodic Mind. The Episodic Mind constitutes the original frame through which our hominid ancestors viewed the world (shown in Fig. 4.1). In this period more than 1.8 million years ago, human consciousness was much like other animals (Donald 1991, p. 163). While it remains the fundamental consciousness for most animal species, humans have further evolved, which we describe in subsequent chapters. The Episodic Mind remains, however, the first layer of our present-day consciousness. It forms the layer of human intersection with the world, the layer of first contact. And we remember our contact in episode experiences in what is called episodic memory. "Episodic memory stores the specific details of [our] situations and life events" (Donald 1991, p. 151). It does not, as procedural memory does, generalize "across situations and life events," nor does it store facts and other knowledge, the purview of our semantic memory. (We return to these three memory systems in Fig. 4.3.)

We are limited in what we can say about the characteristics of our prehistoric, prehuman Episodic Mind phase because we are dependent on the archeological record left to us dating back to more than 1.8 million years ago. None exists from the Episodic Culture because, by Donald's definition, any archeological evidence indicates the next phase of human evolutionary development, the Mimetic Mind, when humans copied (mimicked) and learned from repeating their action experiences to themselves and to others in the group. Therefore, to establish when the Episodic Mind was the only and thus controlling layer of consciousness, we must compare human memory of past episodes to that of other animal species.

Most animal species have some sort of memory of their episodic experience in the world; they have some sort of awareness of their specific actions in the world, and therefore some sort of consciousness. But their awareness of their past episodes of experience is not nearly the same as the human memory of episode experience.

In fact, it was once hypothesized, wrongly, that even the most intelligent animals did not have an episodic memory system, i.e., the memory of details of specific past experiences. It was believed that the animal memory system was based on prototypes or generic extrapolations from their past experience, a process that extracts the

© Springer International Publishing AG, part of Springer Nature 2018
C. Cole, *The Consciousness' Drive*, https://doi.org/10.1007/978-3-319-92457-1_4

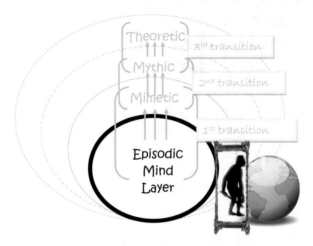

Fig. 4.1 The Episodic Mind and how it frames human intersection with the world

specificity or individuality from these past experiences. This old hypothesis made the animal memory system more like our human procedural memory system—a template for procedures (finding food, building shelters, fighting off enemies, etc.) available to the animal, providing it with basic survival skills.

The new hypothesis about animals is that intelligent animal species have a type of memory for their specific experiences, labeled by Gerald Edelman (1989) in his book *The Remembered Present: A Biological Theory of Consciousness*, the "remembered present."

Even our nearest cousin species, the Neanderthals, had only this limited "remembered present" kind of memory of their specific intersection with the world in past episodes (Lewis-Williams 2002, p. 189). We delve deeper into "remembered present" later in this chapter. For now, suffice to say that the "remembered present" aspect of animal memory of their past experiences is the fundamental feature of primary consciousness.

But humans also have a secondary or higher-order consciousness that is, to a great extent, dependent on the exceptional way humans remember their experiences compared to how animals remember their experiences. What is this essential feature of human episodic memory that distinguishes our secondary consciousness from the more limited memory of episodes that defines the primary consciousness of animals?

To answer this question, this chapter focuses on comparing our memory of experienced episodes to one of the most intelligent species on earth, the scrub jay, shown in Fig. 4.2. The scrub jay is a member of the corvid family (crows, ravens, and jays), mentioned in Chap. 2 as being one of the tiny minority of intelligent animal species that pass the mirror test.

Recent intelligent-animal research has caused us to reevaluate this human versus animal memory of their past experiences. It is now felt species' memory of past episode experience is a continuum, from the less intelligent animals to modern humans, with intelligent animals being in-between. But this in-betweenness has

Fig. 4.2 The western scrub jay (© 2009 Ingrid Taylar. Creative Commons Attribution 2.0 Generic license)

led to very rich discussion about what then is exceptional about human episodic memory and therefore about human secondary consciousness.

Episodic Memory

The episode is the frame through which the ongoing world around us gets inside us. It provides us with an information channel for experiencing the world, and it provides some sort of structure so that we can remember it. Animals must have a bit of this memory system as well, which allows them to learn from their experience. But what is the difference? What makes the human episodic memory system exceptional? In a series of fascinating experiments, researchers have been able to answer some basic questions about what constitutes the exceptionality of human episodic memory. They have done this by observing how the very intelligent scrub jays remember where they have cached or hidden their food for later consumption.

To begin this interspecies comparison, we must first separate out episodic memory from procedural memory. Procedural memory is a much more basic/archaic memory system than episodic memory. We humans and all other animals have procedural memory, which is a skill memory, controlling automatic as opposed to decision-based actions. Animals know how to catch fish because of procedural memory; humans can catch a ball because of procedural memory. We don't remember specific past experiences when we catch a ball. Procedural memory forms the automatic algorithm of how to do these skills. This is very different from the voluntary access episodic memory system, which is the subject of this chapter.

We separate out the human memory systems in Fig. 4.3, a diagram we return to again later in the book. Figure 4.3 places human episodic memory at the top of the memory system hierarchy, which in this book we see as the essence of our exceptional consciousness. The semantic memory system, our knowledge of facts, is also part of our voluntary memory system which we mix into our thinking before we act or react to event stimuli from the outside world. As we shall see, intelligent animals also have this semantic memory layer. Procedural memory is at the bottom of the memory hierarchy and is present in both animals and humans. But the secondary or higher consciousness that only humans have resides in our episodic memory.

Let's focus in on the features of episodic memory. Human episodic memory is the "memory for specific episodes in life, that is, events with a specific time-space locus" (Donald 1991, p. 150). In other words, episodic memory has something to do with a time-bound event or incident we experienced either ourselves or observed others doing in a specific space. The memory of the episode anchors us in unique experience, providing the spot in time and space where each human uniquely and individually intersects with the world. To illustrate an experienced episode, and the importance of our framing of this experience in episodic memory, we utilize an evocative image of an Upper Paleolithic human hunting a bison just as an eclipse occurs, shown in Fig. 4.4. We will use this eclipse episode throughout Part I to describe how humans think. An eclipse episode is evocative because our framing of such an experience, our consciousness of it, is very, very different from any other species.

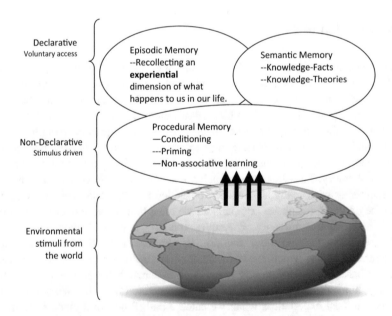

Fig. 4.3 The layers and components of the human memory system that constitute our thinking and consciousness (after Suddendorf and Corballis 2007, p. 301; Squire 1992)

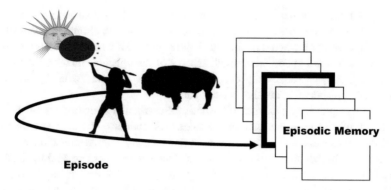

Fig. 4.4 A human hunting a bison during an eclipse and then framing the episode in episodic memory

As Donald (1991, p. 151) says, all animals have a "degree of conscious awareness." We can sense, we can even observe this consciousness in our cats and dogs. And all species have the episode as the basic unit of their memory. But humans do episode-framing differently.

The episode experiences of modern humans are more deeply entrenched in our episodic memory system than episodes experienced by animals are in their memory systems. We frame what we are experiencing/observing better, more deeply, more specifically than any other species. In the Paleolithic episode experience in Fig. 4.4, even if they don't know what it is, humans remember their specific experience of the moon blocking out the sun during an eclipse. This specificity provides a lead-off-point frame for our subsequent observations, allowing us to "maintain attention" to the part of the world we are observing at a given moment, cutting out from the frame, as Vermeer did in painting *The Little Street* in the previous chapter, "non-relevant stimuli" (Wynn and Coolidge 2004, pp. 469–470).

The Scrub Jay Experiments

The working hypothesis for the scrub jay experiments was that the major difference between animals' memory of an experienced episode and modern humans' episodic memory is that animals do not store the memory of the specific aspects of the experienced episode. In effect, they store what happened to them stripped of its specificity, as generic episodes, somewhat like our human procedural memory. In Edelman's (1989) terms, animal episode memory is like a "present memory," without the time-based specificity of a "past memory" that we store in our human episodic memory system.

In the scrub jay experiments, the starting premise for the animal's memory of an experienced episode would have to incorporate what they did, e.g., they buried food, and where they buried their food. Or what type of food they caught and where, e.g., catching salmon in a nearby river where rocks caused the fish to come near the surface. The starting premise did not incorporate the situational aspects of the episode that center on when it happened. This is because it was thought until recently that animals "do not encode temporal" aspects of the episodes they experience (de Kort et al. 2005, p. 160). They encode only the "what" and "where" part of the experienced episode, but not the "when" part.

It was hypothesized that the full what-where-when framework establishes the specificity of the episodic memory structure of modern humans and therefore constitutes some essential difference between primary animal consciousness and secondary or higher human consciousness. Once researchers operationalized the exceptionality of human episodic memory around the "when" it happened, they could devise experiments to test a working hypothesis of the difference between how animals remember episodes based on a "what-where" representation framework versus how humans remember episodes based on a "what-where-when" framework.

To test this hypothesis, researchers took an intelligent animal species, the scrub jay—a type of corvid that passed the mirror test described in Chap. 2. If it were shown that the scrub jay did in fact encode temporal aspects of their experienced episodes—the when—then that would certainly bring the hypothesis they were testing into doubt.

The scrub jay experiments were carried out and reported in Clayton and Dickinson (1998) and Clayton et al. (2003). Their study findings established that scrub jays cache (hide) their food and encode in memory these episodes of caching according to **what** type of food (worm or berry), **where** it was cached, and **when** it was cached. The findings show that the scrub jay not only remembers when it cached the food to avoid food deterioration of the tasty worm, it is able to mix semantic knowledge about food deterioration rates and temperature variance with the when of the episode of caching, so it can recover the cache of worms before it rots. The scrub jays could even see through the researchers' attempts at tricking them. This is a very intelligent bird!

But does the fact that it remembers the "when" during cache-recovery bring into question the exceptionality of human episodic memory compared to intelligent animals?

The Answer

The answer to whether and how human episodic memory is different from intelligent animal species like the scrub jays is summarized in Fig. 4.5. It is a complex answer, involving several different theories.

To start with, there is a continuum of the richness of how experience is coded in the memory of the experience, from (a) the "less intelligent" animals whose memory of their experience does not contain the "when" of the "what-where-when" criterion, to (b) the "intelligent animals" like the scrub jays in the middle of the continuum

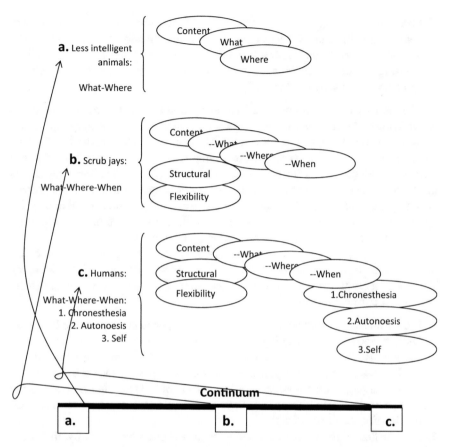

Fig. 4.5 The episode memory continuum between (**a**) less intelligent animals with a generic memory of episodes limited to the "what-where" of food location; (**b**) the so-called intelligent animals like scrub jays with an episodic-like memory that does not contain the individualizing aspects of the "when" present in (**c**) human episodic memory that contains the full "what-where-when" content criterion, with the individualizing aspects of the "when" in (1) Chronesthesia, (2) Autonoesis, and (3) Self

whose memory does contain the "what-where-when" content criterion, and, finally, to (c) the full human episodic memory at the far-right end of the continuum.

We then grade the memory system of (a) less intelligent animals, (b) intelligent animals, and (c) the human episodic memory in terms of the three criteria of human episodic memory of Clayton et al. (2003) (see also, de Kort et al. 2005):

- Content criterion: defined as memory capturing the what-where-when of the experienced episode
- Structural criterion: defined as the content components of the episode event being integrated into a distinct and unique memory for the episode

- Flexibility criterion: defined as the memory of the episode being connected to or embedded in the animal's declarative or semantic memory structure so that new or updated factual and conceptual information, like temperature fluctuations affecting the decay rates for the scrub jays' cached food, can be retroactively applied to previously cached food

The memory system of less intelligent animals does not meet the structural and flexibility criteria, and their memory system only has generic memory representations of experienced episodes containing information on the "what-where" of the what-where-when content criterion, for example, the location (the "where") of a source of food (the "what") (see also, Donald 1991, p. 149). The scrub jay experiments found that intelligent animals have a memory system with all three criteria, including the "when" of the "what-where-when" content criterion. While at the opposite end of the continuum, modern humans have a very rich memory representation of their experienced episodes, meeting all three criteria.

We now bring in a complementary theory of Endel Tulving based on his studies of the amnesiac K.C., who had no episodic memory (Tulving 1972, 2002a, b). Tulving's theory further specifies the "when" part of the what-where-when content criterion of episodic memory:

1. Chronesthesia: "The awareness that the event happened in the past" (de Kort et al. 2005, p. 160; see also, Tulving 1972, 2002a).
2. Autonoesis: The feeling of reexperiencing an episode from one's past during recall of the episode memory, that this memory of a past episode is different both from dreaming or from observing reality in front of us at the moment [such as the "remembered present" stripped of their specificity as most other species remember the past (Edelman 1989)]
3. Self: Realizing that the memory being recalled is one's own memory, that it is a creation of oneself, separate in existence from the rest of the world

Aspect 1 is diminished by the scrub jay experiments because it duplicates the "when" aspect of the what-where-when content criterion. We will return to the nature of the difference in the next chapter. Aspects 2 and 3 are impossible to ascertain in intelligent animals, even for the scrub jays. We assume, as shown in Fig. 4.5, that Aspects 1, 2, and 3 are not fully present in the "when" of the scrub jays' episodic-like memory.

With this assumption, Aspects 1, 2, and 3 therefore become the defining aspects of human episodic memory, and the central feature of the qualitative difference separating human secondary consciousness from the primary consciousness of all other species, even the intelligent animals such as the scrub jays.

But there is something else to say about Aspect 1, namely, the effect of the exceptionality of Aspects 2 and 3 on Aspect 1 and the consequent depth of the human species' emotional connection to their past experience. Because it is so complex, we investigate this on its own in the next chapter.

Chapter 5
Episodic Memory: Subjective Time-Travel

In this chapter, we continue our investigation of how humans exceptionally frame and remember their experiences in the world. Our mind seems to be rooted in episodes of experience. Think about what you think about when your mind is at rest. It is these episode experiences recalled from memory. When there is a matter at hand to attend to, we can focus our mind away from these episode flashes, but once it is over, the matter at hand becomes another one of the episode experiences that flash through our mind; if it is an important event, perhaps for the rest of our lives. These past episodes act as our "on" button, keeping open our channel to the world and experience. The Episodic Mind layer of human consciousness, our experiencing of the world and our memory of it, and how we utilize these memories, constitutes the communication channel between the outside world and what is inside us (Fig. 5.1).

What is this first contact layer of consciousness that channels the outside world into us? How does it work? These are questions we cannot directly answer. We can indirectly identify aspects or criteria of how we represent the outside world inside us by examining what humans remember about their experience in the world, then comparing it to something else.

In Chap. 4, we began comparing how humans remember and use their episodes of experience to the way other animal species do it. Many animal species hide (cache) their food and then cache-recover it later for eating. But there is a lack of depth in their remembering. They know "what" they hid and "where" they hid the food, but it was assumed the memory is stripped of the specific content of the unique experience—the "when" of the experience episode as researchers label it. The intelligent scrub jays proved this assumption wrong, causing researchers to upgrade their evaluation of the scrub jays' episode memory to "episodic-like" (Suddendorf and Corballis 2007, p. 302).

In a separate series of experiments, Endel Tulving (1972, 2002a, b) was able to derive the nature of the memories the amnesiac K.C. lacked to further particularize the "when" content criterion of episodic memory into three aspects:

© Springer International Publishing AG, part of Springer Nature 2018
C. Cole, *The Consciousness' Drive*, https://doi.org/10.1007/978-3-319-92457-1_5

Fig. 5.1 The Episodic
Mind and the time-travel
aspect of episodic memory

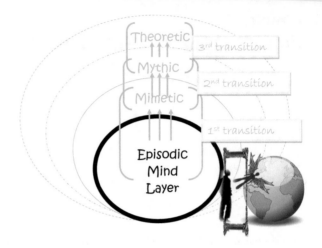

1. The Chronesthesia Aspect: the awareness of the "when"—that the memory
   episode happened in the past
2. The Autonoesis Aspect: the "feeling" we are reexperiencing the past when we
   recall the memory of it
3. The Self Aspect: the awareness that the reexperienced episode is uniquely one's
   own memory

We are a strange species compared to the others on the planet. A group of eight or
so other species are markedly intelligent, and we can see glimmers of our own
consciousness in them, but they are not nearly like us. Here, in these three aspects of
human episodic memory of Endel Tulving's theory, we have the beginnings of a
very real attempt to define the exceptionality of human consciousness.

Tulving's Time-Traveling (Fig. 5.1)

Tulving was well aware of the scrub jay experiments, so he knew the finding that the
scrub jays met the "when" part of the what-where-when content criterion, the key
criterion of human episodic memory. As a result, he shifted his theory's focus away
from the "when" Aspect 1, Chronesthesia, focusing the theory instead on Aspects
2 and 3 (Suddendorf and Corballis 2007). But the extreme nature of Aspects 2 and
3 unhinge human episodic memory from the normal constraints of time and place.
We first expand Aspects 2 and 3 to show their extremeness.

Aspect 2, Autonoetic consciousness, is the awareness by the human doing the
remembering that the memory is separate and different from her so-called online
perception and thinking at the moment, in real time, she is experiencing the world.
This is because the memory of the episode must be reconstructed when it is recalled
from memory, based on the particularities of the episode, including its

- Characters (human and animal)
- Actions (participated in or observed)
- Setting
- Emotional reactions aroused during the episode (Suddendorf and Corballis 2007, p. 301)

As a result of the reconstructing process, the individual feels as if she is reexperiencing the recalled episode while being aware that it is in her mind.

Aspect 3, Self, is the sense that the recalled episode memory is one's own memory, proprietary to oneself. In the same way we have a sense of self that we know is ours, like our arms and our legs are ours (Taylor 1989), we have a sense that the memory of our own experience is a possession of the individual herself and no one else. This sense of proprietorship over the memory of the episode of experience gives the individual the right to engage in the act of self-recognition by objectifying the experience episode (Malafouris 2009, p. 99), through mimicking it mentally to oneself and to others (see next chapter), and in writing and language and other externalizations of the memory.

It is important to emphasize that when a human recalls an episode from her episodic memory, the individual reconstructs the episode memory from its constituent parts. The reconstructing process of Aspect 2 causes the reexperiencing of the episode. Because the individual is doing the mental reconstruction of the episode, the individual uniquely owns the episode, and asserts this ownership in the act of recognizing herself in the episode, which she does by objectifying the episode (Aspect 3). The individual has control over the memory of the episode and, by extension, over the part of the world from which the episode came.

This is an extreme picture of human consciousness that we cannot imagine other animal species coming close to. It is qualitatively different, and is a conceptualization of the nature of human exceptionality as a species. But we will leave these implications to the Conclusion of the book. Here, we return to the particularity of our episodic memory system: time-travel.

It is Tulving's contention that as a result of the makeup of how we store a memory of an experience in our episodic memory, and the extreme strength of our episode memory compared to all other species due to Aspects 2 and 3, humans' memory of the "when" of reexperiencing past experiences (Aspect 1) is unhinged. We mentally or subjectively time-travel. The basis of our consciousness is this time-traveling. Using again the previous chapter's depiction of a prehistoric human's episodic memory of hunting a bison during an eclipse, we diagram Aspects 2 and 3 time-travel effect on Aspect 1 in Fig. 5.2.

What seems on the surface very odd, we hope at the end of this chapter will seem perfectly logical and commonsensical.

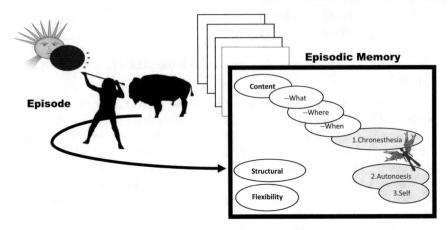

Fig. 5.2 The structure of an episode of a bison hunter during an eclipse as it is represented in the hunter's episodic memory, enabling mental time-traveling

Time-Travel: Heightened Awareness of Our Experience of the World

It is difficult to convey the time-travel aspect of human episodic memory. But it is at the heart of human consciousness and the unique, exceptional way humans relate to the world. We are animals like all the other animal species, so our consciousness is not totally different from these other species, especially the intelligent species like the scrub jays. But we are unhinged from the flow of the world, in terms of time and place, but especially in terms of our consciousness.

We reiterate that human episodic memory is "not about regularities" of our experienced episodes; regularities could be written into algorithms as procedures or as laws of phenomena that are stored in our semantic memory system. Rather, episodic memory is about "the particularities" of specific episodes we have experienced (Suddendorf and Corballis 2007, p. 301). Animals' episodic-like memory is more toward the procedural memory, rote or automatic spectrum of the memory system, i.e., with memory of the generalities and not the specific particularities of the specific episode being remembered.

Even for the scrub jays, there is less reconstructing of their episodes perhaps because there is less experiencing of the richness of the particularities of the original experience when it first occurred. Why is this so, according to Tulving's theory? We return to Aspect 2 and 3 of Tulving's time-travel theory. In Aspect 2, there is more richness to the memory of the episode, thus more of an experience of actually being there in the past episode when remembering it. And in Aspect 3, perhaps because of the skill in remembering the experience of the episode, we feel more ownership of our interaction with the world, that the interface channel, the memories in our episodic memory system, are ours alone—that we recognize our unique self in objectifying the memories. We in fact strengthen the memory in this objectification, for which we need information, and insatiable amount of new information out in the world.

This is an explosive mixture intersecting with the world, isn't it?

Humans pay better attention to what is happening in their experience in the world, perhaps because we can better understand, due to our episodic memory, what is happening. We are not only seeing what we are experiencing, we are categorizing it, so we are seeing-it-as-understanding it. This allows us to have a unique power to establish and concentrate on only what we consider relevant, ignoring what is irrelevant. We are discerning in what we see; we don't just accept everything the world throws at us as equally important. We take ownership in selecting what is important or relevant to us because it is motivated by the self-recognition aspect of our episodic memory.

This uniquely human process of paying attention to and taking ownership of the episode better than any other species "objectifies" or freezes the particularities of the episode in a frame that we can then take out of the world, making it our own, and then storing it in memory as if it were a movie or a painting. But again, it is a movie or painting that we control because we reconstruct the episode during recall of the memory.

Future Time-Travel

Aspects 2 and 3 of the "when" part of the what-where-when criterion of episodic memory emphasize the reconstruction of the past episode from its particularities as we recall it from episodic memory. We have focused on the "objectness" of our uniquely possessing the memory episode, and that we objectify the memory in the act of self-recognition. As a result, we have a ravenous, self-feeding need for new information in the outside world—but of a specific kind. Because it is our object, this self-recognition process, we think we know exactly what new information we need. We take the frame of our previous experience from its place in episodic memory, and use it to direct our information search activities, for the specific information we think we need.

The reconstruction of the episode when we recall it (Aspect 2), and our belief in our right of ownership of the memory episode, allows us to envisage deliberately changing the episode's particularities, and to envisage different scenarios—what ifs. We go back to the memory of the episode and imagine different scenarios. The deliberate changing of these past episodes creates the flexibility, by giving the individual licence, to anticipate and rehearse future events when we recall the episode from memory. This anticipation and simulation of future events— prospection—has been labeled **"constructive episodic simulation"** (Coolidge and Wynn 2009, pp. 44, 218, 222). Schacter and Addis (2007, p. 778), who originally came up with the concept, refer to this as the "constructive episodic simulation hypothesis."

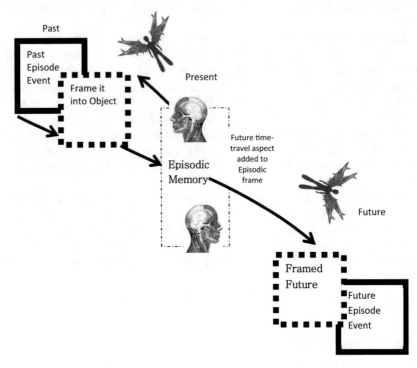

Fig. 5.3 Via episodes of experience stored in and recalled at will from episodic memory, humans are constantly time-traveling back to the past and forward to the future

The constructive episodic simulation hypothesis holds that humans rehearse the future by preexperiencing future events based on constructed and reconstructed versions, not exact replicas, of past episodes from the person's experience and memory of the same or similar episodes. There is indication that the recombinant of components of the past episode in constructing a simulation of a future episode creates a memory of the mental simulation that itself is encoded in memory for later use (Schacter et al. 2017). That the past episode utilized to create the rehearsal for a future episode is constructed rather than played back like a film, gives constructive episodic simulation the flexibility required to simulate the future in the present, which is what is meant by future time-travel.

In Fig. 5.3, we diagram this framed future due to subjective time-travel. There is no doubt that even though time-travel to the past is the first step to accessing and activating the Chronesthesia, Autonoesis, and Self aspects of the "when" part of the what-where-when criterion of human episodic memory, the really "useful" (in the sense of putting food on the table) exceptionality of humans is our ability to time-travel to the future by creating an anticipatory frame. We do this by anticipating a future event, recalling an experienced episode from episodic memory that we believe is similar to the future episode, then utilizing the recalled frame as a sort of planning document.

A prototypical example is the job interview. We all rehearse things like a future job interview by recalling an old job interview episode from episodic memory, and using it as a sort of framing device in the upcoming interview. Let's say that in the already experienced past interview episode the interviewer reacted negatively to one of our answers, but through the simulation of this future interview we dramatically change our old answer and receive a positive reaction from the interviewer. Waves of happy emotion come over us, a totally anticipated and mentally manufactured feeling.

The mental re-simulation of past episodes and the pre-simulation of future episodes—our ability to do so, given to us by our exceptional consciousness—may in fact be the basis of our human concept of time. We do not know this, but our consciousness believes that the past and the future are on the same dimension; it believes that the past and future is a continuum (Suddendorf and Corballis 2007). Evidence from neurological research that similar parts of the human brain are utilized for both retrieving past experiences and simulating future events supports this "same dimension" hypothesis (Schacter and Addis 2007). We so easily time-travel along this continuum, it is more than a learned technique—it is ingrained; which, of course, invites time-traveling even beyond our own life, back through our species' history and forward to our science fiction future after our death.

Let us put forth a preliminary definition of consciousness we have so far, which we will add to in subsequent chapters:

> Human consciousness is a product of our constant mental and subjective time-traveling back to the past and forward to the future as we think about our experiences in the world. This time-travel establishes and reinforces who we are as separate actors in the world, who are different from the ongoing world. By time-traveling we take ownership of our experiences in this world in a continuous act of self-recognition. And we have an incessant information need for new information.

With this temporary definition, I have probably left you with more questions than answers about human consciousness and the topic of this book: the role of information need in how we become aware of and define our separate, individual, and specific place in the world. But I won't leave you floating uncomfortably in this sea of doubt. Over the next several chapters, we further develop a theory that puts mental time-travel in a much larger framework: the framework of our evolution as a species, specifically the evolution of the human brain. This theory will allow us to delve further into the heart of the matter of consciousness and the role of information need and information search in developing this consciousness.

Chapter 6
Episodic-to-Mimetic Transition

At a certain point in human evolutionary development, our Homo erectus prehuman ancestors transitioned from an episode-based consciousness, described in the last two chapters on Episode Mind, to a mimetic-based consciousness that Donald calls the Mimetic Mind (Fig. 6.1). With its new way of thinking about the world and our place in it, the Mimetic Mind produced a radically different culture or society with a heightened emphasis on communication within the group. The transition took a slow, evolutionary pace, beginning roughly 1.8 million years ago and ending, 40,000–60,000 years ago with the emergence of cognitively modern humans. At its fully developed form at the end of the transition, the Mimetic Mind had changed human culture, the way humans organized their living, creating large and complex social groups with "collectively invented and maintained customs, games, skills, and representations ... cultural innovation and new forms of social control" (Donald, 1991, p. 173).

We are less interested in the differences between the Episodic and Mimetic Mind than the evolution of the features the two phases of consciousness had in common. So rather than focusing on the stark changes that occurred in the human society or culture by the end of the Mimetic Mind phase, we focus instead on the development of aspects of human thinking that were there at the beginning, that were already present in the Episodic Mind phase.

We portrayed the Episodic Mind as the first contact layer with the outside world, how we intersect with the world in episodes of experience. The Episodic Mind is the experience layer of human consciousness, the interface channel transferring what is outside us in the world to what is inside us. These experiences are ours alone; we gain self-recognition in thinking about them and objectifying them. The heart of the Mimetic Mind phase is the continued development of this repetitious mimicking to ourselves of our episodes of experiences in a continuous exercise of self-recognition. It is only natural that this self-recognition would eventually extend to mimicking our episode experiences to others in the group, at an ever faster, more sophisticated pace.

© Springer International Publishing AG, part of Springer Nature 2018
C. Cole, *The Consciousness' Drive*, https://doi.org/10.1007/978-3-319-92457-1_6

Fig. 6.1 Donald's (1991)
4-phase, 3-transition theory
of the evolution of the
human mind: 1st transition:
Episodic to Mimetic Mind

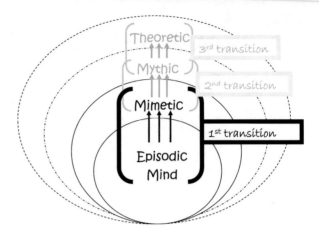

There are two important points of Donald's theory we wish to emphasize:

1. The seed of the transition to the Mimetic Mind was already contained in and transforming the Episodic Mind.
2. The Episodic Mind phase remained as a vestige first-contact layer of human consciousness after the transition to the Mimetic Mind.

It is the intention behind the evolutionary transition that changed.

The Intention Underlying the Episodic to Mimetic Mind Transition

What is the advantage to our species of mentally mimicking and thus reexperiencing our previously experienced episodes? What was the original intention behind mimicking that set off the evolutionary trajectory of human consciousness?

To begin with, the mental mimicking of an episode is different from the experiencing of it, which in turn is different from the facts of the experience as seen and recorded by an all-seeing objective observer. We know this from our courts of law where witnesses are notoriously wrong when it comes to identifying suspects and the order of events that made up the crime episode they happened to have witnessed. In the courts, we must rely on collaborative evidence to back up or "fact-check" what the witness thought he experienced.

The witness experiences the episode and then mimics it when he is in court before the judge. The mimicking changes the original episode of experience.

We can change the outcome in the future by mentally rehearsing and changing features of the past behavior that went wrong in the frame, then utilizing the frame as a plan of action. We devote much of Part II of this book to this future time-traveling. But future time-traveling is surely an unforeseen consequence. Why did our prehistoric ancestors originally mimic or reenact past episodes? What was their overwhelming original intention?

The most logical original intention must have been to understand our experience, or what we observed, in our experiencing of the world around us. There is something in our encoding of our experience that raises questions in our mind causing us to return to the episode, mentally, to mimic or reenact it. We actually don't really know how we experience life in the moment; we believe such and such happened, but we aren't sure; which means mimicking or reenacting it to ourselves has the aim of trying to understand it.

"What just happened?" we are asking ourselves implicitly when we mentally mimic what just happened.

This question, so seemingly simple, does not appear to be a question any other species asks. And surely the answer has to come from somewhere in our memory system requiring us to forge links to these other memory systems, to other episodes we have experienced, for example.

Mimicking an experienced episode to ourselves is inevitably a manipulation of our real-time experiencing of the episode because it brings in this other information from other parts of our memory system. And more importantly for this book, the striving to understand what just happened causes us to seek out further information in the world where the experience happened.

New information, be it from other parts of our memory system or sought for and found in the outside world, changes the original experienced episode. Perhaps this change is a reason why we mimic or reenact it. And in fact, an episode we spend a lot of time thinking about, by mimicking it over and over again, often does change its focal point, and to achieve this change in understanding, may be the reason why we spend so much time on it:

– to get a different view, perspective, or focal point.

We assume, therefore, that the understanding gained by mimicking an experienced episode over and over again, and changing the focal point of the experience, is the essence of backward time-traveling to reexperience an episode.

More Lessons from Vermeer

Did Vermeer paint *The Little Street*, the laneway at the back of his father's tavern The Mechelen, to gain a different focal point of understanding of an episode he had previously experienced, perhaps in childhood?

The Little Street represents an episode in the artist's experience, but there is a restriction on the artist's mimicking it on canvas: He must paint what is there in front of him. Why else paint these particular buildings, these particular people? For this reason, by definition, streetscape paintings are the most literal of painting genres. Among other reasons for this literalness, we the viewer can go back to the place the artist painted and fact-check to see if the painting accurately depicts the scene. This would be particularly so for the contemporaneous patron of Vermeer's who commissioned it, or if it was not commissioned, for the person who eventually bought the painting.

But in painting *The Little Street*, Vermeer dropped the canal behind his father's tavern out of the frame. Was this usual for him to change elements in the episode he was actually mimicking in his paintings? Vermeer painted only three streetscape-type paintings of *The Little Street* ilk. One is lost to us and the third is a *View of Delft*. In the *View of Delft*, we know from contemporaneous sources that Vermeer changed the episode he saw across the harbor by changing the buildings that were actually there at the time. The important buildings were there, but not all of the minor ones. There is a manipulation in the mimicking of the experienced episode to gain a different focal point of the artist's understanding of what he had experienced.

Most of Vermeer's paintings are setups of episodes from everyday life, painted in a room, most probably a room in the house where he lived. In fact, these episodes were created or staged with models and props. Vermeer, who is probably one of the most figurative artists the world has ever produced, added and subtracted details from these carefully staged everyday-experience episodes so that he could achieve the effect he desired. Genre paintings like his were common in Dutch painting at the time: to tell a story with the intention that it would affect the viewer so that she would buy it. This is not a peculiarity of Vermeer. He is, however, an interesting case for our purposes because he was so literal, obsessively so, but the literalness was a manipulation of the actual experience of the episode for the desired effect of trying to understand the episode of experience he was painting. Among his more typical, staged paintings is *The Woman in Blue Reading a Letter*, shown in Fig. 6.2. Let us contemplate this painting for a brief moment.

First of all, Vermeer painted many paintings of women reading letters. In those days, a letter had tremendous import. It announced good news and bad news. So we can only imagine what the letter contained in this particular episode of a woman in a blue jacket caught by the observer standing in front of what looks to be a large wall map. It could be from an episode stored in Vermeer's memory—his mother, perhaps. The woman is about to stop reading because she realizes he (the boy-Vermeer?) was there at the door observing her. We know Vermeer took a long time to paint each painting, possibly as long as a year, and that he actually staged these paintings with models. The model here is perhaps his wife. But the genesis of the idea of these paintings is probably from an episode he really experienced in life. That's why it has such power. But where does this power come from?

Let us assume the episode in Fig. 6.2 was motivated by some episode from memory. Vermeer painted other letter readers. Perhaps Vermeer had many such episode experiences stored in memory, from when he was a little boy, catching his mother reading a letter next to the window. They didn't have good artificial light in those days. Something had struck him about the scene; he had always remembered it for some reason, especially the way the rain-soaked light illuminated the wall behind her and the sheen of the silk in her blue jacket as she read the letter. The letter contained news, but what news? He didn't know; he was only a child and children are told nothing of the world of adults. But Vermeer tried to answer this question the rest of his life. And this search for understanding is the strength of the mimicked

Fig. 6.2 Vermeer's *Woman in Blue Reading a Letter*, c. 1663–1664. Rijkmuseum, Amsterdam. (© circa 1662–1663 (1647–1675) Unknown (Photographer). Creative Commons license. (CC0 1.0))

episode. We don't know this; we are only guessing. The irony here is that because there is so little known about his life, we are dependent on investigating the originating episode of this and Vermeer's other paintings by the artist's mimicked representation of the episode. We are left to understand it by ourselves, from our own memories.

We will return to these emotional substrata of our experienced episodes, and how they are mimicked and communicated to oneself and to others, later in this book. For now, let us go back in time to our 32,000-year-old human ancestors who also left artifacts that mimicked their experienced life episodes. The difference in these mimicked representations of experienced episodes will give us insight into the Mimetic Mind layer of human consciousness.

Mimicking in the Cave

In Chap. 3, we briefly examined one of the most famous cave paintings left to us by our Paleolithic ancestors, which depicted an episode of lions chasing a herd of bison. Like Vermeer, the artist or artists who painted this cave painting changed, even manipulated the episode they themselves had experienced.

Fig. 6.3 A partial view of an episode of the hunt painted on Chauvet Cave 32,000 years ago. (© 2016 Claude Valette. Creative Commons Attribution-Share Alike 4.0 International license)

We have cropped this famous cave painting in Fig. 6.3 to highlight this manipulated aspect of the real-life episode in its mimicked reproduction on the cave wall.

It is hypothesized (because we cannot know the original artist's real intention) that the cave artist was not painting ten or however many lions there are in this particular cave painting—it is difficult to count them for there is such a flurry of heads, some of them incomplete! Rather, he or she wished to depict the rapid motion forward of one or two lions by painting many lions-heads close together, almost unnaturally close together. A herd of lions may walk this close together, but in the running phase of hunting prey they separate out and attack the target animal from different angles. If this was really the cave artist's intention to paint his experience of observing one or two lions' movement over time, he or she is mimicking a feeling of the lions' speed as they chased the bison down, not the actual episode experience itself. To do this repositioning for the mimicking of the intended speed-effect, the artist manipulated the experienced event inside her consciousness, adding information to the episode from other memories and other memory systems.

The mimicked representation of an episode from the artist's life is different from the artist's factual knowledge about the position of lions when they are engaged in the hunt. The mimetic frame, therefore, involves the artist's intention to go beyond a surface representation of the world, to get at a deeper understanding of reality.

This understanding intention is the seed in the Episodic Mind phase of our consciousness' evolution, driving the evolutionary transition of the human mind to the Mimetic Mind phase, and then through the Mimetic Mind phase to the next transition.

Let us break this **understanding intention** down in terms of an evolutionary line trajectory driving the transition:

- From the end of the Episodic Mind and the beginning of the Mimetic Mind
- To the end of the Mimetic Mind phase of human consciousness when it reached its fully developed form—complex social groups with "collectively invented and maintained customs, games, skills, and representations ... cultural innovation and new forms of social control" (Donald, 1991, p. 173)

We will now examine this trajectory more carefully, beginning with our base-diagram of a prehistoric bison hunter about to spear a bison when an eclipse occurs.

The Transition to the Mimetic Mind: Intention Trajectory

Starting with the bison hunting-during-an-eclipses episode we have already used in Chaps. 4 and 5, we illustrate in three figures (Figs. 6.4, 6.5, and 6.6), the evolutionary trajectory of the transition of human consciousness, from the framing of the experienced episode in the Episodic Mind phase of human brain development to the Mimetic Mind frame at the end of the transition.

In Fig. 6.4, a Homo erectus hunter living 1.8 million years ago, at the end of the Episodic Mind phase of human evolutionary development, is about to kill a bison when an eclipse occurs. This forms an episode of experience for this particular individual that he stores in his episodic memory as a complete unit, perhaps with some sort of tag or label such as: "This is what happened to me yesterday." There would be many other framed units of experience stored in his episodic memory, shown in Fig. 6.4 as a sort of disconnected memory system of experienced episodes filed away in memory storage. Without some sort of linkage system, these episodes

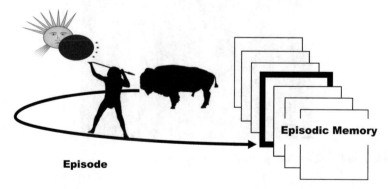

Fig. 6.4 Episodic Mind-basis of the early hominid memory system made up of a series of framed episodes of the hominid's experience with the world

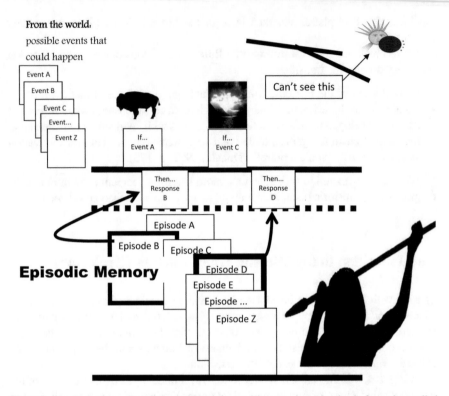

Fig. 6.5 The limitations of an Episodic Mind frame: The experienced episode frame is recalled from episodic memory, but there is no memory of an eclipse so the hunter does not see it

Fig. 6.6 A feeling of foreboding resulting from the eclipse

would operate independently, each on their own. We go into this linkage system in the next chapter. But there is an intermediary phase, serving as a "seed" in the Episodic Mind phase, which causes the transition to the Mimetic Mind phase.

As our hunter ages through life, thousands and thousands of these episode frames would be stored in the hunter's memory, and after a certain age, most of what he met up with in his real-time experience of the world could be matched by a memory episode. We know from our own experience that we react to the world by drawing on our previous experience with what is happening in front of us. The hunter would do the same; he would recall from memory an episode frame of the same phenomenon he had previously experienced.

In its simplest form, a memory built on the unit of the experienced episode and only the experienced episode would be similar to a stimulus–response mechanism, as shown for our bison hunter in Fig. 6.5. This would be somewhat equivalent to the Episodic Mind based on a memory system similar to a less intelligent animal in the "less intelligent animals-scrub jays-modern humans" continuum outlined in Chap. 4. So he would not process the eclipse itself because it had not been written into his response algorithm (his memory of episodes).

The eclipse would be an anomalous experience for the hunter. But let us assume that each episode stored in episodic memory had some flexibility and could cover new episode experiences that were not exactly the same but somewhat similar. How would the hunter then respond to a hunting episode with an eclipse? An eclipse produces a darkened sky, a sudden wind. The bison hunt and the darkened sky may in fact attach themselves to two separate memory episodes, shown in Fig. 6.5. But because it was in the middle of the day and the day was warm with blue skies, he felt and encoded in his episodic memory of the experience a sense of strangeness and foreboding, shown as an up-reaching hand in Fig. 6.6.

What is needed to see and process the eclipse in a Homo erectus hunter who is just transitioning to the Mimetic Mind?

At our current level of development, humans have a semantic memory system that incorporates thinking mechanisms, like "cause and effect," which feed into the recalled episode; the sudden darkness in the middle of the day would incite us to look around for some cause. At a simpler level, if the darkness and the bison episodes were separate experiences, as is the case in Fig. 6.5, he would also need some memory system that would enable linking the two episodes together into a single episode. But these later evolutionary systems and mechanisms indicate a more advanced cognition than existed in the Homo erectus period of human evolution. But we don't need these more sophisticated systems and mechanisms.

The internal, understanding intention "seed" already present in the Episodic Mind phase of human evolutionary development provides a plausible embryonic first pathway for our bison hunter, enabling him and his descendants, many thousands of generations of his descendants because evolution is slow, to see and incorporate anomalies in their experiencing of the world.

Our Episodic Mind layer of consciousness' framing of experience in episodic memory, with its exceptional encoding of the "when" part of the what-where-when criterion of episodic memory, creates a deep sense of separation between ourselves and the world, and a vehicle in the episode memory representation whose structure enables question marks to be attached to the memory experience. So with an eclipse, we ask ourselves: What is the world doing to us? For anomalous or new experiences, the separation our episodic memory gives us incites us to try and understand what happened to us in our experience of the world, even in this early Episodic Mind phase of our cognitive development.

We remember and encode in episodic memory so much of our experience of the episode in our framing of it that our exceptional episodic memory enables us to time-travel back to the episode to examine the experience almost as if it were an object that we can hold up and examine. We mentally mimic the episode, going over and over it, manipulating it so that we can see it from different angles (for new research on this point, see St. Jacques et al. 2017). Part of our obsession with reenacting or mimicking the experienced episode over and over again, is that we encode more of the episode in our episode frame than we are consciously aware of, which leads to questions embedded inside the episode frame, shown in Fig. 6.7. (We return to this issue in much more detail in Part III of this book.)

This is the understanding intention "seed" planted in the Episodic Mind. The seed not only causes the transition to the Mimetic Mind, it is the transitionary drive causing further evolutionary forces to take hold in the Mimetic Mind phase individual at both the individual level and at the level of the group.

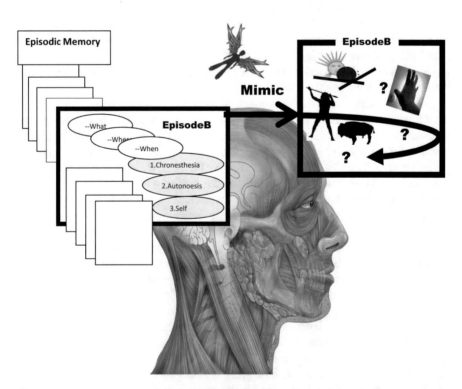

Fig. 6.7 Time-travel to the past, mimicking EpisodeB (bison hunt-eclipse, yesterday), producing question marks for future information need and information search

In Fig. 6.7, the Autonoetic aspect of episodic memory of an experienced episode includes the bison hunter's emotional state as he was experiencing it. The hand grabbing at the blocked sun represents the feeling of foreboding.

Even today, an eclipse evokes feelings of foreboding in us. We are aware of this feeling, and encode it in our memory of it in our own episodic memory. In a way, the foreboding, particularly for the young, is far more a part of the specificity of our intersection with the world during the episode than what is actually happening in the factual sense. We might even not be consciously aware of the fact that the moon is blocking the sun. Instead, we notice the darkening sky it brings, and a sort of heaviness in the air. We can only imagine the effect of such an episode on our prehistoric ancestors. "What was happening that day?" our ancestor asks himself.

To find understanding, the bison hunter is motivated to seek further information in the outside world. As outlined in Fig. 6.8,

1. During the initial experience of the episode, the bison hunter frames the experience and stores it in episodic memory. He does not see or process the eclipse, but there are question marks encoded in the episode in his episodic memory.

    (a) In his mind, he mimics the memory of the initial episode over and over again. Something is not right, he concludes, causing him to seek further information.

2. The hunter returns to the scene of the initial episode and discovers a cliff nearby.

    (a) He looks down from the cliff and sees carcasses of bison at the bottom of the cliff.
    (b) This new information causes him to go back into his memory of the episode, which he mentally mimics again. And he is able to see the episode differently, at a different angle.
    (c) He now remembers hearing the stampeding bison when the darkness occurred. Yes, the bison were stampeding toward the cliff.
    (d) And there was the sound of a flock of birds.

3. In his mimicking of the memory, he mentally sees himself looking up into the sky and, as if seeing it for the first time, he recognizes his own hand reaching up and covering the sun, bringing darkness to the sky.

In this way, through mentally mimicking the experienced episode over and over again, seeking new information, and seeing the episode from new angles, the hunter has time-traveled back to the episode in his own mind and reexperiences the past event. But the motivating intention in mimicking it over and over again, obsessively, was to understand what just happened, so that he can understand it himself.

As the years pass, the bison hunter continues to think about the episode, constantly mentally mimicking it over and over again, shown in Fig. 6.9 as Mimicking 1.

The hunter ages, becomes old. He is made leader of the settlement, perhaps because he is more serious than the others. He is constantly collating all his ideas about what had happened on that day so long ago when he was hunting a bison and his hand covered the sun, darkening the sky, and causing the bison to stampede off

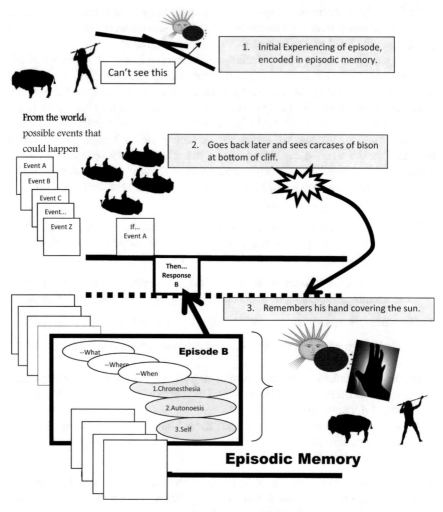

Fig. 6.8 An elaborated vision of episodic memory. (1) The initial experience of the episode encoded in episodic memory. (2) Goes back to scene of episode and sees bison carcasses at base of cliff. (3) Remembers his hand covering sun

the cliff. The hunter now wants to pass on his episode experience to his entire settlement group and he brings the group together for this purpose. It is not a frivolous decision. The hunter has decided the hunting-bison-eclipse episode is important. He picks the day carefully by finding out, over a number of years, the shortest day of the year. He constantly imagined and manipulated the initial episode memory for that future day, positioning his hand in front of the sun at different angles, trying to maximize the effect.

The hunter mimics out the hunting-bison-eclipse episode in front of the group, shown in Fig. 6.9 as Mimicking 2. The group listens to the old hunter, fine-tuned to

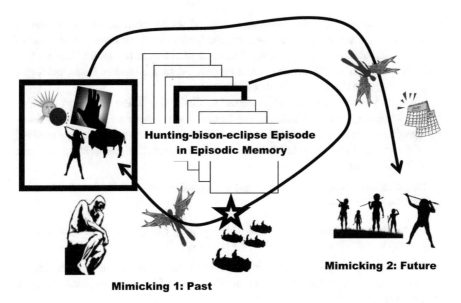

Fig. 6.9 The mimetic frame: The hunter mimics to himself the past experienced episode of the hunting-bison-eclipse in Mimicking 1. Mimicking 1 involves information-seeking behavior, with the hunter going back to the cliff and noticing bison carcasses at the bottom of the cliff. Generations later, the same episode is mimicked in Mimicking 2, with a communicative intention

what the old hunter was communicating by mimicking the act of spearing the bison, then covering the sun with his hand just as the sun went down beyond the mountain. They felt transported, light-headed. They wanted to touch his spear. The hunter could see this reaction. The special day, the shortest day of the year, he would mimic the episode again then, but he rehearsed this future event, just to himself of course, to find out where the best place would be to repeat the ritual, for dramatic effect when he blocked the sun with his hand.

In Mimicking 2, when the same episode is mimicked months, years, and generations later, the unitary intention of understanding the outside world and the hunter's place in it is joined by a second intention: communicating a message for the purposes of group cohesion, adherence to a religion, for social control, or some other intention.

Obviously, our single narrative here of the life of one bison hunter and his memory episode of an eclipse is a metaphor for the evolutionary transition, lasting thousands of generations, from the end of the Episodic Mind phase of human consciousness, to the end of the Mimetic Mind phase when it was in full flight. The seed motivating the transition to this different consciousness was the understanding intention. The internal, subjective time-traveling back to the experienced episode, encoded in the hunter's episodic memory, led to the hunter's internal or mental mimicking of the episode over and over again—the seed that caused, over thousands of generations, the evolutionary transition to Mimetic Mind.

The full-fledged mimicking that characterized the Mimetic Mind phase/layer of human evolutionary development was external mimicking—the communication of the individual of his or her experienced episode to others in the group. There was a different intention in the mimicking, a communication intention based on future time-traveling via the same episode experience.

We would like to emphasize this important distinction in the intentions underlying the mimicking act, one based in the Episodic Mind layer of human consciousness, which we have separately labeled Mimicking 1, and the other a newly evolved intention based in the Mimetic Mind layer of human consciousness, which we have labeled Mimicking 2:

> The Mimicking 1 intention is the individual who experienced the episode searching for an understanding of the episode.

> The Mimicking 2 intention is the person communicating the message of the episode for teaching, influencing others, or for some other objective.

And now, before moving on to the next evolutionary phase of the development of human consciousness, we can update our definition of human consciousness from the previous chapter:

> Human consciousness is a product of our constant subjective time-traveling back to the past and forward to the future as we mimic our experiences stored in episodic memory. We are able to do this by encoding our intersection with the world in our experiences exceptionally well compared to other species because we take ownership of the intersection. The mental time-traveling and the mental mimicking of an experienced episode were originally motivated by the intention of gaining an understanding of the experienced episode, which led to, in the transition to the later stages of the Mimetic Mind, the human wish to mimic the episode to others with either the intention to further others' understanding of the episode, or with the intention of facilitating the influencing of others in the group for the purpose of social cohesion and control of the group. The Episodic Mind and the Mimetic Mind form two different layers in our present-day consciousness, with these two different intentions.

Chapter 7
Framing: The Mimetic-to-Mythic Transition

We have so far talked about the first evolutionary layer of human consciousness, the contact layer with the world in the unit of the episode of experience; and the second layer, where the individual mimics or reexperiences the episode by time-traveling back to the stored representation of the memory in episodic memory. The linking seed is the evolving intention of our prehistoric ancestors, which we hypothesize as being due to the explosive intersection of these ancestors with the world. We have question marks attached to our representation of our intersection experience, which causes us to seek understanding of the world around us and our place in it through a constant time-traveling back to mimic or reexperience the experience via our representation of it in episodic memory.

For the next evolutionary transition, from the Mimetic to Mythic Mind, shown in Fig. 7.1, we need a more powerful time machine, a more powerful intention.

Upgrading Time Machine to Afterlife

We describe a more powerful time machine in this chapter. This more powerful time-machine occurred when humans transitioned from the Mimetic to Mythic Mind, shown in Fig. 7.1. For Donald, this second of three evolutionary transitions of the human brain, which occurred 40,000–60,000 years ago, was the pivotal transition separating us from all other species, specifically our closest cousin species, the Neanderthals.

Humans were directly competing with the Neanderthals 20,000 years ago, in southern Spain, when they went extinct. It was not due to brain size: the Neanderthals, in fact, had bigger brains than humans. And like humans, the Neanderthals lived in groups in a Mimetic-type culture—they communicated with each other, made sophisticated tools for hunting that involved complex mimicking activity. But despite living near humans, even copying them, the Neanderthals failed to make this pivotal transition to the Mythic Mind.

© Springer International Publishing AG, part of Springer Nature 2018
C. Cole, *The Consciousness' Drive*, https://doi.org/10.1007/978-3-319-92457-1_7

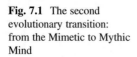

Fig. 7.1 The second
evolutionary transition:
from the Mimetic to Mythic
Mind

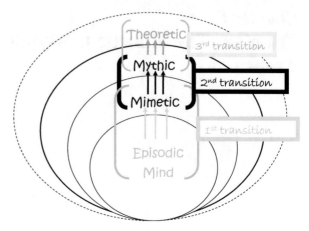

Something had happened that separated the two species in terms of their respective "consciousnesses" (Lewis-Williams 2002, p. 94). While the Mimetic Mind could only describe the human and Neanderthal intersection with the world in a linear fashion, in terms of the episode of their experience, with the Mythic Mind human consciousness evolved to a much broader, more expansive outlook on the world and their place in the world, an outlook that "validated" the human position "in terms of a much wider picture, both in time and space" (McLeish 1996, p. 11).

The transition to the Mythic Mind rendered humans capable of thinking about themselves in terms of "conceptual models of the universe" (Donald 1991, p. 213).

The Greek myths—the Iliad, the Odyssey of Homer, and their transfiguration into the Roman world in Ovid's Metamorphoses—form the foundation of Western Civilization. They are stories constructed on the episode, almost an enlarged episode. Although the myths have gods aplenty interacting, interfering, loving, and controlling mortals, they are not religious stories to us who are alive today. Myths are more open ended than religions. In myths, no one, not even the gods, has answers. As Kenneth McLeish (1996, p. 11) states in his introduction to Peter Grave's *The Greek Myths*, the myths provide a "way" "to think about answers" to questions about "the nature of the universe."

The Mythic Mind

The transition to the Mythic Mind phase of the human brain is based on evidence in the artwork left by humans in various caves spread throughout Europe, created in the Upper Paleolithic period roughly 20,000–41,000 years ago. The transition, of course, started occurring much earlier. In this book, we somewhat arbitrarily place the transition start-point at 60,000 years ago, but we emphasize that the seeds of the transition were there much earlier.

The artists' intention behind the cave paintings is unknown to us, but many researchers, including cognitive anthropologists, are examining the paintings for clues as to the structure of the human brain at the time of painting. One of the oldest paintings, of the stenciled human hands and animals on the cave wall of the El Castillo Cave in northern Spain, shown in Fig. 7.2, dates from 30,000–41,000 years ago. The dates of the various symbols on this wall vary, the oldest being a red dot painted 40,800 years ago. The hand stencils date from around 40,000 years ago; the bison is a later addition. We focus here on the hand stencils, which are considered the oldest cave paintings.

The El Castillo Cave painting illustrates the artist framing a small part of his experience in the world, then storing it in episodic memory; later, he or she came into the cave and mimicked the memory episode on the cave wall. The artist's intention was both to understand the episode, which we labeled the Mimicking 1 intention in the last chapter, and to communicate to and influence others, called the Mimicking 2 intention. We can assume this latter intention here, in the El Castillo Cave, because of how high up on the cave wall the hand stencils were painted. But there is another intention. The cathedral-like aspect of the location of the cave painting indicates something important, grand, and ceremonial. In other words, the place itself, and the positioning of the painted hand stencils high up on the cave wall, in addition to the

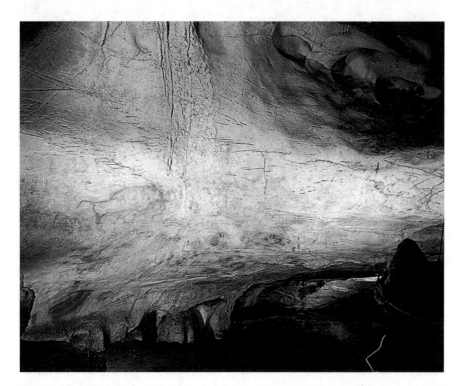

Fig. 7.2 El Castillo Cave in northern Spain, dating from 30,000–41,000 years ago (© 2008 Gabinete de Prensa del Gobierno de Cantabria. Creative Commons Attribution 3.0 Spain license)

understanding and communication intentions, indicate a third, new and different intention of the artist 30,000–40,000 years ago, indicating a new phase of human brain evolution: the Mythic Mind.

The act of painting itself communicates importance, seriousness, because to paint the hand stencils would have been very difficult to do. It would have required the El Castillo Cave artists to construct some sort of scaffolding or ladder apparatus. One is immediately reminded of the famously difficult task of Michelangelo when he painted the Sistine Chapel, shown in Fig. 7.3. Michelangelo, an iconic renaissance man interested in engineering and architecture (the St. Peters dome is one example of his engineering acumen), constructed a special scaffolding for the Sistine Chapel so he could get at the ceiling to paint it—a necessity for a work lasting 4 years (1508–1512 AD).

The similarity of the spatial aspect of the 30,000–40,000-year-old El Castillo Cave painting and Michelangelo's sixteenth-century painting of the Sistine Chapel is interesting for at least two other reasons. The first reason is the height of the two

Fig. 7.3 Michelangelo's Sistine Chapel (1508–1512 AD) (© 2008 Patrick Landy Creative Commons Attribution 3.0 Unported license)

paintings above the floor of the cave and the chapel respectively. Both the Paleolithic cave artist and the Pope who commissioned Michelangelo went to great lengths to place the paintings so that the viewer was forced to look upward. Why? Or maybe the better question is: Toward what?

The second reason is the episodic subject of the Paleolithic cave paintings and Michelangelo's frescos. We have already discussed (in the previous chapter) the episodes of the hunt the cave artists depicted on cave walls of the Chauvet Cave starting 32,000 years ago. The cave artist and Michelangelo are separated by, according to Donald's thesis, an evolutionary phase of human brain development—the cave artist was in the Mythic Mind phase, while Michelangelo was in the Theoretic Mind phase of human brain evolution. Despite this, the two artists' art referred back to the fundamental foundational structure of the human consciousness, the episode—the basic building block upon which all subsequent evolutionary phases are based. We underline this basic point by a more direct view of Michelangelo's Sistine Chapel, shown in Fig. 7.4. Here we see the ceiling alone, and its divisions into episodes of the Old Testament.

If we examine the ceiling's central row of frescos only, there are nine separate frescos. The origins of the universe take up the first three frescos, the origins of man the middle three frescos, and the origin of evil the last three frescos. In the three middle origins-of-man frescos, the episodes depicted are: the creation of Adam, the creation of Eve, and the original sin and the banishment of Adam and Eve from the Garden of Eden. These episodes are taken from Genesis. Indeed, like the frescos of the Sistine Chapel, the message of the Bible is communicated largely through the episode.

Both the Sistine Chapel and the Paleolithic-era El Castillo Cave painting of the stenciled hands, though they are separated by 40,000 years of evolution, are representations of the Mythic Mind layer of human consciousness. There is an evolution within this single transition, however. In the next section, we examine the different intentions we have talked about thus far.

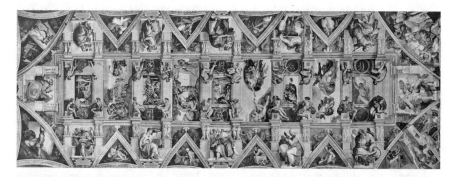

Fig. 7.4 Episodes of the Sistine Chapel (© 2010 Qypchak Creative Commons Attribution-Share Alike 3.0 Unported license)

The Intention of the Mythic Mind

Let us now get into the more difficult aspect of the Mythic Mind, its subject matter and what it says about the underlying intention of the Mythic Mind layer of human consciousness. We list four intentions with examples from different cave paintings.

Many of the episodes the cave artists painted in the Upper Paleolithic Era 15,000–40,000 years ago appear to be based on episodes of animals and hunting. But there are also other types of subjects, some of which appear strange to us. Let's look at the oldest cave art, the stenciled hands of the El Castillo Cave in northern Spain, shown in Fig. 7.2. The approximately 50 stenciled hands evident on this wall and elsewhere in the El Castillo cave could actually be a sort of graffiti, or more precisely, a selfie. There is an "I am here" quality to this painting, reminding us of the mirror test in Chap. 2. What is the artist's intention? We don't know; but let us analyze four of their paintings.

The El Castillo stenciled-hands painting is very different in its intention from Mimicking 1, the understanding intention, or Mimicking 2, the influencing intention of the Mimetic Mind phase of the evolution of human consciousness. The artist(s) who painted the El Castillo hand stencils was exploring his recognition of being separate from the flow of the world; he achieved self-recognition through the objectification of his experience in painting these hand stencils. The self-recognition of the individual artist, that he is separate from the flow of the world, is a fundamental precept of the Episodic Mind layer we talked about in Chap. 2 with the mirror test, and again in Chap. 5 with Tulving's theory of the what-where-when content criterion of episodic memory. Let us give this first intention a label:

1. The self-recognition intention of the individual artist and his or her separateness from the flow of the world, associated with the Episodic Mind layer of human consciousness

For our second cave painting intention, we return to the cave painting in the Chauvet Cave in France, previously shown in Chap. 3 (Fig. 3.9) and in Chap. 6 (Fig. 6.3). We show a different section of this same painting here in Fig. 7.5. This artist was interested in exploring the motion of animals. We previously mentioned that the artist was depicting not the ten or so lions actually painted on the cave wall, but one or two lions only at multiple instances of the hunt, which emphasized the tremendous speed of these lions rushing forward toward the kill. Here in Fig. 7.5, we show the same sort of artistic technique in another section of this same painting, with a rhinoceros seeming to move its horn, in quick motion, up and down, as if it were alive in front of the viewer. We have previously labeled the intention behind this artistic technique of showing motion as:

2. The understanding intention of the individual artist who is trying to understand his experience, associated with the Mimetic Mind layer of human consciousness, specifically Mimicking 1

Our third cave painting (Fig. 7.6), created 25,000 years ago, from the Pech Merle cave in France, shows stenciled female hands above and under two spotted horses.

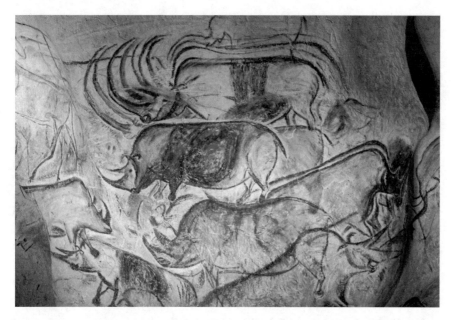

Fig. 7.5 Rhinoceros from Chauvet Cave, 32,000 years ago (© 2016 Patilpv25. Creative Commons Attribution-Share Alike 4.0 International license)

Fig. 7.6 Female artist hand stencils in Pech Merle cave in France, circa 25,000 years ago (© 2009 HTO, Kersti Nebelsiek. Creative Commons license)

According to present-day paleontologists, the stenciled hands are thought to be grasping onto the cave wall, even cracks in the cave wall, which the 25,000-year-old humans believed was where one world met another. The paleontologists go further in their analysis, but new evidence has come to light creating a controversy.

The first hypothesis is that the spotted horses were due to shaman-artists who painted the horses with spots as some sort of spiritual or religious act. The leading proponents of this interpretation are Jean Clottes and David Lewis-Williams (1998) in their book *The Shamans of Prehistory: Trance and Magic in the Painted Caves.* (For the contrary view, see Alpert 2013) According to their thesis, in a darkened cave deprived of light, the shaman goes into a trance, and crosses over into another world with his hand on a crack on the cave wall. Images of animals appear to him; and these mysterious spots appear as a sort of film over the animal in the shaman's mind's eye, induced by the visual deformation caused by the trance and the darkened conditions in the cave. There are at least two possible intentions behind this complex subject matter. Because of the large space for groups in front of the spotted horses painting, we believe this example represents:

3. The influencing or communication intention associated with the Mimetic Mind layer of human consciousness (Mimicking 2), to influence a group in a ritual

For the fourth example of Paleolithic cave painting intention, we jump forward within the Upper Paleolithic Era to 15,000–20,000 years ago, to the Lascaux Cave in France, with an image that shows the evolution of the artist's intention in the full flowering of the Mythic Mind. In Fig. 7.7, a dead man is lying in front of a bison, but there is also a bird on a pole in the foreground. The human figure is thought

Fig. 7.7 Lascaux Cave, France. Man with bison, 15,000–20,000 years ago (© 2005 Peter80. GNU Free Documentation License)

to be a shaman. The bird on a pole signifies the shaman's spiritual journey after death (because the bird carries the shaman's soul upward).

There are many intentions motivating the subject matter of this complex, full-flowering of the Mythic Mind phase of human consciousness. The artist-shaman objectified in the painting his unique experience in the world, in an act of self-recognition. In addition, he or she mimicked or reenacted a dreamed, perhaps hallucinated, episode at the individual artist level, for the sake of understanding the episode (Mimicking 1). We also assume some sort of ceremony accompanied the cave painting, giving life to it at the group level, for communicating a message for purposes of cohering the group together, or for some other influencing intention (Mimicking 2).

But there is evidence here in this landmark work of art of a greater, more powerful intention than simply mimicking an episode of the artist's experience. The painting is conceptualizing, not the answers given by a religion, but rather the artist's questions about what happens to her after she is dead, by taking an episode of dreamed or hallucinated experience, and traveling beyond the here and now of the physical world. The bird-on-the-pole painting therefore indicates this new intention:

4. The search for meaning intention of the artist associated with the Mythic Mind layer of human consciousness in its full strength

These components of the bird-on-the-pole cave painting combined together show a much higher symbolic content than the other three cave paintings in this section. The search for understanding that took place in the Mimetic Mind phase was a necessary intermediary step, but the search for meaning intention we see in the painting depicted in Fig. 7.7 is the fuel for a far more powerful time-machine. How is this so?

The Episodic Mind, through recalling the memory of a past episode experience and then mimicking the past experience, allows the individual to time-travel back to her past, and to reexperience the past. In doing so, the episode of experience, and then time-traveling back to reexperience the past event by recalling the episode from episodic memory, reframes "far space as near space" (which in the physical world, are "separately represented" in different parts of the brain (Berti and Frassinetti 2000, p. 415)). But the Mythic Mind frees the memory from the constraints of the physical reality of experience of the artist that determines what "far space" is. It can fuel the individual backward in time to even before she was born, and forward in time to the afterlife in the artist's future after she is dead.

But isn't this more powerful time-machine, fueled by the search for meaning intention, the logical extension of the understanding intention of the Mimetic Mind?

The Understanding Versus Meaning Intention

What is the difference between the search for understanding and the search for meaning intention? Understanding as we have discussed it thus far, in terms of understanding the individual's experiencing of the world in an episode, answers the question: What just happened? While meaning is a paradigmatic view of the world into which episodes experienced in life fit together and gain meaning. There is an aspect of: Why did this happen? (As we will see in the next chapter, the Theoretic Mind also asks: Why did this happen?)

We will try to do better in our explanation of this difference, and the more powerful time-travel machine that the search for meaning provides, in the following sections.

First, the Frame Has Changed

The Fig. 7.7 Lascaux Cave painting of a man with a bird on a pole lying next to a bison, dates from 15,000–20,000 years ago. It is a different era than the much older hand stencils of the Fig. 7.2 painting from the El Castillo Cave, dating from 35,000 years ago, and the Fig. 7.6 painting from the Pech Merle Cave dating from 25,000 years ago. There is evolution of human consciousness—how and what humans think about the world and their relationship to the world.

The Lascaux Cave painting is based on an episode of man killing a bison with a spear, who is also killed in the encounter (i.e., the spear is broken and the man is lying on the ground). But the episode is also different from the other, earlier cave paintings in other ways. The older cave paintings are more a description of the episode of experience. While the Lascaux Cave painting contains symbolism that is qualitatively different than those earlier cave paintings because the various components represented in the painting come together not in a linear frame of either the Episodic or Mimetic Mind but rather in an overall paradigmatic frame of a belief system—emblematic of the Mythic Mind in full bloom.

These are two different modes of thinking or consciousness, the narrative and the paradigmatic, as Jerome Bruner (1986) labels them, and they are qualitatively different one from the other (Donald 1991, p. 256). The Episodic and Mimetic Mind phases of human consciousness were narrative-based, story-like quality of an episode—this happened, then that happened, followed by this happening. While the paradigmatic frame of the Mythic Mind integrates all episodes and their narrative into a universal perspective of the artist's conceptualization of his/her place, and his/her group's place in the world and the universe.

The Mythic Mind marked the radical transition to the paradigmatic mode of thinking and consciousness. This is the big evolutionary break, according to Donald, which definitively and qualitatively separated humans from all other species, specifically our nearest cousin species, the Neanderthals, as shown in Fig. 7.8.

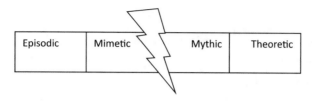

Fig. 7.8 Donald's four phases of human brain evolution; with the primary disruptive transition being from the Mimetic Mind, which is based on linear narrative, to the Mythic Mind, which is paradigmatic

Second, the New Frame Enables Us to See New Things

At a certain point in the Mimetic Culture, the linear narrative of the episode became "not enough." Its frame's borders burst open into the Mythic Mind frame, which has as its central fuel the search for meaning intention. This is a much more powerful time-machine. Now freed from the constraints of the Episodic and Mimetic Minds' need for narrative linearity, the Mythic Mind completely transformed not only how humans framed their interaction with the ongoing world, but what they could now put in the frame. The transition to the Mythic Mind allowed humans to see more.

We diagram this fundamental transition in how the frame underlying human consciousness changed what humans could see in their framing of the world from the Episodic and Mimetic Minds, in Fig. 7.9, to the Mythic Mind, in Fig. 7.10. These two diagrams return us to our example of a hunter hunting a bison when a solar eclipse occurs, bringing a sudden darkness in the middle of the day.

Let us divide the whole episode into units called events. In Fig. 7.9, the hunter is in the midst of a hunting episode, which he is very familiar with. Then the eclipse suddenly occurs, pushing him out of this familiar episode. There is no unifying paradigmatic conceptualization of what is happening in this anomalous environmental event.

There are a number of response events that could now occur in the hunter's consciousness, the range of possible responses delineating how he could respond to the stimulus event of the eclipse. We represent these possible alternative responses, in Fig. 7.9, by a cascading series of boxes. But it depends on the hunter's interpretation, which in turn is dependent on his previous experience with the ongoing world. Event A precipitates a Response B in the hunter based on this past experience.

As an example, Event A could be the bison attacking the hunter. This had happened to the hunter on previous occasions so he was familiar with this possibility. He would have a previous experience in episodic memory to refer to in his response. Event B could be the bison rejoining the herd, which makes it too dangerous for the hunter to continue the hunt. This precipitates the hunter's response of quitting the activity of hunting. This also had previously happened to the hunter. Event C is something else that the hunter had observed once before—a bison feeding its calf. All these events that could have happened that fateful day, elicit responses from the

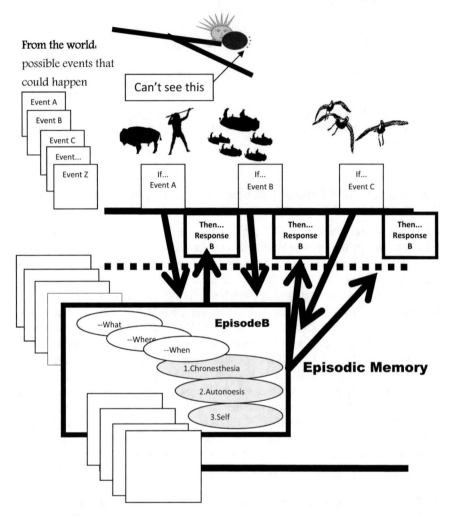

Fig. 7.9 Narrative frame before during Episodic and Mimetic Mind phases of the evolution of human consciousness

hunter according to the hunter's previous experience episodes stored in his episodic memory.

Then there were the events of that fateful day as it actually happened, when the eclipse occurred. This was entirely out of the experience of the hunter. The previous experience episodes of hunting a bison he had stored in episodic memory did not suffice.

The hunter stood there, experiencing the natural phenomenon of the eclipse but not understanding it. Bands of shadows appeared on the ground coming toward him. The sky became intensely blue. The hunter either hid his face, covering it with his hand; or he went into himself, becoming almost unconscious with fright. After a

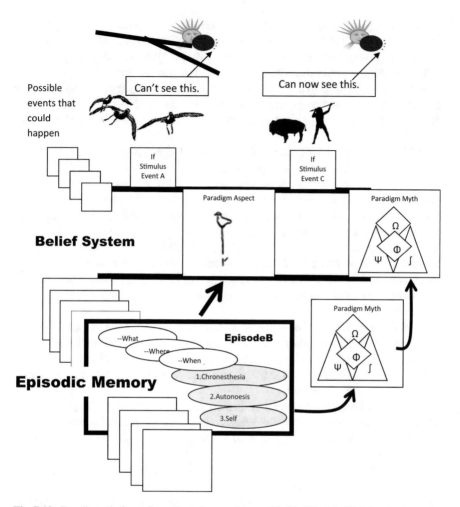

Fig. 7.10 Paradigmatic frame formation after transition to Mythic Mind enabled the shaman-artist to see more in the world than could be seen through the frame of the Mimetic Mind, in this case the moon blocking the sun during an eclipse

time, he dared to look up. It was totally dark, cold. The sky appeared to have a different texture. He reached his hand up into the sky to grab at it for some reason. Then he stayed crouched behind the rock. After 30 min, it felt warm again. The sky was back to normal. The episode ended in real time.

In the ensuing days, the hunter often mentally time-traveled back to the episode and mimicked it in his own mind, sometimes from different angles, with the intention of gaining understanding of it. He mimicked it to others in the group with this same understanding intention, who in turn mimicked what they themselves had seen back to him. The hunter even returned to the rocks and the cliff where the episode had happened.

He went up to the edge of the cliff and looked down. He couldn't believe his eyes! He saw carcasses of bison at the bottom of the cliff. It cued his memory, making him remember the sound of the bison stampeding over the ground during the episode. He had forgotten that until now. Then he remembered that the precipitating sound was actually a flock of birds in the trees next to him. He suddenly remembered the flock of birds. This was before the sky grew dark. The flock of birds, he remembered, made a pattern against the darkening sky. "Where were they going?" he asked himself.

In his mimicking of the eclipse episode over and over again to himself, he always time-traveled back to the same experienced episode, Episode B in Fig. 7.9, which was so richly encoded in his episodic memory in the "when" aspects Chronesthesia, Autonesis and Self. But he still could not see, because he did not understand (it was not in the frame), what was actually happening with the eclipse. He was confined within his experience frame. He found by mimicking the episode, and returning to seek more information at the scene of the experience, that he could enrich his awareness of what was actually in his experience frame. But he still didn't under-stand, nor was he even aware of the eclipse part of his long ago experience. Nor did his children or others in the group. The episode continued to be mimicked for thousands of years.

Then for whatever reason—perhaps climate change forced the human species to adapt, which sharpened their mind—a threshold was reached and the frames of the Episodic and Mimetic Mind layers burst open, causing the transition to the Mythic Mind. The narrative frame of the Episodic and Mimetic Mind layers of human consciousness was not enough.

A new cognitively modern human shaman took up the old hunter's episode story. When does a story become a myth? When an extra unseen, parallel world is invoked to explain the unexplainable. In Fig. 7.10, we diagram the Mythic Mind frame of this new, cognitive modern human shaman.

The Mythic Mind frame is no longer a narrative frame that plots in a linear line the events that made up the episode of the bison hunt—the type of frame found in the Episodic and Mimetic Mind phases of human brain development. In the new Mythic Mind phase of human consciousness, the frame through which humans viewed and processed the ongoing world became more complex, paradigmatic, filled with aspects or features of a constructed view of the world based on the myth.

The Mythic Mind gave the shaman-artist a new capability. "What is really going on here," she asked herself. The myth the artist-shaman was dealing with was her relationship with the world, including what was unseen. The key to her unlocking the eclipse episode was the sound of the birds.

There had recently been another eclipse. The artist-shaman too had noticed a flock of birds aroused to flight even before the eclipse had occurred, followed by a stampeding herd of bison. "It's coming, it's coming!" she said to herself. The artist-shaman was struck by how her own episode experience coincided with the old hunter story she had heard since she was a child. In her own experiencing of this similar episode, the artist-shaman could now see new aspects of the eclipse the old hunter ancestor's story had missed: most importantly, the moon blocking the sun. The artist now believed that the moon blocking the sun created an opening in the sky to the unseen, parallel world that controlled nature, which the flock of birds had flown into and visited. The bird-on-a-pole became a symbol of this aspect of the old hunter's originating episode, a new aspect of the myth.

The myth containing these various aspects of the old hunter's originating episode, and the new insight to the episode added by the artist-shaman thousands of years later, now formed a logical system of thinking about the world, a sort of paradigm.

The paradigmatic Mythic Mind frame, made up of various component aspects of the myth, could incorporate more complexity than the simple narrative thinking frame of earlier phases of human brain development. It allowed the cognitively modern human to see beyond appearances, to what was unseen by the naked eye. Through time-traveling with the more powerful time-machine of the Mythic Mind, back to the past episode of the artist-shaman's experience, the human examined the world and her place in it with a new eye, which enabled her to dig down vertically into her consciousness. Indeed, this vertical-focus may be the reason for the artist-shaman flourishing within the group, and the group as a whole flourishing compared to other groups. So this new frame for looking at the world, the Mythic Mind, may have been naturally selected for.

This new powerful cognitive architecture also contained the seeds of the next phase of human brain development—a myth is a paradigm, a sort of theory, after all—enabling the transition to the theories and models of the Theoretic Mind, which we will examine in the next chapter.

Chapter 8
Framing: The Mythic-to-Theoretic Transition

We have now reached the third and final transition in the evolution of human consciousness, according to Donald's (1991) theory, the transition from the Mythic Mind to the Theoretic Mind, shown in Fig. 8.1. But as in the other two transitions, the seed of the Theoretic Mind was present long before in the Mythic Mind. The communal myths of the Mythic Mind we described in the last chapter formed a paradigmatic layer to human consciousness, enabling humans to frame what they experienced in more than a linear narrative. The Theoretic Mind also has this paradigmatic frame. But there is something very different, something very new in the Theoretic Mind consciousness.

The Theoretic Mind emanates from the human knowledge system, whereas the Mythic Mind emanates from the human belief system. The knowledge system was always there in semantic memory, in embryonic form, but reached some sort of threshold about 5000 years ago with the development of writing. Writing over time enabled the creation of the external storage of knowledge, and through models and theories, the ability to think about and communicate this knowledge in a formal way of thinking (Donald 1998, p. 14).

The Theoretic Mind enabled humans to notice, observe and systematically accumulate and organize, through agree-upon models and theories, factual knowledge about the world from the ground up, often experienced through framing devices. Often the frame for carrying out these knowledge investigations is very small. We highlight an example of a small framing device, the pinprick-sized lens of the seventeenth-century microbiologist Antony van Leeuwenhoek, shown in Fig. 8.2. We will use Leeuwenhoek as an example of the Theoretic Mind at work.

© Springer International Publishing AG, part of Springer Nature 2018
C. Cole, *The Consciousness' Drive*, https://doi.org/10.1007/978-3-319-92457-1_8

Fig. 8.1 The third
evolutionary transition:
Mythic Mind to Theoretic
Mind transition

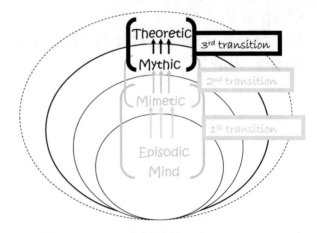

Fig. 8.2 Antony van
Leeuwenhoek's
microscope. The tiny,
pinprick lens highlighted.
The specimen being
observed was stuck on the
point near the lens. The lens
magnified the specimen
200 times its size (© 2008
Jeroen Rouwkema.
Attribution-ShareAlike 3.0
Unported)

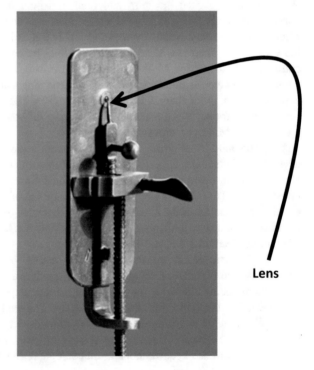

Leeuwenhoek's Framing Lens

Leeuwenhoek first became interested in amplifying a small part of the world in an
experience while crossing a lake in a boat. In viewing the algae on the lake's surface,
he suddenly realized that there was another world of life hidden from view. He
wanted to see the life he detected there. He couldn't do it with the naked eye; only via

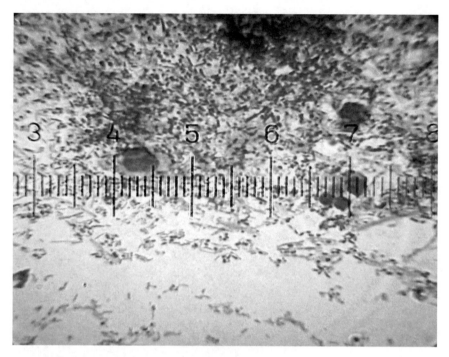

Fig. 8.3 Bacteria from food remnants (plaque) on human teeth (© 2010 Bob Baylock Creative Commons Attribution-Share Alike 3.0 Unported license)

the amplified frame provided by a lens. He then became fascinated, the story goes, with lens-making and microscope-making.

He himself fabricated these lenses for his handmade microscopes. As described by Brian Ford (1991), Leeuwenhoek first melted some glass into globules, polished it into a lens, and then put the lens into a pinprick-sized hole he drilled into a brass plate. To observe the micro-object under the lens, Leeuwenhoek held the hole up to the sun. Because of the extreme magnification capability of his lenses, van Leeuwenhoek, if not the first to have seen it, was the first to have recorded seeing bacteria (Fig. 8.3). Leeuwenhoek's legacy, in addition to his lens-making, was his obsessive recording and communication of his observations.

Van Leeuwenhoek wrote to the Royal Society on September 17, 1683 giving them the details of how he had discovered animalcules (bacteria) while examining the white stuff—the plaque—between his own teeth. Under his lens, which magnified the plaque 200 times, he noticed little alive things he called animalcules that were moving in the plaque. He found an old man who had never brushed his teeth in his life and there in this copious plaque found even more animalcules. Bacteria from teeth plaque is shown in Fig. 8.3.

Leeuwenhoek did not invent the microscope. In fact, van Leeuwenhoek visited London in 1688 and saw the inventor Robert Hook's compound microscope and was inspired by it. Hook's microscope, shown in Fig. 8.4, looks far more like modern-

Fig. 8.4 Seventeenth-century compound microscope similar to Hooke's microscope. Whipple Museum, Cambridge, UK (© 2004 Andrew Dunn. Creative Commons Attribution-Share Alike 2.0 Generic)

day microscopes than van Leeuwenhoek's shown in Fig. 8.2. With Hook's microscope, we can imagine ourselves placing our eye next to the top of the microscope and looking down the tube to whatever microorganism was on the tray-like metal circular plate. We can see the usefulness of Hook's light apparatus beside the tube that, with the aid of a circular metal object beside the flame that magnified and focused the light on the object, directed intense light on the small part of the world being examined.

The Theoretic Mind Frame

The historical puzzle that has intrigued art historians is whether Leeuwenhoek and the painter Vermeer were friends, and whether these two historical figures, both famous for their use of framing devices, actually influenced each other or not.

Philip Steadman (2001) in his book on Vermeer goes through the pros and cons on this issue. We have two pieces of textual evidence for this. Both Vermeer and van Leeuwenhoek were born in Delft in the same month, a fact that was recorded on the same page in the New Church's baptismal registry. A coincidence perhaps. But we have another more interesting document.

At Vermeer's death in 1675, Vermeer's widow Catherina Bolnes was bankrupt, so creditors claimed the Vermeer paintings. Vermeer's widow wanted to keep a painting called The Art of Painting, and tried transferring ownership of it to her mother, Maria Thins, with whom she, Vermeer, and their seven surviving children had lived with while the painter was alive. For some reason, van Leeuwenhoek was appointed the trustee for the Vermeer estate. In this interesting second document, Leeuwenhoek ruled the transfer was a ruse and the painting had to go to the creditors.

In the twenty-first century, we see the world through documentary evidence. In the seventeenth century, we have to infer Vermeer's way of seeing, thinking, and communicating about the world via his paintings. Oddly, our view is that Vermeer saw the world in a scientific manner, partly because of the enticing possibility of his association with Leeuwenhoek, particularly van Leeuwenhoek's lenses and Vermeer's (probable) utilization of the camera obscura to frame the scenes he painted.

Let's look more closely at the possibility these two world figures were friends and worked together—in fact they were part of a very small movement—to change our notion of how we frame the world through the precise objectification (description) of our experience in the world.

Objectification Through Description of Experience

To begin with, the two men were both sons of silk traders who lived in close proximity to each other. Vermeer lived as a boy on the Market Square in the center of Delft. Leeuwenhoek's birth was registered under the name Thonis Phillipszoon, which he soon changed to Antoni van Leeuwenhoek. Leeuwenhoek means "Lion's Gate" in Dutch, which is the location of van Leeuwenhoek's house when he was born. In Fig. 8.5, we show a picture of 7 Lion's Gate from about that time—it is among the group of houses in front of the double-towered gate. Actually, this map, the *Kaart Figuratief* by Dirck van Bleyswijck, published in 1678, is not a map as we know it but rather a combination of map and aerial view. The Dutch were obsessed with maps in the seventeenth century, their Golden Age when their merchants were scouring the world for products and markets. Maps and commerce around the world went hand-in-hand with the frame of the scientific mind. Vermeer shared in the Dutch Republic's advanced scientific culture, according to Svetlana Alpers (1983) in her book *The Art of Describing*. In fact, Vermeer used maps as props in roughly 11 of his paintings.

Figure 8.6 shows a map of Delft from the seventeenth century to situate where these two men lived. Leeuwenhoek's home is near the Lion's Gate at the top right-hand corner of Delft on this map. Vermeer's boyhood home, in his father's tavern The Mechelen, is located on the Central Market in front of the New Church, the large white space in the middle of the map. The Schiedam and Rotterdam Gates are at the

Fig. 8.5 van Leeuwenhoek's birth place, according to Bouricius (1925), between the numbers 33 and 34 on the map, the Lion's Gate in Delft. Map: Kaart Figuratief by Dirck van Bleyswijck, 1678 (Detail of map: © 2005 Douglas Anderson. Creative Commons License)

bottom right-hand corner of the map, where Delft's harbor was located. To get a better image of the Lion's Gate, what it was like, we have a detailed painting of these two gates, shown in Fig. 8.7.

The painting in Fig. 8.7 is, of course, Vermeer's masterpiece, *View of Delft*. It is believed Vermeer painted the scene of these two gates from the second floor of a house across the harbor. If he used the camera obscura for this painting, it would have been an incredible feat of engineering to have constructed a camera obscura large enough for this huge separation between the framing device of the camera obscura and the scene being painted across the harbor. The lenses for this camera would have been particularly difficult to get just right. Did Vermeer seek the help of the preeminent lens-maker in the world of their time, Antony van Leeuwenhoek?

Vermeer and van Leeuwenhoek's Intention: Understanding

Svetlana Alpers (1983), in her book *The Art of Describing*, investigates the similarity of the Theoretic Mind of Vermeer and Leeuwenhoek, the intention that motivated their framing the world via the lens. It is the art and science of describing the world rather than narrating, she states. In the case of Vermeer, there is almost a secret,

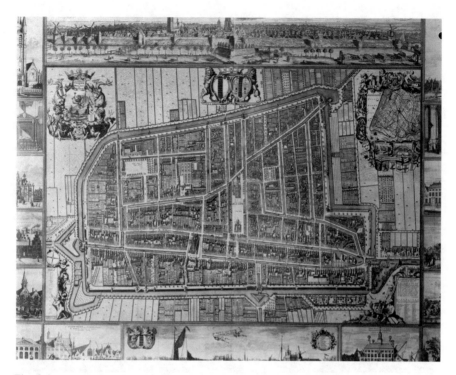

Fig. 8.6 A map of seventeenth-century Delft. Kaart Figuratief by Dirck van Bleyswijck, 1678 (© 1966 A.J. van der Wal Creative Commons Attribution-Share Alike 4.0 International license)

undercover world away from the loud actions of heated emotions and religious themes. And in the case of Leeuwenhoek, his intention was to look at and understand, through obsessive description, the world that is there, almost silently there, hidden, parallel to the human surface world of action and thoughts.

To both, the lens framed the entry to an understanding of the real world.

And yet, Alpers (1983) conjectures, Vermeer and Leeuwenhoek believed that we, humans, actively see the world through an interface of our own making, made up of our eyes, which they considered optical devices, as well as our mind—made up of intellectual or mental constructs of our own making—that act as vehicles or channels linking us and the outside world. Robert Huerta (2003) labels this "mental lensing" in his book *Giants of Delft: Johannes Vermeer and the Natural Philosophers: The Parallel Search for Knowledge during the Age of Discovery*:

> Artists and scientists of the time conceptualized the intellect as both a "conceptual and visual lens to bring into focus features of the reality that were unclear to their contemporaries." (Huerta 2003, p. 72)

Vermeer's technique to make the viewer's eye "see" depth perception in his paintings—with dancing light—were accomplished using the famous globules of shiny white paint he placed in his carpets. Vermeer asked what was really there in the real world, and how he could use painting technique to "confuse" the viewer into

Fig. 8.7 Vermeer's *View of Delft*, painted 1660–1661, showing the Schiedam and Rotterdam Gates, the gates next to the Lion's Gate where Leeuwenhoek was born. Royal Picture Gallery Mauritshuis, The Hague (© 2011 www.mauritshuis.nl Creative Commons CC0 1.0 Universal Public Domain Dedication)

seeing it. Alpers (1983, pp. 31–32) calls Vermeer's globules "painted equivalents of the circles of confusion, diffused circles of light." The globules "confused" the viewer's eye into seeing the depth perception like in the real world. (We can see the white globules in the View of Delft in Fig. 8.7, on the side of the boat and again in the wall of the gate in front of it.)

Leeuwenhoek, likewise, prepped his specimens so that he could see and describe them; he used dark-ground illumination so that the specimen popped out when viewed through the microscope (Dobell 1958). He also stained his specimens to improve contrast. And he sectioned his specimens for better viewing under a microscope; he was one of the first to do this. As a result, no one else at the time could see what Leeuwenhoek could see through his microscope lens, according to Huerta (2003). van Leeuwenhoek further manipulated the specimen in its lighting. When viewing globules of blood, for example, he arranged the lighting so that, in Leeuwenhoek's own words, ". . . the globules in the blood are as sharp and clean as one can distinguish sand grains on a piece of black taffeta" (quoted in Dobell 1958, p. 331). He couldn't help himself with the "taffeta" reference: he had earned his living in the silk trade.

So Leeuwenhoek's genius resided in how he framed what he saw to make it more observable; the fineness of his lens-making was without equal at the time—and how he manipulated the small part of the world as if it were his alone, objectifying his experience, because the episode of observing his specimens was his own personal intersection with the world. As a result of this framing and his objectification of the world he observed, he was able to see things nobody else saw.

But the third aspect of Leeuwenhoek's genius, and another aspect of the scientific method and the Theoretic Mind, was his rigorous accounting of what he saw. His written reports, including illustrations done by professional illustrators, were rigorously communicated to his scientific peers in over 300 letters to the Royal Society in London. There was an agreed-upon paradigmatic frame for communicating knowledge to others in the scientific community of the time, a hallmark of the Theoretic Mind.

A theory or model is a paradigmatic perspective, rather than a descriptive, linear perspective, on the part of the world the scientist experiences through his senses, with or without the aid of scientific instruments. It has foundational assumptions, proven propositional statements, and incorporates cause and effect relations that have been more or less confirmed by others who have replicated the study as it was precisely described in a report. Theory both predicts findings in exactly replicated studies by others, and explains why the observed phenomena occur.

Leeuwenhoek set his observations of bacteria within the framework of two major prevailing theories. The spontaneous generation theory (animals developed spontaneously in mud at the bottom of ponds) and the preformation theory (an embryo was preformed and only grew larger in development to adulthood). Needless to say, he was on the wrong side of science on both counts. But Leeuwenhoek's objectification of his scientific experiences under the microscope, in written reports and theoretical constructs, provided the empirical evidence that would later, in the nineteenth century, develop into cell theory.

The Theoretic Mind's objectification of the experience of the individual scientist observing part of the world, and his reporting of that experience through a paradigmatic theory representing the scientific community's consensus on a given topic at a moment in time, is the basis of knowledge construction.

The Theoretic Mind: The Objectification of Experience into Knowledge

We jump now roughly 300 years in time to a later stage of the Theoretic Mind. Karl Popper (1975) encapsulates the scientific method as it stands today in his concept of 3-Worlds, illustrated in Fig. 8.8.

World 1 is the Material/Physical world itself, including episode experiences of scientific observation. World 1 is reality, the target of all scientific study. World 3 is the Objective Knowledge store—the theories and models of all humankind

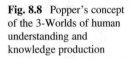

Fig. 8.8 Popper's concept of the 3-Worlds of human understanding and knowledge production

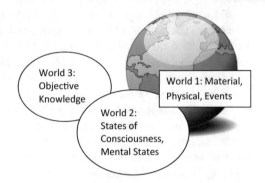

deposited in books, articles, etc. And finally, World 2 is the intersection of these two worlds: the States of Consciousness and the Mental States of individual scientists as they grasp for understanding and formulate new knowledge. The interaction between this world, World 2 and World 3, the world of documents, books and theories and models that are written down, is the essential topic of information science (Brookes 1980, p. 128).

The modus operandi of these Theoretic Mind scientific investigations, according to Popper, is to disprove or falsify the theories and models of our objective knowledge depository in World 3, which is done by constantly referring our objective knowledge back to World 1, the physical-material world. Eventually, the falsification thrust of scientific inquiry shifts the scientific paradigm of research in a particular field at a given moment in time, known as a "paradigm shift," which Kuhn (1962) describes in his groundbreaking book *The Structure of Scientific Revolutions*. The Theoretic Mind, like the Mythic Mind, is a paradigmatic consciousness, but instead of belief-based, the Theoretic Mind is knowledge-based.

The Knowledge-Based Paradigmatic Mind

In the Theoretic Mind, humans have found a way to bring group consensus on "knowledge" together into a paradigmatic structure frame based on multicomponent theories and models. These theories and models are built to be extremely flexible, leaving room for new knowledge to enter the frame. It means also that all knowledge is constantly open to being challenged, then either confirmed or refuted if the knowledge is proven to be wrong. The extreme utility of the paradigmatic frame of the Theoretic Mind is its flexibility, its ability to absorb new knowledge, and to jettison old knowledge when it is refuted.

The objectification of the world into these human knowledge frames, in a constant deconstruction and reconstruction process, is the hallmark of the Theoretic Mind. In Fig. 8.9, we utilize Leeuwenhoek as an example of the Theoretic Mind at work, diagraming the evolution of his paradigmatic frame controlling his scientific observations under his lens. Leeuwenhoek has a succession of iterations of his

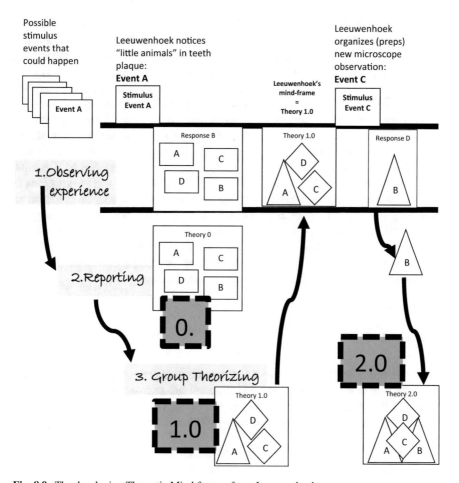

Fig. 8.9 The developing Theoretic Mind frame of van Leeuwenhoek

paradigmatic frame through which he views his scientific experiences, which we will call Theory 0, Theory 1.0, and finally Theory 2.0.

Theory 0

Leeuwenhoek begins his observations without a theoretical perspective, so we'll call this part of the process Theory 0, but he nonetheless has various scientific techniques and assumptions in his viewing frame: (1) he begins with his observing experience; (2) he then reports his findings; and, finally, (3) he along with his entire scientific community theorizes about the findings.

1. Observing experience: Leeuwenhoek notices his famous description of bacteria as animalcules or "little animals" in some teeth plaque. This experience event is Event A in Fig. 8.9. Event A is one of a great number of possible events that could have occurred, indicated by the chain of boxes on the left-hand side of the figure. Leeuwenhoek's observation response is Response B, which has some scientific principles and tenets, but they are not incorporated into any theory.
2. Leeuwenhoek reports his observation in a letter to the Royal Society in London, using the scientific principles and assumptions of the moment. After all, he wanted to communicate his observation in a language the readers of the letter, who were researchers in his field, would understand and respond to. Over the course of the following months, other scientists report their own observations to their own experiments, some in reaction to Leeuwenhoek's original observation.
3. Group theorizing: Leeuwenhoek's observations are framed in old theories by the scientific community as a whole, discussed in private communications between members, and in public letters to the Royal Society. A new developing theory begins to take shape. Leeuwenhoek sets his new experiments in this latest iteration of the developing theory, called Theory 1.0.

Theory 1.0

Many months after the initial Event A observation experience, Leeuwenhoek prepares for a new observation experience through his microscope lens, with a firm, Theory 1.0, paradigmatic frame for the observation episode. Governed by the Theory 1.0 frame, he preps the specimens, and carefully positions a lighting apparatus next to the lens.

The new observing experience occurs, Event C. It is important to note that Event C is one of many possible events that could have occurred during the observation experience. Leeuwenhoek's experience would have been different if he had prepped the specimens differently, or he had put a more intense light beside the lens, or if the specimens had come from a different plaque source.

Theory 2.0

In Response D at the far right-hand side of the Fig. 8.9, Leeuwenhoek is surprised by what he sees. The developing Theory 1.0, the mind-frame through which he started the Event C observation experience, began to shift in light of Leeuwenhoek's new findings (in the bottom right-hand corner of Fig. 8.9). He sees something very particular under his microscope lens that he wants other scientists in his group to see.

2. Reporting

Leeuwenhoek hires an illustrator to draw or map out what he sees under the microscope in Event C. He reports in minute detail everything he observed in Event C in letters to the Royal Society in London.

3. Theorizing

Leeuwenhoek and the other scientists who read his letters to the Royal Society begin to theorize about the bacteria in the teeth plaque he has just observed, mapped, and reported to the Royal Society in London. They conclude that the new thing Leeuwenhoek observed fits in well with their developing theory. The theory is now more complete, i.e., answers more questions, shown in the bottom right-hand corner of Fig. 8.9.

Conclusion

The lenses of both Vermeer, in his camera obscura, and van Leeuwenhoek, in his hand-held microscope, enabled these two pioneers of our own Theoretic Culture to frame and observe a small part of the world, for greater understanding of that small part of the world. They objectified the small part of the world by prepping or manipulating the part of the world they observed with innovative techniques and technology. But this is only the first and minor part of gaining self-recognition via objectifying their experience in the world.

Ultimately, the paradigmatic or theoretic frame enabled humans to predict and explain the world around us, further turning the world into "knowledge." Knowledge objectifies the human experience in the world, turning not only the experience but the world itself into an object that we can manipulate, enhance, degrade, or destroy. Their techniques, however, were always in service to the frame provided by the Theoretic Mind, the intention of which is the search for understanding of the truth— the true reality of the world. We return to this discussion about the intention underlying knowledge construction in Part III of this book.

But before ending Part I, we conclude with a definition of human consciousness as it has evolved in the Theoretic Culture.

Part I
Conclusion

We have come to the end of Part I where we set out to investigate, describe, and begin to explain the exceptionality of human consciousness—how we experience the world and our place in the world, and how we think about this experience. We structured our investigation on Merlin Donald's 4-phase theory of the evolution of the human mind, from the Episodic to the Mimetic to the Mythic and to our present-day Theoretic Mind. These four phases of the evolution of human consciousness remain "like an onion" (Donald (1991, p. 141), as vestige layers of our consciousness today, shown in Fig. 1. Together these four evolutionary layers determine how human consciousness frames our perspective on the world and our place in that world, defining what we think about and how we think.

It is a remarkable story, our evolutionary development. Humans started out in the Episodic Mind phase as just another animal species. But there was something different about them. Like other species, they framed their experiences of the world in units of the episode, then stored these episodes in a form of episodic memory—the memory of experience. Perhaps our episodic memory was always unique; or perhaps, somewhere along the way, human episodic memory evolved differently than other species, pushing humans far ahead in evolutionary terms. In Part I, we have placed the "seed" of human uniqueness in how we store our experiences in episodic memory: we are uniquely aware that the memory is in the past (Chronesthesia, in Fig. 1), that we are reexperiencing the past when we recall it from memory (Autonoesis), and that the experience and the memory of it is uniquely the individual's and hers alone (Self). From this seed, everything else that contributed to our unique consciousness arose over the hundreds of thousands of years of evolution. In any case, our consciousness is different from any other species. Exceptional.

We are now ready to operationally define human consciousness for the purpose of this book. It is a very rough definition, crude and steeped in the oil and fumes of our rapidly disappearing—to be replaced by AI and robots—petrol-based industrial age.

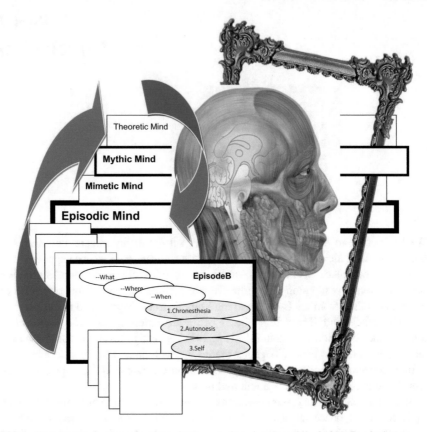

Fig. 1 Human consciousness framing what we see, based on Donald's 4-phase/levels theory

Definition of Consciousness: The Combustion Engine

In this book, we are interested in information need and information search from a broad human consciousness perspective. Here, we compare human consciousness to an internal combustion engine. We start with our base diagram of the structure of human consciousness—Donald's (1991) four layers: the Episodic Mind, the Mimetic Mind, the Mythic Mind, and the Theoretic Mind—shown in Fig. 1.

At the top of Fig. 1 are the four layers of our present-day consciousness; at the bottom of figure is Endel Tulving's three-aspect theory of episodic memory. The Tulving theory is a very dynamic conception of this vital part of our consciousness—the interface vehicle or channel between what is outside us in the world and what is inside us. Within this episodic memory are the engine's

- Pistons, and the
- Sparkplug that ignites the combustion process when human consciousness comes into contact with the outside world.

In addition, as the subject of this book is information need, we consider the individual's intention in searching for information, which is the engine's

• Fuel.

We will discuss each of these in turn in the following sections.

Pistons

The essence of Tulving's theory is that humans engage in time-travel to a past episode via its storage in episodic memory. More important, humans can also time-travel to the future, manipulating the stored memory of the episode as a rehearsal or planning device for a future episode experience.

Time-travel seems so bizarre an idea, but if you think about it we really do go back in time through our episodic memory system to relive, reenact, at the very least mimic an episode we have just experienced, or even experienced many years before. In telling your spouse about your day, we are accessing episodic memory and mimicking the episode out loud. We often exaggerate such stories, especially with the years. So we often mentally manipulate the episode memory, look at it from different angles, even change the episode's scenario or narrative.

Future time-travel seems even odder an idea until we think about it. The future, again, is accessed through the past episode representation stored in our episodic memory. Via these already experienced episodes, we extrapolate, using them as mental rehearsals for future episode experiences. We do these rehearsal scenarios in our head almost as a matter of course: for an upcoming birthday; and even making a list of items when we go to the grocery store, aren't we in a certain sense rehearsing a future episode of our experience?

If we take an overview of it, mental time-travel backward and forward is done through each of Donald's four layers of consciousness, starting from a past memory stored in episodic memory, as in the following:

Time-travel to the past:

1. Episodic Mind layer: The individual mentally time-travels to a past experienced episode stored in memory.

   a. Mimetic Mind layer: The individual mentally mimics this past experienced episode to herself and to others in the group.

      • Mythic Mind layer: The individual projects a past experienced episode as an existential experience, for example, a religious experience of a real or imagined conversation with some religious figure.

         Theoretic Mind layer: The individual mentally returns to an episode of a scientific experiment gone wrong, in order to figure out what went wrong. In the social sciences, the researcher may interview subjects and return to these interviews by mentally time-traveling back to the interview situation.

Time-travel to the future:

1. Episodic Mind layer: The individual mentally accesses a previously experienced episode as a rehearsal for a future experience with the same or similar episode. Going to the dentist's office, for example, everything seems familiar when we walk in.

   a. Mimetic Mind layer: For a projected future encounter with the same or a similar episode, the individual mentally mimics or reenacts possible scenarios, particularly if the future episode is important. There are awareness levels for this mimicking. The less important a future episode is, the less we are aware of mimicking it before it happens.

      • Mythic Mind layer: The individual mentally projects his or her ascendance to heaven after death.

      Theoretic Mind layer: The scientist mentally time-travels to the future to control the future, for example, the scientist Leeuwenhoek planning and prepping the bacteria sample for a future experiment.

Time-traveling both backward and forward, and by interweaving between Donald's four layers, forms the engine's up-and-down moving pistons that drive our consciousness. To give a partial impression only, in Fig. 2 we diagram with a winged-figure this two-pronged time-traveling, in-between the four layers, and backward and forward in time.

But the interweaving between the four layers, and backward and forward in time, is the least of what constitutes the pistons in the consciousness engine. There is much more mental backward and forward time-traveling driving the piston action of the consciousness engine.

Remember, even future mental time-travel involves first accessing a past memory episode from episodic memory. Mentally time-traveling backward and using the episode as a frame or schema for what we are to do next is a matter of our everyday existence, for everything we are about to do. We are constantly, in fact, traveling back in time, picking up an appropriate episode memory, then using that memory to predict and guide us in the action we are about to carry out, however trivial. Entering a new room, for example, because it is so common an episode, so trivial, it is almost automatic—without our awareness. We travel back to a room frame stored in episodic memory and then utilize this room frame before we open the door to enter the new room. As we are physically moving around the room, we are still using this frame. So the past episode frame is also, and almost simultaneously, a future representation as well, of what we are about to do on an almost constant basis. In fact, one could say that we almost constantly "live" in the future. And for a normal, everyday intersection with the world, we don't in fact experience these episode experiences in the present, or at least the "present" in these episodes is very minimal. We are on autopilot.

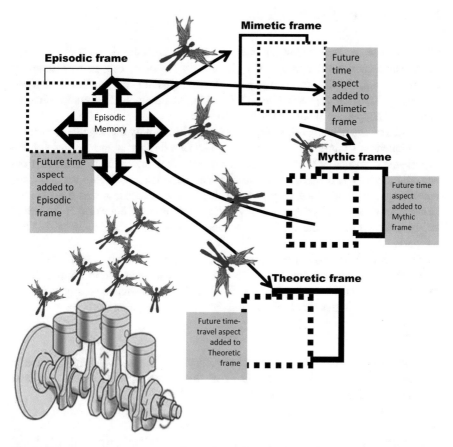

Fig. 2 Human consciousness compared to an internal combustion engine, starting with the pistons of the consciousness engine in the lower left-hand corner of the figure

Part II goes much more into this future time-travel fact of our consciousness. The point we wish to make here is that this constant backward and forward traveling in time is a fact of our consciousness. It is how we frame the ongoing world in real time, *as we are experiencing or intersecting with it.* It is the constant up and down of pistons in a car engine—the driving force in human consciousness.

But for the moment, let's move on to the second major point we wish to emphasize in this Part I Conclusion, which is the combustion that occurs in human consciousness that keeps the pistons going up and down. Its intensity and strength is so much greater than in any other species that it is different in nature.

SparkPlug and Combustion

We have seen in Chap. 4 that the human ability to mentally time-travel back to a previously experienced episode, via our memory system, can also be done by intelligent animals like the scrub jays. But humans do this mental time-travel differently, not simply quantitatively different but qualitatively different in its nature than all other species. What makes this difference?

Endel Tulving describes three aspects of episodic memory that together constitute the uniqueness of human consciousness: (1) Chronesthesia: the "when" of the experienced episode; (2) Autonoesis: awareness that the memory recalled from episodic memory is being reconstructed by the individual and is different from her real-time perception of the ongoing world; (3) Self: awareness that the memory being reconstructed is her own memory of her intersection of the world in the unit of an episode, and hers alone, and that she therefore has proprietary ownership of this memory.

These three aspects of human episodic memory are incendiary, creating combustion; they form the sparkplug—the transferring device—that allows the transfer of information from the outside world inside us into human consciousness. This intense ownership of the human intersection with the world is exceptional among species, in terms of

1. Time:

- Humans can reframe time by reconstructing their intersection with the world, moving it back and forth in a time continuum, even to "before birth and after death." (Suddendorf and Corballis 2007, p. 301)

2. Space:

- Humans can reframe "far space as near space" inside their own heads (Berti and Frassinetti 2000, p. 415; see also, Malafouris 2009, p. 97)

A corollary of this exceptional human ownership of their intersection with the world is ownership of and thus permission to mentally objectify the intersection, via the experienced episode stored in episodic memory, and ultimately to objectify the world itself. It is this object-making quality to the episode intersection that creates the unique and spectacular combustibility agent between humans and the world.

The evolutionary development of the human brain through Donald's four phases describes an ever-increasing intensification of this human ownership of their intersection with the world. With the development of writing in the Theoretic Mind, man's objectification of the world in knowledge symbols and equations, in theories, models and algorithms, on the Internet and in books and articles, has dramatically intensified the sense of proprietorship given to us by the representation of our intersection with the world in episodic memory, and by corollary extension the world itself, and on both an individual and on a species level. This is the essence of human exceptionality as a species, and the foundation of our unique and special consciousness. For good and for bad!

Now for the fuel fueling this intense combustibility, which is information need and the subject of this book.

Fuel

The fuel of the engine of human consciousness is the search for self-recognition of the Episodic Mind layer, the search for understanding of the Mimetic Mind layer, and then the more powerful time-travel machine: the search for meaning of the Mythic Mind layer. These describe the intentions underlying why humans travel back in time to reenact an experienced episode. The understanding intention was the seed forcing the developmental transition to the Mimetic Mind phase of human brain evolution. The search for meaning was a more powerful fuel fueling a more powerful Mythic Mind time-machine.

The transition from the linear to the paradigmatic way of thinking, which provided the seed for the transition to the new consciousness in the Mythic Mind phase, was, according to Donald (1991), the pivotal step in human evolution, the one that turned us into cognitively modern humans and separated us for good from our closest cousin species the Neanderthals. This new paradigmatic consciousness, in turn, enabled the third and so far last transition to the Theoretic Mind. In Part I, however, we take the odd position that the essence of the Theoretic Mind is the search for understanding the world, frequently with technological enhancement, not the search for meaning. Yet, the search for meaning intention is the more powerful fuel for the backward and forward of our consciousness engine's time-traveling pistons—a fine distinction that forms the thesis of this book, which we fully articulate in Part III.

There it is—a rough definition of consciousness. But however flawed it may be, it provides us with an operational definition of consciousness that is extremely useful for our purposes.

Consciousness-Based Information Search

We end Part I with the extremely practical objective of this book, which is that information search systems should be designed taking a consciousness-based perspective. Now they obey a narrow interpretation of Popper's 3-World vision of knowledge construction, shown in Fig. 3a. According to this narrow interpretation of Popper, the central interaction of information search is the interaction between the individual searcher's grasping for understanding (World 2) of elements in the objective knowledge store (World 3). The searcher then only goes back to World 1, the world of the material-physical, social and human episodic experience events, to refute or confirm the theories, models, and hypotheses of the searcher.

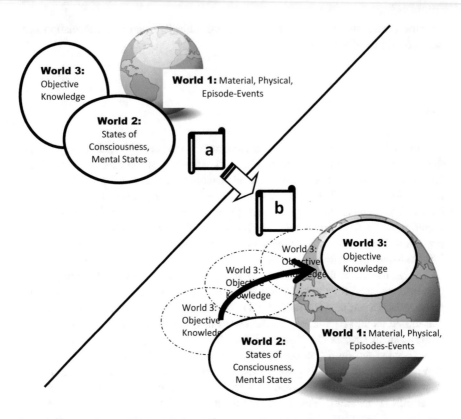

Fig. 3 The switch in paradigm frame in information search, from (**a**) a focus on the interaction between Popper's World 3 and World 2, to (**b**) World 3 merging into World 1 resulting in information search as the experiencing of an episode

This is a transactional focus on the transfer of information between the knowledge store in World 3 and the mental states, human consciousness, and grasping at understanding in World 2. In other words, the information search transaction is shifted away from World 1, the real world itself—the world of the physical and material world, and most importantly, the world of human experiencing in the world.

A consciousness-based search system, on the other hand, switches the focus of information system design to facilitating information transfer between World 1, the physical and material world, and the world of experiencing episode events, and World 2, the world of human consciousness and mental states. With a consciousness-based vision, World 3 becomes part of World 1, and new knowledge production is viewed through the lens of the searcher experiencing an episode in life, as shown in Fig. 3b.

Information search in this new paradigm is now an episode of the searcher's experiencing of the world, and therefore part of the intention structure of human consciousness. So a search engine based on this consciousness perspective will build into its design how and why humans as a species intersect with the outside world of information. There are layers of consciousness so there are layers of different intentions. It is how we frame the world, our place in that world, and the nature of the information need intention that drives us to search for information. The two dominant intentions are the search for understanding and the more powerful search for meaning. The two are linked, as we will investigate in Part III. But we must first deal, in Part II, with the central problem of information search for new knowledge construction due to our exceptional consciousness.

Part II
The Framing Problem

Introduction to Part II

Part II addresses the problem of human consciousness's exceptional ability at framing our experience. The frames are a good thing, giving us a tremendous advantage; we are an exceptionally efficient species.

The paradigmatic framing described in Part I creates theories about the world that we use constantly in real time as we live and experience the flow of the world around us. Because of these theories, we can immediately hone in on what is important in what we are seeing and experiencing, and ignore the rest of the world outside of the frame.

And with enough technology, and if we really wanted to, we could limit our behavior so that all our experience in the world fits into our frames—or someone else's frames if we admired them enough. We would then be able to anticipate everything that happens to us so that we can lead a perfectly safe life. Our frames give us this potential ability. Science fiction is rife with such scenarios of life.

But there is a greater problem than this George Orwell (1961) vision of the future.

In purely practical terms, if we create a social world that fits perfectly into our frames, we shut down access to new information, essential for the production of new knowledge. In effect, our exceptional frames can close down the open information loop that is necessary between us and the world. The resulting stasis would eventually lead to atrophy, the end of our species' ability to recognize and seek out new information in the environment, necessary so that we can adapt to change and survive as a species.

We have to really know the framing problem before we can prevent it. Part II takes a serious look at it.

Chapter 9 starts off by defining the problem with Marvin Minsky's (1975) frame theory, which forms the conceptual center of this book. Minsky summarizes the theme of this book: humans are an exceptional species because of the way we can frame our episode intersections with the world, store them in memory and then recall them later to anticipate or rehearse our experience in the world in real time. In effect,

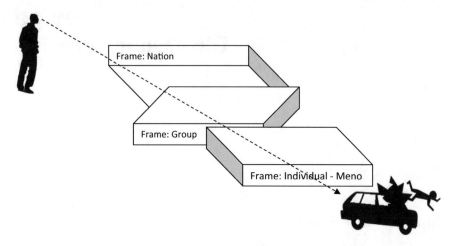

Fig. 1 Human framing levels: the Nation, the Group, and the Individual leading to Meno's Paradox

through our frames we pre-experience most if not all of our experience. Minsky's iconic theory is one of the fundaments of artificial intelligence and its goal to capture what and how humans think in an AI machine. In our book, we divide frames into levels of frames, shown in Fig. 1.

Figure 1 shows a man "viewing" the episode of a real-life traffic accident through levels of frames recalled from memory: through a nation-level frame, a group-level frame, and then through an individual-level frame. These frame levels are based on our own past experiences and our own conceptualization of ourselves, who we are, and our place in the world. The frames shape what we see in our experience. We spend the rest of Part II giving examples in full chapters of the negative side of these levels of framing.

Chapter 10 sets out the individual-level consequences of Minsky's frame theory. This negative consequence is famously encapsulated in a very old paradox of Plato, called the Meno's Paradox.

> How can you come to know that which you don't already know? You can't know what it is you don't know. So you won't recognize it even if you happen to come across it.

If this paradox is true, How then do we come to know new information, new things? The Meno's Paradox has intrigued thinkers over the last 2500 years, including our century's cognitive psychologists, starting in 1932 with Bartlett (1932).

In Chap. 11, we investigate the group-level frame. Comparing the group they belong to with outside groups enables individual members to categorize features of their inside group. We are x because the other group is not x. These comparisons are according to the same feature, so most frequently the comparisons are our group is "bigger," "better," "smarter," etc., than the other group. We give as an example Elfreda Chatman's (2000) research into dirt-eaters in the southern USA who avoid outsider information that contradicts the core values and beliefs of their dirt-eating group.

In Chap. 12, we investigate the nation-level frame with the example of the Nazi ideological frame and its hold over German citizens from 1933 to 1945. The nation-level frame is distinguished from the group-level frame by the efficiency and resources at its disposal, legitimized by bureaucratic structures that systematize the organization of national activity. The most notable historical example is the inhuman act of the Final Solution perpetrated by the Nazis in 1933–1945. We emphasize the hold of the nation frame over the German population, and their avoidance of information outside the Nazi frame.

In the Conclusion to Part II, we relate the problem of frames, which disconnect the searcher from finding new information in the outside world, to the information search situation. We humans can become imprisoned in the closed information loops of our frames. Information that contradicts the frame is either not seen or is avoided.

Chapter 9
Problem Setup: Minsky's Frame Theory

In Part I, we investigated the exceptionality of human consciousness in terms of how humans frame their intersection with the ongoing world in the unit of the episode. As shown in Fig. 9.1, it is a combustible intersection, causing memory time-traveling backward to a remembered past and forward to a predicted future. This release from time and space is the basis of our exceptionality as a species. However, there is a problem with this exceptional framing ability which is the investigation we undertake here in Part II.

We begin the investigation by setting up the problem utilizing Marvin Minsky's (1975, 1986) frame theory, one of the touchstones of the psychological modeling of what and how humans think as we experience and navigate our way through the world around us. Minsky's intention in his theory was to model human thinking so that it could be reproduced in AI and put in a machine—a human-thinking robot. According to Minsky, humans negotiate their navigation through the world via the intermediary "frames" of experience they recall from memory.

The memory frame contains "expectations" about a situation or episode or object in a person's life that he or she is about to encounter, which includes information about how to deal with "surprises" in what is about to happen. The memory frame, therefore, allows us to predict the future—that is, the episode of life we are just about to experience in real time—based on our past experience. Minsky's is in a long line of such memory-based theories, beginning with Frederic Bartlett's groundbreaking 1932 book *Remembering*. These frames provide pre-determined scripts, scenarios, or experience schemata that give us pre-knowledge and thus pre-understanding of our real-time experiences before they are actually experienced. Our frames enable us to see-as-understanding, as shown in Fig. 9.2. The understanding can be wrong; it is our understanding based on what the frame has in it or knows.

The memory frame we invoke to understand what we are seeing is an extremely beneficial product of our mental time-traveling to the future, which becomes a guiding framework for seeing the present. The frame is a predicted future of what is happening to us in real time—in the case of Fig. 9.2, witnessing a car accident—based on our experiences with the same or similar episodes from our past. Our

© Springer International Publishing AG, part of Springer Nature 2018

C. Cole, *The Consciousness' Drive*, https://doi.org/10.1007/978-3-319-92457-1_9

Fig. 9.1 Human consciousness frames our intersection with the world. It is so intense that it causes combustion and human mental or subjective time-travel

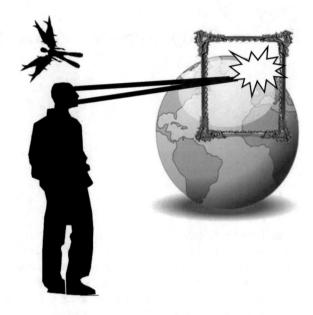

Fig. 9.2 Seeing-as-understanding, via a memory frame, a car accident episode occurring in real time

frames are extremely helpful to us in getting through life with as few cuts and bruises as possible. The problem lies in the frequency of our time-traveling, its ubiquity.

The Problem of Time-Travel

The problem of time-travel associated with human consciousness is that we are so good at it. It has become so automatic that we don't think we are doing it. But, in fact, we mentally time-travel more than we realize, backward to the subjective past and forward to the predicted future. Our consciousness is set up that way.

If we could record what we think about all day, we in fact think about past episodes constantly. We go over and over again the first time we met our spouse, the death of a parent, or child that haunts every waking moment of the present, or the role we played in someone else's unhappiness that we regret, and any number of other major events in our life. How often do we do this per day, per minute? This must increase as we get older, as we accumulate more and more memories, but there are reasons to think that time-travel back to past episode experience is our "on" motor.

Time-travel to the future is another matter. Future time-travel must be rare, we think. We use past experienced episodes as rehearsal frames to guide us in controlling our behavior for important future events, like an upcoming job interview. An old job interview episode might serve to figure out what type of questions we will be asked, including what went wrong then that we can correct and plan for in the interview next week. We may even imagine the future job interview scenario with the correction in place, testing out various different scenarios in our head. We create a script of the likely questions. Yes, that sort of time-travel to the future we accept doing now and then.

And when we're young especially, we live in the future, envisaging happy lives in marriage and career. That we also admit to. It is like when we are in the car driving to a destination. We admit to thinking about our future destination; a sort of in-the-car daydream of how the destination episode would go. And when we get to the destination, we may check our actual experience of it against our expectation of it back in the car. This is the sort of future time-traveling that we know we do on a regular basis.

The alert reader is now into future time-travel, the concept of it, and asks: What is planning ahead for anything if not future time-travel? At work, we create the same sort of future scenarios for the next year—if the economy grows by 2% our company should grow by x%—and we constantly check real-time performance against the predicted future. We all admit to that sort of future time-traveling. And at a broader level, at the level of our species, aren't all our scientific models and theories predictions of the future based on past experience. Yes, we admit to that. We take pride in it, our ability to predict, even explain, the future via our Theoretic Mind layer models and theories.

But no one, if you asked them, would say that he or she experiences life primarily through the intermediary of a predicted future frame that generalizes or categorizes our experience. That seems counterintuitive. At the most basic day-to-day operation of living our lives, we feel as though we are just responding spontaneously to stimuli from the world around us. A person asks us a question, we answer it. A car veers in front of us, we turn the wheel in the opposite direction.

But this is not so. Our whole life, be it the big or small decisions we make every minute of the day, actually each of our actions is permeated by future time-travel. This low-level, everyday future time-travelling is what Minsky's frame theory is about. It is a hallmark of our species that makes us exceptional, because future time-travel takes us out of the reacting-life into another kind of living. Through our frames containing pre-knowledge and pre-understanding of the future, we **see-the-world-as-understanding**. In effect, the frame constitutes a theory of the episode we are just about to experience.

Minsky's Frame Theory

We focus on two of Minsky's example frames to explain his frame theory: an "entering a room" frame and a "going to a child's birthday party" frame. In the "entering a room" frame, which is a spatial almost perceptual example, Minsky was influenced by Eleanor Rosch's (1973) seminal work on category formation in her book *On the Internal Structure of Perceptual and Semantic Categories*. It is how we categorize our experience through reference to prototypes of the category stored in our memory system.

When we enter a room we have never been in before, it is like any number of spatial situations that form the foundational existence of humans moving through the physical world. We are always entering such spaces—entering an airplane, entering a car, entering a school, etc. We are used to it, good at it. But let us further examine this entering a new room situation. How exactly do we think about it when we are actually doing it?

Figure 9.3 shows a man at the door of a room he is about to enter; and on the right side of the figure is the empty room itself behind that same door. The man then enters the room and is facing the far wall with the window. The door behind him and the three other walls are not in his visual range; but when he suddenly turns back, the door behind him and the wall that surrounds it are instantly in front of him, in full view, at both the perceptual and cognitive level, meaning the room is both a physical space and a concept. In a sense, the man immediately and automatically understands what he sees when he turns around, even though he has never seen this particular wall and door before. They appear to him without any apparent perceptual input. It's

Fig. 9.3 A man at an open door about to enter an unfamiliar room

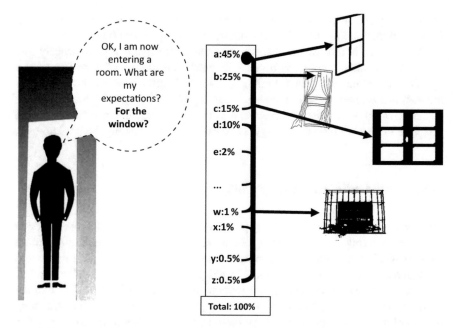

Fig. 9.4 Window feature slot in prototype frame for "entering a room." The circle is the default setting (the most probable window the man will find in the actual room)

almost as if he understood the room before he saw it (in the perceptual sense of seeing). This is the Minsky concept of our frames and future time-travel.

As a result of his time-traveling, with each new turn the man makes, the new wall in front of him does not have to be discovered, either perceptually or conceptually; rather, it only has to be refreshed in his mind, even though it is the first time in his life he has seen this particular wall.

Don't we really "expect" what we are about to see? What we are seeing in real time is initially only a memory image of a prototypical room. Attached to this memory image is a set of hypotheses about the real room we are just entering that we check against what is really there, just to make sure we are on track.

We make this expectation explicit in Fig. 9.4. Here we have the same man at the door of the same unfamiliar room he is about to enter. He recalls a prototype frame from memory of a room, which creates expectations for the various features of the room he is about to enter. Figure 9.4 gives an example of an expectation set for the window feature in the room he is about to enter, i.e., before he sees the actual window in the room. There is a default setting for the most probable window he will see in the room, but there are other alternative assignments in the expectation set for this particular feature; and each of these alternative assignments is assigned lesser probabilities of occurring, but they are also almost instantaneously and automatically available to the frame. In the example shown, there are 26 possible alternative assignments in the window feature slot in this particular man's "entering a room" frame. For this middle-class, North American male, the "w" window-with-prison bar assignment probability is very low, given here at 1%. Another man, another woman from a different culture would have a different prototype room frame.

This strange ability of the man to understand the room, instantaneously and automatically, upon entering is because he enters the room with a prototype of a room already in mind, which according to Eleanor Rosch are all instances of rooms the man has entered in his life averaged into a prototypical room. The fact that he doesn't have to see or discover each wall, each new floor, each new ceiling for the first time saves both time and energy. He sees-it-as-understanding; he pre-knows it.

Going to a Child's Birthday Party

Minsky's "going to a child's birthday party" frame example is much more elaborate than the "entering a room" frame just described. Entering an unfamiliar room requires what is essentially a perceptual frame for guiding our physical movement through space. The "going to a child's birthday party" frame, on the other hand, is filled with complex sociological and psychological twists and turns. But like the room frame, the "going to a child's birthday party" frame involves time-traveling backward to a stereotype frame of the episode, then mentally time-traveling in the frame forward in time. We instantiate the frame before we commence the real-time experiencing of the episode, then use the frame as a guide for experiencing the episode in real time, for an episode that may last many hours, days, even weeks.

Broadly speaking, attached to each such frame is:

- Information about how to use the frame
- What we can expect to happen next
- What we can do if these expectations are not met

An outline of the "going to a child's birthday party" frame is shown in Fig. 9.5. The frame outlined is for a middle-class North American birthday party, and is specific to that culture. (For Minsky's (1986) own itemization of this frame, see his book *The Society of the Mind*.)

The frame is divided into upper and lower levels. At the top of the frame are the upper level parameters of the frame that are fundamental and almost always true about "going to a child's birthday party." At the bottom of the frame are aspect slots of the frame, which are variable and must be filled in by the specific details of the birthday party. In Fig. 9.5, we give three examples (a, b, c) where the frame has alternative possibilities attached to these lower-level aspect slots. The aspect slots, in turn, link to subframes that set out alternative behavior routines. In the case of (a), for example, the subframe would indicate finding out if you, the parent, had made the mistake or not about the date of the child's birthday party because "no one's there" when you arrive at the party.

One can see at once that the birthday party scenario illustrated in Fig. 9.5 is not at all complete. Thus the need for access to subframes in a frame network of all this human's knowledge and experience, which builds into the frame diverse alternative

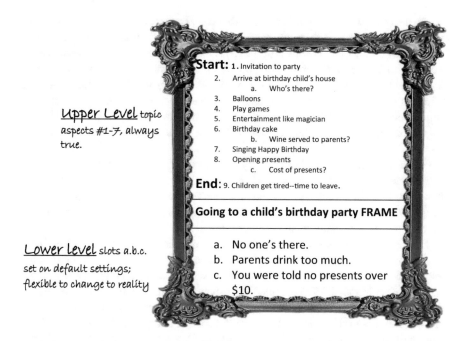

Start: 1. Invitation to party
2.   Arrive at birthday child's house
        a.   Who's there?
3.   Balloons
4.   Play games
5.   Entertainment like magician
6.   Birthday cake
        b.   Wine served to parents?
7.   Singing Happy Birthday
8.   Opening presents
        c.   Cost of presents?

End: 9. Children get tired--time to leave.

Going to a child's birthday party FRAME

a.   No one's there.
b.   Parents drink too much.
c.   You were told no presents over $10.

Upper Level topic aspects #1-7, always true.

Lower Level slots a.b.c. set on default settings; flexible to change to reality

Fig. 9.5 Minsky's frame "going to a child's birthday party," with two levels to the frame: Upper Level and Lower Level slots that are flexible and connected to subframes

aspects and decision–action scenarios. These alternative scenarios, in turn, have their own frames in the network. Take, for example, the point of arriving at the birthday child's house (see 2. in Fig. 9.5).

You arrive at the party and there is no one there. Or so it seems. For an average parent, this scenario would be unexpected but it would certainly be within the realm of possibilities. There could be a "surprise" aspect to it; that the other children and parents will soon come out from behind a wall and shout "surprise" because it is also your birthday, or you have the wrong street address or the wrong date or start-time. Any of these subroutine frames would be built into the "going to a child's birthday party" frame in its lower-level aspect slots. These subframes would tell you, the parent, how to act and what to expect. If it's the wrong date and time, for example, the frame asks" Whose mistake is it? Is it yours or the host's? If it's yours, you have to assure your own child with an excuse for your mistake, something that won't frighten the child. Do you want to indicate to the child you are invincible or that you are human, vulnerable to error and that errors are part of life?

Minsky's "going to a child's birthday party" frame rings true. One can easily imagine running through it from Start to End almost on autopilot, easily taking into account slight variations in the real-time episode via the default slots in the lower half of the frame. Why couldn't we then build this AI into a robot so that we wouldn't have to accompany our child to the birthday party?

The idea of creating a "child-caring" robot based on a frame theory conception of AI is not so farfetched. If there are, say, 10,000 basic situations in an average life that make up our life, then it would be relatively easy to script a robot with the AI necessary to mimic such a human life, albeit a life that was relegated only to routine situations. So we are talking about a robot programmed for a routine life. The definition of "routine" would gradually expand. Soon the most sophisticated human activities could be AI-framed into a robot, for example, a robot who is programmed to break our children out of drug dependency or any other behavioral problem.

The frame, with its built-in flexibility and its connection to a network of frames, each connected with their own network, and so on, is a paradigmatic way of thinking about life. It is something our Mythic and Theoretic Mind layers of consciousness are used to dealing with. So Minsky conceptualized human thinking in his frame theory. It mimics the way we think—our human consciousness.

If these preconfigured episodes of all human experience could be duplicated in AI frames and inserted in a robot, would these robots be imitating human consciousness? This is a very big question. We have set up the exceptionality of human consciousness in Part I. We describe the problem here in Part II. We are setting up the problem theoretically (based on Minsky's frame theory) in this chapter. Let's then diagram the problem the same as we did for our exceptionality in Part I of this book, with similar diagrams of human thinking. (Doing so will enable us to better explain the solution to the problem in Part III of the book.)

Diagramming Frame Theory's Conceptualization of Human Consciousness

A common theme in this book is diagramming human thinking in terms of stimulus events that occur outside of us in the world, and our human response to these events. In the last such diagram in Part I, we diagrammed paradigmatic Theoretic Mind layer thinking for Leeuwenhoek, the seventeenth-century microbiologist and possible collaborator of Vermeer. Here, in Fig. 9.6, we diagram the "going to child's birthday party" in a paradigmatic frame. The frame is formed from our first experience of the episode situation, and then generalized from all our experiences with this type of life episode, including our viewings of it on TV and in the movies. The stereotyping or generalizing of the episode is a form of theory-making: we theorize the episode into a paradigmatic-type frame based on what Minsky calls "stereotyped situations." Then for each subsequent stimulus event in the person's life of the "going to a child's birthday party" episode-event, the theory frame of the episode is recalled from memory to predict and guide the real-time unfolding of the episode. We basically already pre-know what will happen before it happens based on our memory frame. We then see the unfolding episode-as-understanding. Minsky's frame theory explains the economy and efficiency inherent in human seeing and experiencing life via this conceptualization of seeing-as-understanding.

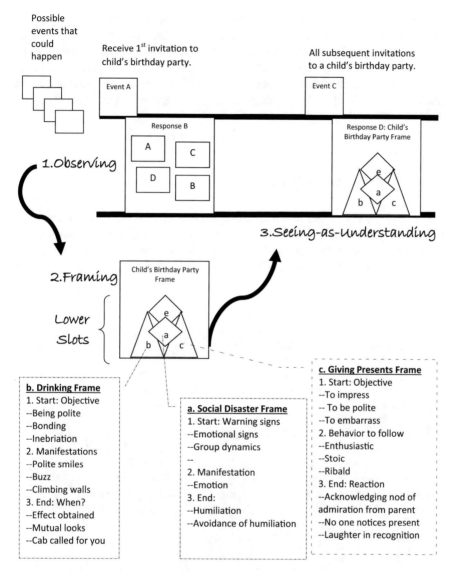

Fig. 9.6 Paradigmatic frame of "going to a child's birthday party," recalled to see-as-understanding all future episodes of "going to a child's birthday party"

The frame has to be very flexible; it has to be sensitive to variation in the specific situation as it unfolds in real time. Lower-level slots that determine flexibility in the specific aspects of the frame become more varied, more sophisticated as our prototype for the episode frame evolves with age. Therefore, access to related frames are increasingly put into the frame, which enables the instantiation of evermore sensitive aspect slots in the frame's lower level.

For Fig. 9.6, aspect slot (b), the frame poses the question: "Is there drinking by the parents at the child's birthday party?" This aspect slot links directly to a "drinking in general" frame, which is also derived from the person's life. This linkage to other frames in a frame network forms an interconnected and ever-growing (as we age) network of frames that determine our experience of life, who we are, and the way we think. Thus the ability of the paradigmatic frame at capturing human exceptionality and the consciousness of the unique individual!

What Are We Really Seeing?

What are we really seeing in a real-time episode of life? In Fig. 9.7, we show the experiencing of a real-time episode of a car accident directed through the intermediary of a predicted future frame of reference. This means we see and experience the world-as-understanding it; the seeing is not direct but mediated through a memory

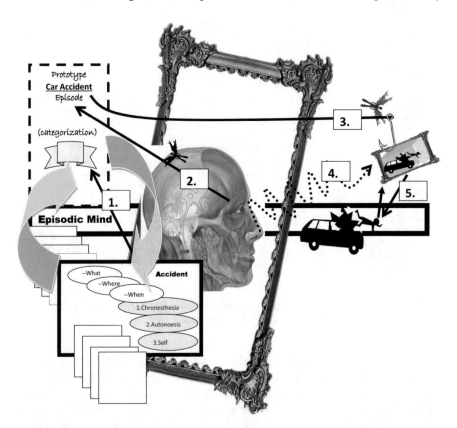

Fig. 9.7 Time-traveling via predicted future "car accident" episode frame, forming a prototype of the episode, which is subsequently used to guide seeing-as-understanding of real-time car accidents

frame—in the case of Fig. 9.7, a frame based on a car accident recalled from our memory system (including what we have experienced second-hand via film, TV, and the Internet). It is how we categorize the chaotic stimuli coming at us from the outside world. (I have gone into categorization in much more detail in my previous book (Cole 2012)). Prototype framing of episodes in life is a categorization activity. Here in Fig. 9.7, we include the categorization-into-prototype frame of a "car accident" as being attached to episodic memory, which is where specific life episodes are stored; prototype episode frames are generalized or generic representations of specific types of episodes in life stored in episodic memory. The arrows in Fig. 9.7, therefore, go both ways between prototype episode storage and episodic memory because, and this is the point of this chapter, prototype episode frames **shape** how the individual sees and understands real-time episodes.

Where Minsky's prototype frames and Tulving's episodic memory frames join is in the feature assignments in the lower half of the prototype frame for, in the case of Fig. 9.7, witnessing a car accident. The feature assignments are set on the default, but there are other assignments turned on in the expectation set for each feature of the frame. In Fig. 9.4, as an example, there are 26 assignments in the window feature expectation set. Here in these expectation feature sets is where the scenario construction takes place.

In quick, blink-of-an-eye generative cognitive processes, different scenarios attached to the assignments are simulated or tried-out against the actual episode until the most probable one is decided on. This simulation procedure aligns the generic prototype frame to the real-time episode taking place in front of the individual witnessing the accident. It is this real-time instantiation of a subframe into the principal frame of "witnessing a car accident" that creates the specific memory of the episode in the witness's episodic memory. It creates ownership of the generic episode of the car accident, one of the primary conditions of episodic memory outlined in Part I (The three criteria of episodic memory: Chronesthesia, Autonoesis, and Self, are shown again in Fig. 9.7). The subframes accessed via the feature slots in the lower level of the prototype frame create a constructed and simulated future frame that guides the seeing-as-understanding of the real-time experiencing of the episode in life, such as a witnessing a car accident.

In Fig. 9.7, (1) the man has previously formed a prototype frame for the episode, based on the prototype case of his experience of the same or similar episodes in his life. The man's eye sees the car accident and (2) automatically recalls a prototype frame for a car accident. (3) The prototype frame is a predicted future frame that guides the individual's seeing-as-understanding of the real-time car accident. (4) The man sees-as-understanding via the prototype episode for the car accident, not the real-time car accident in front of him. (5) The prototype frame checks its default slot assignments against the real-time car accident episode, leading to real-time revision of the frame's default slot assignments in the lower level of the frame.

The frames are not perfect. As shown time and again in real-life court cases, witnesses to car accidents are notoriously unreliable because witnesses see-as-understanding the real-time accident through the predicted future frame they recall from prototype memory. The accident is seen as if we have already experienced it.

The Problem: Living Life in the Predicted Future Frame

Minsky's conceptualization of our experiencing life through the intermediary of a predicted future frame establishes a very efficient way to see, experience, and to quickly react to what the world throws at us. From the point of view of the survival of our species, the predicted future frame saves cognitive time and energy, establishing a focus—establishing what is relevant in the world from what is noise—which gives us an exceptional advantage over all other species.

Where is the problem? How can the predicted future framing of everything in life's experience be a bad thing? The problem is that the prototype frames with their default settings bias what we see and experience in the world to what we have seen and experienced before. We have a theory frame of all experiences. Over time, and with the buildup in confidence that these predicted future frames are dependable, or if we are made afraid to veer from what is expected of us, we cease testing the theory of the particular episode against the real-time experience. In fact, it becomes so comfortable to pre-experience the world in our mind, mentally, rather than experiencing the world directly, that the world becomes lodged on the wrong side of the frame, in the inner side of it in our own head, as shown in Fig. 9.8.

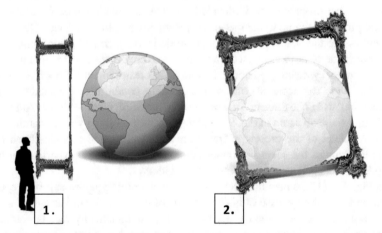

Fig. 9.8 The predicted future framing problem: (1) Instead of seeing the world through the frame, (2) real-time experiencing of the world shifts into the inner side of the frame. Our experiencing of the world is on the wrong side of the frame!

Chapter 10
Individual Frame Level: Meno's Paradox

Minsky's frame theory portrays a human consciousness that condemns humans to experiencing the world through prototype or predicted future frames. When we intersect with the real world, we automatically recall a prototype frame of the episode we are about to experience in real time. We "enter" this experience. Minsky gives the examples of "entering an unknown room" or "going to a child's birthday party." The prototype frame predicts the episode of experience we are about to undergo, allowing us to see-the-world-as-understanding rather than directly experiencing the cacophony of real-world existence. Visualize yourself out in the world, on the street, without a frame directing your actions. A car to your right honks its horn; a woman in a window is shaking a rug clean of its dust; an airplane overhead gleams in the sky, etc. It is rare that we do this. It is probably good for us as we walk through a forest, or through a meadow. Thinking about nothing; living in the moment. But in these moments, we have no frame in place, no standard of what is relevant and what is irrelevant. It is chaos. We are not built like that, our species.

The frame structuring our way of thinking is a very efficient consciousness. Our predetermined prototype frame for the particular phenomenon we are facing in real time allows us only to focus on what in our intersection with the world is relevant, based on our past experience with the same or similar phenomena.

The problematic side is that the constructed world we see through the frame becomes so strong and real-like, it can control what we see and experience in the real world; it becomes a safe and predictable substitute for the rough and tumble of real-world experience. Shown in Fig. 10.1, the constructed world becomes lodged inside the frame—it becomes what we see in the real world—while the outside world is kept at arm's length. It is a safe place, predictable and efficient. And as our real-time experiencing of the world fades further and further away, we experience life through an echo of the real world, not the real world itself.

There are different levels of the frame problem. At the nation level, which we describe later in Part II, the ideological frame of an all-powerful government can become inculcated into the civilian population, leading to mass, almost suicidal destruction and death. We illustrate the nation-frame with the example of Nazi Germany in World War II.

© Springer International Publishing AG, part of Springer Nature 2018

C. Cole, *The Consciousness' Drive*, https://doi.org/10.1007/978-3-319-92457-1_10

Fig. 10.1 The individual's experiencing of life becomes lodged inside the predicted future frame, resulting in the real experiencing of the world being kept at arm's length

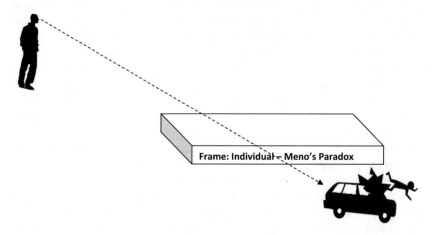

Fig. 10.2 The framing problem at the individual level and Meno's Paradox

At the group level, described in the next chapter, the group creates a frame of day-to-day existence that excludes dissonant outside information. This particularly affects disadvantaged groups in our society. We use the example of Elfreda Chatman's study of the small world of dirt-eaters and their avoidance of out-of-frame information from the outside world, even when this information would help them improve their living conditions.

In this chapter, shown in Fig. 10.2, we investigate the ramifications of the framing problem in terms of the individual consciousness which condemns each one of us to experience life not directly but through experience once removed, in our predicted future frames. It is an existential problem, the reverse side of positive side of our consciousness coin described in Part I of this book. This existential problem of our relationship to the world has been a focus of thinkers since Plato and Meno's Paradox.

The Framing Problem at the Existential Level

The alert reader will realize that we are about to enter the realm of epistemology: how we come to know—the nature and origin of knowledge. We believe we experience the world directly and not secondhand, once removed. We assume that we cognitively process the world around us, i.e., that we think about it, make decisions concerning what actions to take—the same way we perceive the world in touch, smell, and sight, which is to say directly, without an intermediary curating what we see and experience. We pay for an item at the cashier the same way we feel a cool spring breeze on our skin, or the sudden heat of the stove warning us to take our hand away.

But sometimes we sense another parallel world, or it is as if we're disconnected from the world, when we sense a déjà vu, or during a religious or spiritual experience, or in times of great grief or joy. In these precious moments, we get the strange feeling that most of the time we are merely seeing and experiencing a surface world. Then we ask ourselves: What is the full, complete world? In fact, this vague awareness of a gap between ourselves and the world, due to our Mythic Mind layer of consciousness, may be the basis of our difference, our uniqueness, our exceptionality as a species.

It is the root cause of our search for meaning.

Our species has always felt this gap, our species' essential unease. Plato expressed it in his Allegory of the Cave written 2500 years ago. As discussed in Part I of this book, it is even possible—and we can only infer this intention—that even our Paleolithic ancestors were expressing their disconnectedness from existence as far back as 15,000–40,000 years ago when they painted on cave walls the supernatural quality of the animals they hunted, and the bird symbol on a pole signifying passage to a parallel existence, perhaps the afterlife.

Plato's Allegory of the Cave

The idea that we live in a fabricated interface experience rather than in real experience has long fascinated Western civilization. Plato (2000), in his *Allegory of the Cave* (*The Republic*, Book VII), shown in Fig. 10.3, portrayed humans as prisoners of their consciousness, shackled to chairs in a cave, who believe that the shadows they are watching on the cave wall in front of them are their real experience. The prisoners' shackles prevent them from looking behind them and to the side, in

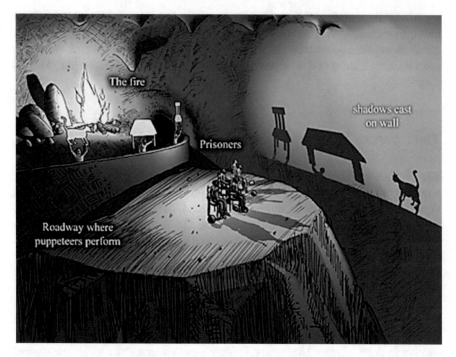

Fig. 10.3 Plato's *Allegory of the Cave*: What we are mistaking for our experiencing of the world and reality is only shadows of the real world on the cave wall (© 2016 John D'Alembert. Creative Commons Attribution-Share Alike 4.0 International license)

fact, anywhere else except straight ahead, so they cannot see they are being duped. Situated out-of-sight behind the prisoners are the puppeteers. Behind the puppeteers is a light source, a great fire, which shines light on the images the puppeteers hold up to produce the shadows on the cave wall. The shadow images are "the illusions that dominate the human condition" (Abensour 2007, p. 965).

There are diverse interpretations of what the puppeteers represent. There is an epistemological interpretation (e.g., Heidegger and Salder 2002) and a political interpretation (e.g., Arendt 1990; see also, Abensour 2007) of this cave allegory. The political interpretation, exemplified by the Nazis' hold over their civilian population when they were losing World War II, despite heavy civilian losses and famine, we examine later in Part II (see Chap. 12).

In the epistemological interpretation, the prisoners are being played by their own consciousness. Their consciousness dupes them—us!—into thinking they are experiencing and seeing what is real when in fact they are seeing and experiencing only shadows of existence on the cave wall.[1]

---

[1]There are alternative interpretations of Plato's *Allegory of the Cave*. Plato gives a rationalism explanation of what constitutes the real world (in his Theory of the Ideal Forms). Aristotle argues against rationalism. And it is Aristotle's empiricism argument and the categorization of human experience that forms the basis of Minsky's prototype frames.

The cleverness and efficiency of our human consciousness leaves us in a conundrum, a paradox. It gives us stability and a sense of mastery of our world. But we have to see and experience new things in the world, to catch the changes so we can adapt to them and survive as a species. We have always done this, and we have been exceptionally successful at doing this. But because we only see and experience the world via our predicted future frames, which we use as guides to organize and control our real-time experience, we live in the framework they impose. We are constrained to see and experience only what our frames tell us to see and experience.

How then do we come to see and know what is outside of the frames in the real world, i.e., the nonconstructed world, which is different from that which we already know? It was Meno who asked Socrates this question, which Plato (2000) wrote down.

The Meno Paradox

In Plato's written account, Socrates was walking with Meno, a wealthy young nobleman from Thessaly (a province just south of Macedonia), who was accompanied everywhere by an entourage of slaves and hangers-on. Socrates begins their conversation by contrasting Thessaly for its wealth and learning, especially in science, with the abysmal state of learning in Athens, specifically the teaching of virtue and the good. This prompts Meno to ask Socrates the question: Can one learn to be a virtuous person, or must virtue be innate?

Socrates himself professed ignorance about such things. He asked Meno to tell him. The two men went on and on in their dialogue with Socrates prodding Meno to come up with a definition of virtue. At one point, Meno felt completely uncertain, which he complained about. Meno said he thought he knew what virtue was before they began talking that day, at least he was sure he could give examples of it, and that he could even teach it to others, but now he no longer knew what it was. This uncertainty was a teaching technique of Socrates, called apoira.

It is in this state of apoira or knowing nothing that Meno asks Socrates what is considered one of the foundational questions of all philosophy and psychology:

> How can you try to find out about something, Socrates, if you haven't got the faintest idea what it is? I mean, how can you put before your mind a thing **that you have no knowledge of**, in order to try to find out about it? And even supposing you did come across it, how would you know that **that** was **it**, if you didn't know what it was to begin with? (Meno 80d, in Plato 2005, p. 100)

Stated broadly, the paradox asks: How do we come to know that which we don't already know? Because we can't know what we don't know. If we don't know it before, we won't be able to recognize it if we come across it. And if we do recognize it, we already know it.

On the surface, Meno's Paradox seems nonsensical. We believe we are constantly seeing new things in the environment, and we equate this with new knowledge.

When we are reading a book on a new topic, for example, we simply read one thing, then we know it, then we read another thing, then we know that, and so on and until we know everything about the topic as it is contained in this particular book. Brenda Dervin (Dervin and Nilan 1986) has called this the "brick" upon "brick" perspective of knowledge acquisition. But this is not how we gain new knowledge.

The frames are built to be efficient, leading us through life experience smartly, so that we can make quick decisions, know how to deal with sudden danger, and survive in a hostile world. They are not structured to easily accept change—new information and new knowledge. We see and remember information that ties in to what we already know and believe—that is already in our frames of experience. We are in fact imprisoned by our frames, prevented from seeing the new information requisite for acquiring new knowledge from the world.

The predicted future frames we use to guide us in our experiencing of the world put us into a closed information loop of seeing and experiencing the world, shown in Fig. 10.4.

The constraint placed on our seeing by our frame-constructed consciousness is on the whole a good thing. It allows us to be very efficient. There is a lot of tra-la-la going on in the world that is not useful to pay attention to, so it's better to ignore this

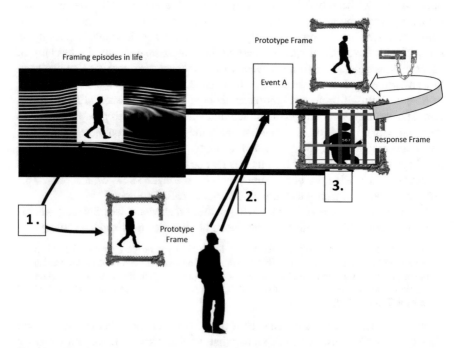

Fig. 10.4 We are imprisoned by our frames in a closed information system feedback loop, in terms of what we subsequently see and experience. (1) We frame our experience in a prototype frame for the episode. (2) Our next intersection with the same Event A episode in the world. (3) We are imprisoned by the closed information feedback loop of our future predicted guide frame for this subsequent episode

white noise. That is why as a species we are so good at staying focused and concentrating on the important things.

And it is very comforting to live within our frames. It is like living in a very secure room we have grown to love. With a lovely fireplace in winter to keep us warm. There are extra blankets in the cupboard. The fridge is stocked with food; and we know how to replenish it with our "going to the supermarket" episode frame.

But this tendency of ours to construct our lives within our secure and well-worn frames has a dark side. We can become easily induced into staying within the confines of secure and comfortable frames; it is our natural tendency, our default position; but our self-imprisonment can become truly dangerous at the group or nation level.

Figure 10.4 represents this dark side of our framing ability: our frames imprison us in a vicious cycle of rehashing the same old thing—turning us into a predictable stimulus–response mechanism. We respond or react to a stimulus from the world according to our frame, which can be manipulated by an ideology. We cannot see and experience anything outside the frame because our frames control and constrain what we see and experience. Life becomes a closed system onto itself, confined to what is inside the frame. It becomes a locked door, a prison. The negative or dark side of our species' ability at framing our world is the subject of the next two chapters.

Chapter 11
Group Frame Level: Information Avoidance

In the previous chapter, we investigated the negative effect of human framing of their experience in the world at the individual level. Our mental frames imprison us in what we already know, which prevents us from coming to know that which we don't already know. In this chapter, we move up from the individual frame to the problem posed by our group frame, shown in Fig. 11.1.

If you think about it, we define ourselves in terms of the groups we belong to. We belong to ethnic groups, religious groups, social groups like the girl scouts, or political affiliation groups that represent our views on how society should be organized. We also belong to amorphous, informally organized groups like social class. Our group affiliations not only represent our personal characteristics or beliefs in relation to other groups, they even help us to recognize or consolidate in ourselves who we actually are and what we believe as individuals. They thus participate in the self-recognition intention of our individual consciousness.

The 15,000–40,000-year-old cave paintings at Chauvet and Lascaux are possibly examples of group actualization and/or consolidation ceremonies that were intended to create or strengthen group solidarity, on the part of either the artists themselves, or others in the group who ritualized episodes of experience in cave ceremonies associated with the paintings perhaps to consolidate their control over the group. We can see how group processes, centered on self-recognition, benefited our species.

Our intergroup categorization of human social, political, and economic activities and behavior allowed us, via predetermined group category frames, to react quickly and effectively to the vagaries, hostile and otherwise, in the human physical and social environment. This can be a positive force of human experience when we coalesce as a group around an issue and find together a group solution to problems that negatively affect our experience in the world.

We focus in this chapter on the negative side of defining our individual consciousness in terms of group categorization processes, specifically in terms of discrimination by groups against another group, isolating the latter into their small worlds. Groups actualize and consolidate negative individual characteristics of themselves through this discrimination process. These individual characteristics

© Springer International Publishing AG, part of Springer Nature 2018
C. Cole, *The Consciousness' Drive*, https://doi.org/10.1007/978-3-319-92457-1_11

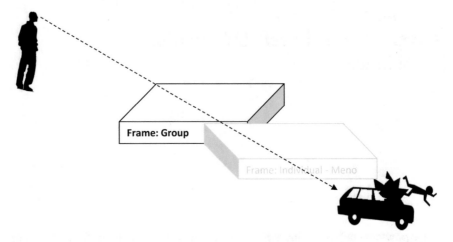

Fig. 11.1 Group frame: seeing reality through the group frame

become ingrained in the discriminated against group, even protected, causing the group members to reject or avoid information that contradicts the characteristics, values, and beliefs of the group.

That is the negative effect of discrimination. We will get to an example of that at the end of this chapter. But there is a positive effect of discrimination from the point of view of our species' self-recognition intention. Discrimination is an essential phase of categorizing the outside world in terms of our individual consciousness. We will get to this first. At the beginning of this chapter, we focus on the dynamics of group categorization as they concern processes that actualize or define the belief dimensions of the individual's consciousness.

We define what a group frame is, in two steps:

1. The formation of the group frame—how and why it is formed.

   • We will briefly describe intergroup dynamics as part of the self-actualization or self-recognition of the individual's consciousness.

2. The negative consequence of the group frame, via the process of discrimination, leads to information avoidance by the discriminated-against group.

   • We use Elfreda Chatman's (1990, 1996) theory of small worlds and her study of dirt-eaters in the southern USA as an example of information avoidance in groups.

Formation of Group Frame

In the sections that follow, we rely on a foundational article on group formation and group dynamics of Tajfel and Turner (1979). To start with, they distinguish between the individual behavior when two individuals meet and their behavior together involving **"interpersonal behavior,"** and two individuals meeting and their behavior together involving **"intergroup behavior."** This is an important definitional distinction.

Interpersonal behavior is the interaction of two or more individuals strictly as individuals. In its purest form, the nearest approximation of interpersonal behavior is between two spouses. In most cases, we assume the pair has pushed their separate group-identifications out of their relationship, or at least these group affiliations have been decided and are nonissues. We are talking about assumptions making up the "purest" case here, which does not necessarily conform to reality. Likewise, intergroup behavior also does not exist in its purest form; the nearest approximation would be between two soldiers from opposite sides of a battle who meet on the battlefield as representatives of opposing ideologies. In this "purest" case of intergroup interaction, individual members of the opposing groups become "undifferentiated items in a unified social category" (Tajfel 1981, p. 243). What this means, in other words, is that the two soldiers from opposing sides are purely (in theory) only units of the social category and not individuals.

There are touching stories about soldiers on two sides of a conflict coming together for a Christmas feast (e.g., *Joyeux Noël*, a French film made in 2005 concerns the December 1914 World War I event where the two enemy sides came together to celebrate Christmas), but mostly soldiers manage to keep interpersonal dynamics out of the battle, partly because it is rare for soldiers from opposing camps to talk to each other, and partly because it is more difficult to kill the enemy if he or she is thought of as a person. Tajfel and Turner put these two positions on opposite ends of a continuum, shown in Fig. 11.2.

The continuum clarifies the distinction that intergroup behavior between two people coming from opposing group categories is very different from two individuals reacting together interpersonally based purely on their individual characteristics such as (in theory) two spouses or partners in a marriage.

Within the context of a group, the individual subsumes herself into being a member of a category or prototype both for the member herself and for members of an opposing group. In an intergroup interaction, a member of a group categorizes a meeting with an opposing group member similarly to categorizing any environmental stimulus, which we will briefly review here.

Fig. 11.2 Continuum: interpersonal (e.g., spouses interacting) to intergroup (soldiers from opposing sides of a conflict interacting)

Categorizing a Stimulus Experience: Interpersonal End of Continuum

We begin first on the other side of the continuum, on the interpersonal end of Fig. 11.2; then we will progress with the categorization process for the intergroup end of the Fig. 11.2 continuum, which is the main topic of this chapter.

Interpersonal Categorization We have examined categorization involving an interpersonal-type stimulus in much more detail in my first book on information need (Cole 2012). We re-utilize a diagram from that book here, shown in Fig. 11.3. The figure shows an individual's process of categorizing a stimulus from the outside world and deciding between two prototype categories. There is a "discriminating" and then "identification" phase to this process.

Figure 11.3 describes a categorization process for a physical object—similar to Minsky's "entering an unknown room" example discussed earlier in Part II, in Chap. 9. When "entering an unknown room," an individual recalls from memory a prototype frame for this action, but also recalls, and has at ready, other possible prototype frames in case it is not a room behind the door he is about to open. It could be a balcony. It could be another corridor. For each of these other possibilities, he recalls competing alternative prototype frames to cover every exigency based on his previous experience. His memory system cannot leave him in the lurch and must

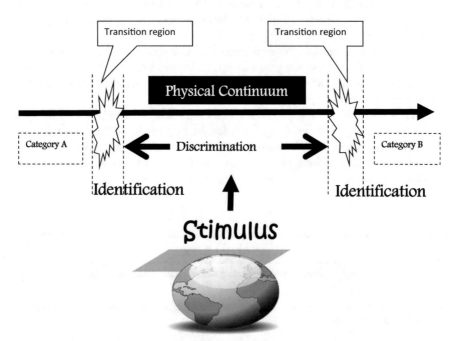

Fig. 11.3 Discrimination and identification in an individual's categorization of a stimulus from the outside world (from Cole 2012, p. 124, Fig. 12.5)

provide him with backup Plan B, with quick access to many more plans if so needed. In Fig. 11.3, we have only two alternative prototype categories: Category A and Category B.

In Fig. 11.4, for an interpersonal categorization process, we expand Fig. 11.3's representation of the categorization process for a more complicated stimulus from the outside world: the more complicated Minsky example of prototype framing of a life experience: "going to a child's birthday party." The stimulus sets off the categorization process. Here, another parent and friend, in exactly the same groups as "our individual," says something to "our individual." Fig. 11.4 describes the categorization of a stimulus from the outside world as it is entering our individual's consciousness. This is a purely interpersonal example—we strip the example of all intergroup dynamics.

The two key categorization phases are first "discrimination" then "identification" (Harnad 1987a, b).

The other parent-friend starts off the categorization process with the stimulus, asking our individual the question: "Are you doing anything next Sunday?"

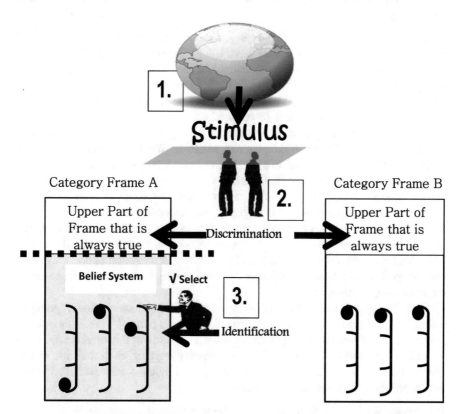

Fig. 11.4 Categorization phases: (1) Stimulus from outside world. (2) Discrimination between Category A and Category B. (3) Identification phases of categorization process

Discrimination is the phase of the categorization process where the outside stim-ulus, in this case the "friend's" invitation, is matched to every episode category frame in our individual's memory system. Is the memory category "in" or "out" as matching the invitation frame? Our individual must reduce the set of possible alternatives to the most likely, to a manageable number.

In our individual's mind, the invitation clearly veers between a child's birthday party and an adult birthday party, but our individual cannot ask the so-called friend which outright. He or she must fish for clues. This is because our individual's spouse had flirted with the inviting friend and in our individual's eyes it was possible there was something more going on here.

Our individual answers the invitation: "I am free next Sunday. My spouse has something planned but can probably cancel it. What do you have in mind?"

The so-called friend answers: "As our two children are friends, could you babysit mine for a couple of hours next Sunday. They can play together so I assume it's all the same to you. I will reciprocate the favour, of course, at a date of your choosing. By the way, your spouse mentioned being tired, needing a break. Let's honour that. She does all the hard lifting in your family. That's what I hear. Can you do the baby sitting on your own?"

Identification is the phase of the categorization process where the number of possible alternative category frames have been reduced to a manageable number (in the discrimination phase) and our individual must now specify the stimulus by filling in the specific features of the stimulus that are variant in the lower level of the prototype frame, as shown in Fig. 11.4. Our individual, in this identification phase, identifies the variant and salient features of the outside stimulus (the invitation) matched to features in the category episode prototype frame our individual has selected as the most likely for this stimulus situation. What are the critical features in the lower level of the frame? In Fig. 11.4, we have labeled this lower level of the selected prototype frame as the "belief system" of our individual because the feature assignments are based on probability assumptions, not certainty. Our individual "believes" each feature to be the most likely, with more or less certainty.

Our individual can seek information to further this identification of category process. For example, our individual asks the friend doing the inviting: "My spouse mentioned it's your birthday Sunday, and your baby's, so why don't I bring my child over to your house Sunday. My spouse loves parties and will cancel the other engagement to be there too."

Is the life episode that is now happening to our individual mainly about "going to a child's birthday party" or "going to a friend's birthday party?" Or is it "the spouse going to a friend's birthday party without you?" Life is full of this murkiness, and in a certain sense, those who can decipher what really is going on in their life at any given moment, and can therefore be properly guided by the correct predicted future prototype frame, will succeed best in life.

Intergroup End of Continuum: Categorizing a Stimulus Experience
We will now shift away from interpersonal categorization between two individuals without group affiliation, to intergroup categorization between two members of

different category groups who categorize their interaction according to a group prototype. In the example we give here, the inside group member is a 20-year-old African-American male and the outside group member is a white, female plain-clothes police officer. The two are about to begin an interaction and we chart the categorization phases from the African-American male's point of view. We outline his categorization process in Fig. 11.5.

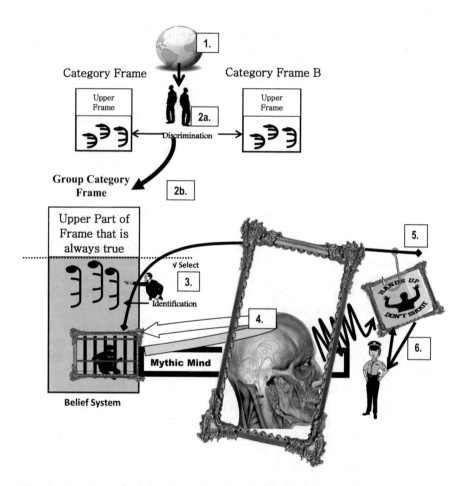

Fig. 11.5 Intergroup categorization process: (1) Stimulus from the outside world initiates categorization. (2a) Discrimination phase starts as interpersonal categorization, but quickly (2b) switches to intergroup categorization when negative bias kicks in against the outside group member. (3) Identification phase of group categorization process, but the default slots remain firmly set because the inside group member is (4) imprisoned in the closed loop of his belief system. (5) The inside group member produces a predetermined future frame, creating an expectation frame based on the bias against the outside group category, which in turn leads to (6) the breakdown of the inside group member's checking the future predicted intergroup category frame against the real-time experience of the episode

For intergroup categorization, we refer to Tajfel (Tajfel and Turner 1979; Tajfel 1982), whose theory utilizes the same terms to describe the phases of intergroup categorization as Harnad uses in the previous section to describe interpersonal categorization. Following the Fig. 11.5 numbering system:

The stimulus initiates the interaction, which sets off

1. The "discrimination" categorization phase, which is followed by
2. The "identification" categorization phase.

Our inside group member working on his car watches the outside group member approach him out of the corner of his eye, which starts the interaction stimulus. The inside group member must decide how to categorize the interaction through discrimination and identification processes.

1. **The stimulus:** As the female approaching our inside group member is 6-feet tall but otherwise unremarkable, our inside group member begins the categorization process as an episode prototype, so as an interpersonal interaction.
2. **Discrimination:** In the discrimination phase, the inside group member mentally establishes "discrete and discontinuous" category frames from which he selects the most appropriate category for the specific stimulus situation being experienced (Tajfel and Turner 1979, p. 39). The African-American man asks: Is the woman approaching him someone in need of help with her car or is she going to ask for directions, which will make the interaction interpersonal (to a large extent). So there could be a multitude of possible episode situations, some of which our man brings forward to the front of his mind. Figure 11.5 shows frames for two prototype episode categories only: Category Frame A and Category Frame B. But there are other possible alternative prototype category frames in the mix that are not shown in Fig. 11.5.

   In the initial discrimination phase of categorization, the individual deals with the invariant and most salient features of the episode prototype category frames in the upper level of Category Frame A and Category Frame B. These are features of the two prototype episode frames that are always true for these episodes. If the features of the approaching stimulus do not match these "always true" features of a prototype category frame, the frame is discarded from consideration during this discrimination phase. Let us say that "a woman asking him for a donation" is excluded in this phase while a "woman in some sort of law enforcement action like a bailiff or perhaps an undercover police officer" is kept in the categorization mix. We return to our example.

   With measured movement, the tall, young woman outside member shows our inside group member a police badge, thus proclaiming her group category affiliation. For our inside member, the episode immediately changes from an interpersonal situation to an intergroup situation.

   Tajfel refers to Sherif's (1966, p. 62) definition of intergroup behavior as the "actors' identification of themselves and the others as belonging to different social categories" (Tajfel and Turner 1979, p. 40). The male African-American in the interaction becomes the inside group member of one social category, and the female police office becomes the outside member of a different social group category.

Why does an interpersonal categorization process turn into an intergroup categorization process when members of two different social categories who oppose each other on some issue come together and meet head to head? The answer lies in the term "discrimination." Discrimination is the first phase of the categorization process for both Harnad for interpersonal categorization and Tajfel for intergroup categorization. But they mean slightly different things.

In our Harnad interpersonal categorization example of an invitation to "a child's birthday party," the individual receiving the invitation must "discriminate" between various possible alternative episode frames, any one of which could explain the stimulus event—the other parent-friend's invitation to the "child's birthday party." All possible alternative explanations for the invitation constitute a set. Each possible alternative in the set could serve as a guiding frame for the individual to react to the stimulus in an appropriate and efficient way. The first part of the discrimination phase is creating the complete set of possible alternative episode frames from which the individual must select the one that is most relevant or appropriate.

The first phase of discrimination is categorizing the stimulus by establishing separate categories that identify the stimulus, then establishing the set of possible alternative members of the category set and subtracting from the set the unlikely possibilities. We categorize our experience by deciding what's in and what's out of the set.

Both Harnad for interpersonal categorization and Tajfel for intergroup categorization use the term "discrimination" to mean "distinguishing" or "differentiating" categories as separate categories, then putting them in or out of the set of possible alternative members being seriously considered to explain the stimulus. This is phase 2 in Fig. 11.4 for interpersonal categorization and phase 2a in Fig. 11.5 for intergroup categorization.

But for Tajfel's intergroup categorization, there is a 2b (in Fig. 11.5), a second part of this discrimination first phase. Ironically, this second phase constitutes the primary definition of the term "discrimination" in present-day society: "bias." In other words, intergroup categorization includes a bias of the inside group member toward the outside group member in either a positive or negative direction. In the case we are currently describing, the African-American male inside group member holds a negative bias toward the outside group member in front of him, the female police officer.

The categorization process is now firmly out of interpersonal categorization because the outside group member as an individual person has become depersonalized and dehumanized in the discrimination first phase of the categorization process.

3. **Identification:** We next enter the "identification" phase of the categorization process, indicated as phase 3 in Fig. 11.5. The identification phase of categorization concerns the identification of the variant and less salient features of the social category of the outside member located in the lower level of the inside

member's group category frame. These lower level frame features are established along certain relational dimensions defined by the inside group member's belief system—what the belief system believes about the outside social category in relation to the inside group member's social category. They are set on default slots for quick and efficient reaction to the stimulus based on the inside group member's past experience with the outside group category in front of him.

For purely interpersonal categorization, the default slots in the lower level of the selected category frame are not firmly set; there are other possible assignments for the feature in the feature set; and these are easily substituted for the default if appropriate. But for intergroup categorization, this identification phase is immediate because the default slots for these features are much more firmly in place. With the default slots more firmly set, there is far less uncertainty for intergroup category "identification." They are hardened, according to Tajfel (1982), along "salient [feature] dimensions" (Commins and Lockwood 1979, pp. 281–282). These "salient dimensions" are relational. That is, they define the relation between the inside and outside social categories, which vary according to the inside group category and the outside group category involved in the interaction. They are hardened in a closed loop inside the belief system of the inside group member.

The intergroup categorization process is imprisoned in a closed information loop inside the inside group member's belief system, shown as phase 4 in Fig. 11.5. The belief system, located in the Mythic Mind layer of human consciousness (see Part I of this book), controls the inside group member's social identity as a member of a group versus other outside groups in society.

The result of the closed loop for intergroup categorization during interaction between a member of the inside group and a member of an outside group is similar to the predetermined category prototype frames described in Chap. 9 (particularly in Fig. 9.7). The difference is that the individual framing of prototype category episodes is located in the Episodic Mind layer of human consciousness while the intergroup categorization process described in this chapter is located in the Mythic Mind layer of human consciousness, the belief system layer of human consciousness (in other words, in the inside group's foundational stories).

The group frame constrains our view of the world to what we already believe in; and this constraint is along certain value dimensions features of the group category frame that "biases" the individual member's perspective when interacting with an outside group member. In our example, the inside group member (the young, African-American male) recalls from memory the police officer social category frame and then uses it to predict and guide his behavior in the real-time interaction with the police officer, shown as phase 5 in Fig. 11.5.

Information from the real-time interaction with the police officer in the outside world—for instance if she smiles and acts in a kindly manner—that contradicts the "bias" of the group frame, is shown as phase 6 in Fig. 11.5. But we are, because of our group affiliation, imprisoned in a closed information loop of the values of our belief system. But why is this so?

This is certainly a negative consequence of the group frame.

The Negative Consequence of the Group Frame

The breakdown in reality checking shown in Phase 6 in Fig. 11.5 is the result of an inside group member meeting an outside group member, and the intergroup category frame being firmly stuck on its default slots, imprisoning the inside group member in a closed information loop during the categorization process. The inside group member is then prevented from observing contradictory information in the real-time interaction experience from the outside group member—such as the female police officer smiling or giving off other signs of conciliatory intention. The inside group member stops paying attention to exactly what is said by the outside group member. The bias of the closed loop is worsened if the same intergroup categorization breakdown also occurs from the other side, the outside group member.

The consequences of this double-barreled, self-induced closed-loop blindness to new and contradictory information in the real-time experiencing of an episode can be disastrous, leading to preventable violence and even death.

What is the evolutionary advantage to the human species of this phenomenon? Surely it leads to negative consequences for the human species. But no. There is a much greater categorization at work, from the point of view of the individual's human consciousness. Because it is in groups, through the intergroup categorization process, that humans have the cognitive tools to discriminate, identify, and classify incoming data from the outside world into categories of beliefs and values, we self-define or self-recognize in groups. This is the core of our consciousness, in effect permitting us to self-identify our own small world in the much larger world around us.

Elfreda Chatman illustrated her small world theory case studies of marginalized groups in American society, of which we have selected one: dirt-eaters.

Dirt-eating (or geophagy) is normative behavior in the small world of a group of mostly young, rural African-American women living in single-parent households in the southern USA. The custom is passed down from mother to daughter. They believe dirt has medicinal properties, especially during pregnancy. The dirt tastes good but the dirt tastes even better when it is smoked in a chimney. The outside world looks down on the dirt-eaters, considering them ignorant and, ironically, dirty. The dirt-eaters know this. In the face of such antipathy, their small world defined ". . . normative behaviour," according to Chatman (2000, p. 13), which "provides a predictable, routine, and manageable approach to everyday reality." Outside information is avoided, so the small world is kept secret. The outsiders would tell them to stop eating dirt, a normative value or belief the young women live by, that orders their small world existence. The core value of this small world:

I am a dirt-eater.

One can replace any number of small world labels that would represent most of us. We are excited by our membership in this select club. It is often a secret affiliation. We don't tell anyone. If they only knew! With 63% of white American males voting for Trump in the 2016 American election, a small world suddenly becomes a majority world (Trump was projected to lose the election):

I am a Trump voter.

There is a second benefit of closing the loop during the intergroup categorization process. Once our small world groups are formed, we are at equilibrium with the world. We know who our friends are—they are like us in that they hold the same values and beliefs that form our core self. And in the larger world outside us, which is unsafe, scary, anomalous, and unpredictable, we know who our enemies are. The intergroup frames allow us to neutralize this chaos.

The group frames create stable categories for friends versus enemies, defining how we should react when we meet members of outside groups. Within our small worlds, our frames invoke security, uniformity of experience, and above all predictability as we make our way through the larger world in time and space. Our small world is the vessel in which we identify, encapsulate, and defend our core values and beliefs. We are in a certain sense at peace in this equilibrium between our small world and the larger world around us (Chatman 1999).

The equilibrium must be protected at all costs from contradictory information, even if the contradictory information is beneficial to our real interests. Information avoidance is a "self-protective behaviour" to protect the inside group member's small world (Chatman 1996, pp. 197–198). We avoid information because it may "demand a change in beliefs," "demand undesired action," or it "may cause unpleasant emotions or diminish pleasant emotions" (Sweeny et al. 2010, p. 342). We seek information that confirms our attitudes and beliefs (Smith et al. 2008). And this information dynamic intensifies when people are "most motivated to defend their worldview" (Jonas et al. 2003).

Conclusion

The thesis of this chapter is that group dynamics positively contribute to the self-recognition of individual consciousness, but they lead to information avoidance on a much greater scale, and with more resilience, than we are able to as individuals.

Not only do our group categorization frames become lodged on the inside of the frame through which we interface or view the outside world, which keeps the world and new information at arm's length, the resulting closed information loop that is controlled by the frame becomes even tighter: the individual actively keeps at bay the outside world of new, contradictory information, as shown in Fig. 11.6.

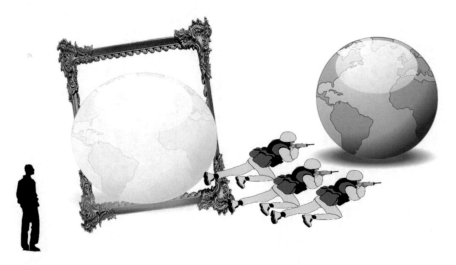

Fig. 11.6 Frame problem: Group frame increases keeping world at arm's length to actively avoid the world and new information. We'll fight it off, literally till death

These conceptualizations of the value and belief dimensions of the group are so important, so vital to us, that we avoid contradictory information at all costs, even if we know the information is helpful or useful. Literally, we'll fight to the death to maintain the small world we have created for ourselves inside our group frame.

Chapter 12
Nation Frame Level: The Dark Side

We are now at the most dangerous frame level of all, the nation frame, shown in Fig. 12.1, which, in the nineteenth century and especially in the twentieth century, became harnessed to the resources and industrial efficiency of the modern nation-state. These nation-states—the Soviet Union, Communist China, Nazi Germany—devoted, as their top priority, huge state-wide manpower and administrative resources to enforcing conformity to an ideological frame. Truly horrendous acts have been committed in the name of such frames.

The touchstone for all writings on this issue is Plato's *Allegory of the Cave*, written in the fourth century BC. The Allegory has both an epistemological and political interpretation. We previously described Plato's cave allegory's epistemological interpretation: that we as individuals live life indirectly through mental constructs—the shadows on the cave wall—rather than experiencing life directly in the world.

The political interpretation of Plato's cave allegory is that the shadows on the cave wall are deliberately constructed by the state to trick its own citizens into believing a false reality is real, lulling them into passive acceptance of state laws and regulations that actually serve the state's own ends. These ends could be an elite or dictator's desire for power and wealth; or it could be in the service of an ideology.

Plato wrote the *Allegory of the Cave* when the Athenian state had executed his mentor Socrates in 399 BC for the crime of not worshiping the city's gods, and for corrupting youth. This brutal state-sanctioned act against one of its most prominent teacher-citizens caused Plato to switch careers from that of a rising 28-year-old politician to a philosopher-teacher, founder of the West's first university in 387 BC. The *Allegory of the Cave*, with its steadfast focus on the disconnect between a constructed reality and what is real has riveted and perplexed humankind for almost 2500 years. Let's take another look at it, with another diagram interpretation of the Allegory in Fig. 12.2.

© Springer International Publishing AG, part of Springer Nature 2018   143
C. Cole, *The Consciousness' Drive*, https://doi.org/10.1007/978-3-319-92457-1_12

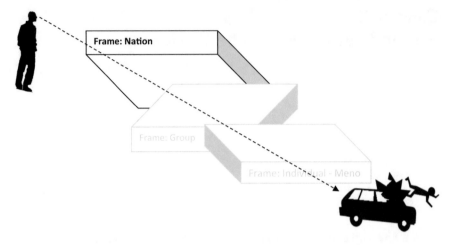

Fig. 12.1 Nation-level frame as a prism through which we see a constructed version of an episode experienced in real life

Figure 12.2 depicts a visualization of the *Allegory of the Cave*, wherein humans are "prisoners" sitting shackled to a bench, forced to look at the reflections on the cave wall in front of them. The citizen-prisoners have been told, and they believe, that these shadows are their real experiences of life. They are prevented from looking behind them or the sides by the shackles, so they don't realize they are being duped. Behind them, puppet showmen can be seen creating the images on the cave wall. Behind the puppeteers is a fire, which produces the light that projects the puppeteers' creations onto the cave wall. This is a closed information loop because what is real, real experience, what is really going on in terms of the citizens' governance, is kept out of their view. But there is an escape ladder, an "ascent to the sunlight" and real experience, i.e., the citizen must be complicit in her own imprisonment for the system to work.

In the previous chapter, we described intergroup categorization, and the actualization of our self-concept that occurs when we compare the beliefs and values of our ingroup frame to the beliefs and values of outsider groups. In other words, we become more powerful as individuals inside the group.

The nation-state can actually magnify the closed information loop centered on the beliefs and values of the group member through carefully constructed propaganda expressions of those beliefs and values, and the violent intimidation of citizens who do not stay within the frame. Because the manipulation is based on, and in fact plays on the core values and beliefs of the individual, the transfer of our control over our experiencing of the world, to puppeteers-propagandists hired by the state to project false shadows on the cave wall, is consensual. The consent, rooted in the benefit accruing to the individual citizen through the strengthening of the citizen's self-concept, makes the control stronger.

Fig. 12.2 Plato's *Allegory of the Cave*: Prisoners duped by state into mistaking shadows on the wall for reality. But there is a possibility of escape, into the sunlight (© 1996 Veldkamp, Gabriele and Maurer, Markus Creative Commons Attribution-Share Alike 3.0 Unported license)

The Nazi Rise to Power

There have been many times in human history, and in recent history, when information has been deliberately controlled by the state for the purpose of keeping the population passive and pliable. In the present era alone, states such as North Korea have carefully constructed frameworks for social discourse and for how their citizenry must live, creating deliberately closed systems of living.

In the Nazi era in Germany, Joseph Goebbels' propaganda machine excited the population's support of the race-centered policies of the Nazi regime against Jews, but also against the Nazi Party's political opponents, particularly the communists. The communists were extremely useful to Goebbels, providing the Nazis with the spectre of an ever-present menace to security and public order, reason enough in the eyes of many Germans—the Nazis fell just short of getting a majority of the vote in the March 5, 1933 election—to abrogate the rights of all German citizens.

A particularly successful episode of state-controlled framing of real-life events centered on the Reichstag fire of February 27, 1933, shown in Fig. 12.3. Before the fire, the Nazis had failed to win a majority government in the July and November 1932 elections, which forced them to form a coalition government with the

Fig. 12.3 Reichstag fire February 27, 1933 in Berlin [© 1933 Unknown CC BY-SA 3.0 de. Source: German Federal Archive (Deutsches Bundesarchiv)]

Zentrumspartei (Center Party), a center-right party who believed they could tame the Nazis. In Hitler's eyes, this need to rely on democratic negotiation put the Nazis in a straightjacket.

Then on February 27, 1933, the Reichstag fire broke out. Conveniently, a Dutch communist called Marius van der Lubbe was captured by the police, who immediately and without any fuss confessed to setting the fire. The confession was so ludicrous to Berlin's police chief that he refused to believe it. But the ruse worked.

On February 28, 1933, the day after the fire, the Nazis succeeded in getting passed the Reichstag Fire Decree, giving the national government ministry portfolio they controlled the right to take over the state governments, including the state police forces. Leading KPD (Communist Party) officials were immediately rounded up and arrested. Through careful Nazi manipulation of the framing of the Reichstag Fire event, and the threat it posed to Germany's citizens, the Nazis now had the excuse, and the will to use it, to increase their seat total in the March 5, 1933 elections.

The March 5, 1933 elections were disappointing for the Nazis; although they increased their seat total, the other parties still won the majority of the seats and thus in coalitions had the power to vote the Nazis down. But Hitler was almost there. Using the tools provided them under the Reichstag Fire Decree, the Nazis arrested the 81 KPD elected members who had just won their seats in the Reichstag. They scheduled the vote on the Enabling Act, which would give Hitler almost complete control over all levers of government, for 3 weeks hence, for March 24, 1933.

On March 24, 1933, Chancellor Hitler convened the Reichstag to pass the Enabling Act. During the vote, the Nazi Party's paramilitary units, the SS and SA, physically surrounded Reichstag representatives from the other parties, and through this intimidating show of force was able to get the required 2/3 majority for the Act to pass. Hitler immediately eliminated all parties in the Reichstag except the Nazi Party. The Nazis' ascension to power was now complete. Via the ruse of a communist plot to overthrow the German state, Hitler had succeeded in turning an intergroup categorization frame based on the principles of the Nazi Party into something potentially far more powerful: the frame of the nation-state.

The facts of all Hitler's legal, semi-legal, and outright illegal maneuvrings to gain power were at the time hidden from all but those in the know; only the threat-of-communism shadows on Plato's cave wall were shown or visible to the vast majority of the German people. But the realization of the nation-frame of the Nazi German state that followed could not have been done without the complicit agreement of the German citizens.

The nation-state frame devised by Hitler was so effectively wound around the German people's core values and beliefs, that the closed information loop became stronger via continuous frame propaganda and persecution of dissidence. Outside group members were continuously called out and discriminated against, and as a result the nation-frame's ethnicity feature became locked on its default slot vis-à-vis the outside groups, particularly the Jews. The obsessional focus on the Jews as the problem of the German nation shifted, with the Wannsee Conference in January 20, 1942, into the Final Solution.

Valuable German resources were switched away from the war effort to the carrying out of the Final Solution (Pasher 2014). Germany would have lost the war anyway, even without the Final Solution draining resources away from the war effort, so there were other factors that made defeat inevitable. The point is that the Final Solution remained a priority in the Nazi government's mind until the very end, with the German army and its civilian population being complicit in it, collaborating in Hitler's anti-Semitic aims.

Himmler acknowledged this in a speech given in October 1943 when he spoke of the role of the Jewish massacre in creating a "blood bond" to tie the German military leadership "to the Nazi cause" (Cesarani 2016, p. 665). And it was broader than this: Goebbels wrote in his diary in March 1943 that the Jewish slaughter reinforced the bond between nation and its people. Such was the power of the ethnicity feature of the nation-state frame Hitler had created to imprison Germany's citizens in a closed loop based on the ethnicity feature of the German nation frame. Volksgemeinschaft was used by the Nazis to mean the mystical unity of the Volk or people's community.

The Volksgemeinschaft nation-frame devised by the Nazis induced unparalleled information avoidance on the part of the German people in the face of unparalleled evil acts committed by the Nazi regime in their name, shutting down the German population's ability to see what was happening right in front of them.

In Fig. 12.4, we show the layout of Dachau, just 10 miles outside of Munich. An estimated 32,000 Dachau prisoners never returned to daily life. They were executed.

Fig. 12.4 Information avoidance: Dachau: The evidence mounts of the Final Solution as work camps turned to death camps like Dachau outside Munich. Photo left: (© 2016 Diego Delso CC-BY-SA. Photo right: © May 3 1945 T/4 Sidney Blau, 163rd Signal Photo Company, Army Signal CorpsUSHMM CC-Zero license)

The German people didn't see these camps for what they were in a nation-act of information avoidance without parallel. Let us look at this information avoidance in greater detail. In a way, the German citizens were lulled into information avoidance by the shadow produced on the cave wall over the front gate of Dachau:

"ARBEIT MACHT FREI" (Work makes you free.)

ARBEIT MACHT FREI answers the question we all ask ourselves at one time or another: Do we live to work or do we work to live? We live to work, the Dachau gate proclaims, which is a valid philosophy of life. But did the shadows on the cave wall saying "ARBEIT MACHT FREI" lull the Germans who passed the gate each day into complicit thinking that the camps were indeed only work camps?

Dachau started out in 1933 as a work camp for political dissidents, trade unionists who protested against the Nazi state, and social outcasts, including Gypsies and homosexuals. The camp's detainees were forced to work digging in gravel pits, constructing buildings and roads, and, after World War II started, working in munitions factories they were bused to for the German war effort. It is one of the tenets of the German nation frame that work is an end in itself; that it makes you a good citizen. You live to work not work to live. Dachau's crematorium was finished in August 1938 to gas the ill and prisoners too weak to work.

On the night of November 9–10, 1938, Kristallnacht ("Night of the broken glass") occurred where Jewish businesses were ransacked and 11,000 Jews were arrested and sent to Dachau. Over the course of the next 7 years, 11,000 German and Austrian Jews were executed there. Despite the evidence for all Munich residents to see—the round-up of their German neighbors and the Jewish population's permanent disappearance, as well as the civilian population's participation in the day-to-day servicing of the 6000–30,000 prison population at Dachau (supplying the camp with food and materials, etc.)—Dachau's transformation from work to death camp was information avoided by the civilian German population.

We illustrate the Nazi-created Volksgemeinschaft frame for the German nation-state in Fig. 12.5. Volksgemeinschaft was used by the Nazis to mean the mystical unity of the German Volk or people's community. There is a distinct concern for ethnic purity of the German Volk underpinning Volksgemeinschaft, in opposition to clearly defined outsider groups that had infiltrated the German nation (Gemeinschaftsfremde or Community Aliens). Reference to these outsider groups reinforced the definition of "real" German citizens inside the Volksgemeinschaft group. The Nazi-created nation frame is located partly in the Mythic Mind layer of human consciousness, specifically the belief system incorporating the core beliefs and values of Volksgemeinschaft. And partly in the Theoretic Mind layer of human consciousness.

As Hitler acknowledged as he fought for control of the national power apparatus in the decisive 1932–1933 German elections, being the leader of the Nazi group movement wasn't enough. He needed the knowledge and power of the nation to rally its people and resources into systems of action based on a bureaucratic model of organizing people to achieve a specific goal, in this case the Final Solution. The bureaucratic structure, with the individual bureaucrat relentlessly and efficiently

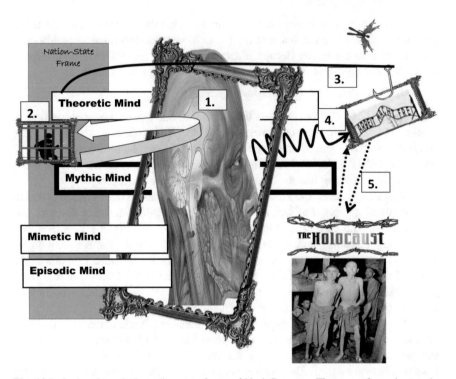

Fig. 12.5 Seeing through the nation-state frame of Nazi Germany. The group frame is upped a 1000-fold by the resources, management systems, and bureaucratic organization of the nation-state: (1) The inside group member is (2) imprisoned in the closed loop of his belief and value system. (3) The inside group member produces a predetermined future frame, creating an expectation and guidance frame of action based on the bias against the outside group category, the Jews. (4) The inside group member sees only the frame. (5) A breakdown, because of information avoidance, of the inside group member's checking of his predicted future frame against the real-time experience of the episode. What the Americans found April 29, 1945, Liberation Day at Dachau (Photo bottom right: © 1945 George Mallinder. CC-Zero license)

carrying out the Nazi administration policies, turned evil into its own routine momentum. Hannah Arendt (1963) called this "the banality of evil."

With the nation frame as their controlling guide, telling them what they would see in their experience, the individual bureaucrat who was part of the Final Solution administrative structure, as well as the average German citizen living in the vicinity of Dachau and the other concentration work camps, avoided information that would contradict the "ARBEIT MACHT FREI" slogan above the Dachau gate. The individual member of the Nazi nation-state was imprisoned in a closed information loop based on the beliefs and values enunciated in the Nazi propaganda; particularly the anti-Semitism used by Goebbels to cement the national frame based on the German value system of Volksgemeinschaft.

But it takes the self-recognition processes operating in the most basic layer of human consciousness, the Episodic Mind layer, to make the whole thing work. In other words, the individual must be complicit in this acceptance of the shadows on the cave wall as being their real experience. Accepting the Nazi propaganda as real, and recognizing himself or herself in the Nazi distortion of experience in the world, strengthened the individual's own self-identify.

Like the support of the Japanese population for their nation's World War II effort until the bombing of Hiroshima, the nation frame the Nazis constructed was successful in its goal of rallying the German people into believing its representation of reality in cleverly manipulated shadows on the cave wall, based on the Nazis' skewed vision of the core beliefs and values of the German nation-state. The power of this nation frame over the German people lasted intact until the Allies changed strategy, from avoiding bombing the German civilian population, to the direct undermining of the German population's faith in the legitimacy of Hitler's frame with the controversial bombing (because of its brutal cruelty) of the civilian population of Dresden in February 13–15, 1945, the devastation of which is shown in Fig. 12.6. The Nazi nation frame finally collapsed, releasing the German population imprisoned in its hold.

Fig. 12.6 Allied bombing of civilian population of Dresden, February 13–15, 1945 [© 1945 Unknown (Bundesarchiv, Bild 146-1994-041-07). CC BY-SA 3.0 de]

Part II
Conclusion

In Part II, we have investigated three levels of frames through which we humans see and understand the world around us and our place in that world:

1. The nation-state frame
2. The group frame
3. The individual frame based on the episode

The frame levels provide the categorization interface through which what is outside the individual in the world is channeled inside the individual. The power of the 3-frame levels resides in their central role in making sense of the chaotic stream of data coming at humans from the outside world. They determine how and what we think about. They determine our human consciousness.

The frames are categorization schemes directly connected to human action. That is, we recall these frames from memory before the same or a similar experience is expected or predicted to occur. They anticipate or predict the future—thus our term "predicted future frames." The selected predicted future frame then determines and guides the individual through his or her real-time experience of the same or similar episode.

The frame network is extremely precise and exceptionally flexible in its predictions of the future because not only is each feature in the lower level of the selected frame set to a default assignment, giving the individual an immediate course of action, but each feature also has alternative slot assignments. These alternative assignments are available to the frame if the default is not the right one for the real-time experience, giving the individual numerous other guidance options for the real-time experience. In addition, one frame can quickly switch to another in the frame network, through immediate interframe connections built into the feature assignments. In this way, the individual has almost immediate access to all his or her experience, categorized for immediate action. A hostile parent sitting beside an individual at a child's birthday party can immediately be accommodated by another interconnected frame in the first person's network—let's call it: "what to do in case of a hostile parent" frame—which is linked to a feature in the lower level of the "going to a child's birthday party" frame. In this way, the most unexpected anomaly in the script of behavior the frame provides can be accommodated by the frame network.

But the frame network plays a more important function than a guidance-to-action categorization system that encompasses the individual's total life experience. The group-level and nation-level frames categorize the individual's social episodes of experience into a self-concept that allows the individual to establish a relation with the outside world. Via the conceptualization of the individual's core beliefs and values, which is established through intergroup and inter-nation categorization processes, the individual establishes this relation between a concept of self, a concept of the world, and a concept of her place in that world.

In Fig. 1, we insert the 3-frame levels just described in the last three chapters, in the same generic diagram of the human memory system used earlier in the book (Part I, Chap. 4, Fig. 4.3). The frame system is at the center of human consciousness, linking our semantic knowledge network, and all our procedural knowledge together

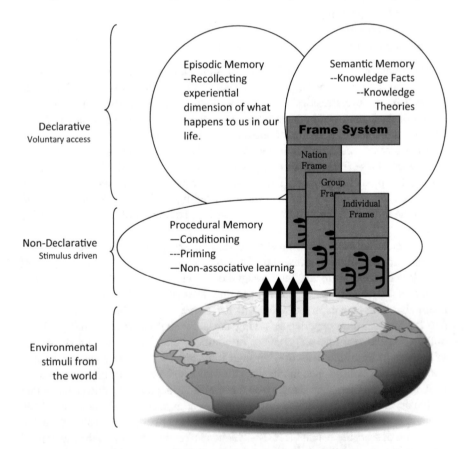

Fig. 1 Three frame levels inserted in the layers and components of the human memory system that constitute our thinking and consciousness (after Suddendorf and Corballis 2007, p. 301; Squire 1992)

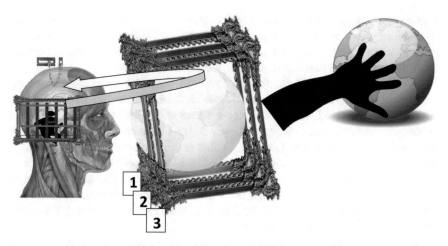

Fig. 2 Three frame levels imprison individuals in closed information loops and new information avoidance: (1) Nation-level frame. (2) Group-level frame and (3) Individual-level frame

into a grand index of who we are in relation to the world and our place in it. The 3-frame system is the channel through which information outside us in the world gets inside us as individual humans. The 3-frame system is directly connected to a database of all we have experienced in that world. The frame system is at the center of how we think and what we think about.

The problem with the frames is that they are so integral to our individual sense of self and our relation with the outside world that humans can cease directly experiencing the chaos and the anomalies of the outside world. Instead, we choose to live our experience of the world once removed, second-hand—through the shadows on the cave wall as Plato describes in his *Allegory of the Cave*. Direct contact with information in the real world that may contradict the frames and threaten the individual's equilibrium is avoided, kept at arm's length as shown in Fig. 2. The pitfall is that the equilibrium provided to the individual by her frames is the first concern, and must be protected at all costs; leading to the individual becoming compliant, even complicit in group or nation-state sponsored acts of terrorism (e.g., the Nazis' Final Solution). So the individual shuts down information need for new, possibly contradictory-to-the frame information, and becomes a prisoner in her own closed information loop.

The Frame Problem of Closed Information Loops

The essence of the efficacy of the frame system is that they are invoked to provide expectations of the future that guide future action. When we are about to enter an unknown room, the room frame is then continuously in our mind predicting and guiding us through our time in that room. Thus our term: predicted future frame. Theoretically, we are supposed to constantly be checking our frame against the reality we are experiencing. But it is more comfortable operating within our default slots. And we can be persuaded, even frightened into doing so.

The Nazi-created nation frame investigated in Chap. 12 is the most egregious example of the imprisonment effect of a closed information loop created by a frame. The Nazi state took advantage of the core values and beliefs of the Germans as a group, manipulating and exaggerating them for its own ends, but with the compliance and complicity of the Germans in this manipulation. The nation frame is perhaps the most powerful frame because of its power to effectuate its objectives, in terms of marshalling manpower and resources in bureaucratic systems. It has legal authority over the state police, army, and the national communication channels. The bureaucratic systems devised by the Nazis became their own driving force that served to dehumanize the individual act.

The group frame level investigated in Chap. 11 actualizes and strengthens the core beliefs and values of the individual, through the intergroup categorization process. We define our self-concept through the ingroup in comparison to outsider groups. We cannot define these core values and beliefs in isolation. "I think therefore I am" becomes "I think as a member of a group, therefore I am." At least, this is the statement we make at this point in our book. (We step somewhat back from the statement in Part III.)

The individual frame investigated in Chaps. 9 and 10 categorizes the individual's intersection experience with the world, as we are traveling through space and time, in the unit of the episode. As we continue to experience the world, these episodes harden into categories of experience called episode prototypes. It is these prototype episodes we recall from memory when we anticipate we are just about to commence a similar episode experience. The predicted future prototype episode frame is intimately connected to the group-level frames of the individual, of which there may be more than one, as well as the nation-state level frame for that individual. The frame levels provide a solid front in guiding us through our real-time experiencing of each intersection we have with the world.

In Fig. 3, we have linked together all three levels of the frames in a summary diagram of the closed information loops that together or singly prevent us from seeing new information in the outside world, including when we conduct an information search with a new knowledge production objective using the Internet. In Fig. 3, we have associated each frame level with a different evolutionary mind layer of human consciousness. The episode frame level we associate with the Episodic Mind and Mimetic Mind layers of human consciousness. The group frame level we associate with the Mythic Mind. And the nation-state frame level we associate with the Theoretic Mind. All three frame levels are present in the individual's intersection with the world in real time, providing future predicted frames guiding our actions. Individuals are comfortable experiencing the world through these frame system intermediaries or interfaces. We are in equilibrium with ourselves and the outside world when we stick to the frame prediction. As a

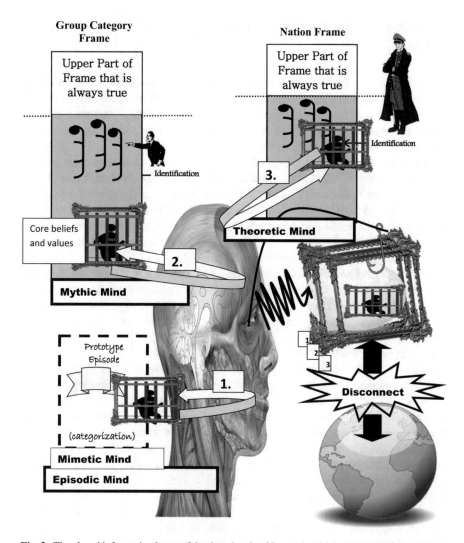

Fig. 3 The closed information loops of the three levels of frames in which we are imprisoned create a disconnect between our framed experience and real experience of the individual's intersection with the world. The 3-frame levels are: (1) the individual frame closed information loop; (2) the group frame closed information loop; and (3) the nation frame closed information loop

result, we can easily become imprisoned in closed information loops inside the frames, and disconnected from the real world.

For information need during information search of an information system, this places us firmly inside the Meno Paradox:

> If we see and recognize in the world only what we already know, what is in our frames, how do we come to know that which we do not already know?

Modeling the Problem for Information Need and Information Search

We are now at the end of Part II in a position to model the problem posed by our 3-frame levels for information need and information search when our objective is the production of new knowledge. Here, we overlay this problem statement onto the model of information search from the human consciousness perspective, previously illustrated in Part I's Conclusion, Fig. 3.

We ended Part I with the conclusion that information search systems and the conceptual basis of information need and information search should take a consciousness-based perspective. This is different from current information search-engine-system design which is transactional—the information searcher is assumed to know what she needs and commands the system for the needed information. This is the problem: our 3-frame levels imprison us in closed information loops that prevent us from knowing our real information need.

We repeat the Part I model diagram (Part I, Conclusion, Fig. 3) here in Fig. 4a and b, extending it (Fig. 4c) to take into account Part II's statement of the problem.

The information science perspective on search engine design is that the search engine should facilitate humans communicating with "accumulated recorded knowledge" (Hjorland 2017, p. 1797). As stated in Part I, this perspective is modeled by Popper's (1975) 3-World model of knowledge construction, shown in Fig. 4a, with the transactional focus on the transfer of information between World 3, the world of objective knowledge available in books, articles, and on websites/pages on the Internet, and World 2, the world of human consciousness and mental states. The current design focus de-emphasizes Popper's World 1, the real world itself and the human experiencing of that world, as the focus of information search.

A consciousness-based search system, on the other hand, considers World 3 part of World 1, as shown in Fig. 4b. With a consciousness-based perspective, World 3 becomes part of World 1, so information need, information search, and information transfer are viewed through the lens of the individual experiencing a new information episode. Information search in this new paradigm is now an episode of the searcher's experiencing of the world. It is now part of how and why we frame the world and our place in that world and the motivational nature of the information need that drives us to search for information in the world.

Shown in Fig. 4c, the problem for information need and information search, and the problem for the design of information search systems in this consciousness-based perspective, is the closed information loops in which the individual searcher is imprisoned during the search. The closed information loops disconnect the searcher from seeing new, contradictory-to-the-frames information in the outside world. In the case of information search using an Internet search engine, the outside world is the results list provided to the searcher by the search engine.

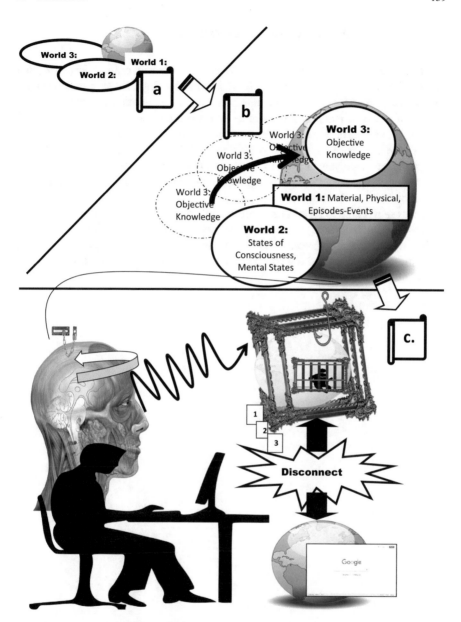

Fig. 4 Experiential conception of information search: Popper's (**a**) 3-Worlds becomes (**b**) only 2-Worlds. (**a**) Popper's focus on the interaction between World 3 and World 2. (**b**) Merging World 3 into World 1 with the redefinition of information search as the experiencing of an episode. (**c**) The disconnect problem of our frames' closed information loops on seeing and experiencing new information in the world and when conducting a Google information search (Google search page: © 2018 Google Reprinted with Permission)

Consciousness-Based Information Search

We have come to the end of Part II where we set out to investigate, describe, and explain the underlying problem for information need and information search caused by our exceptional human ability to intersect with and experience the world through frames of our own making. The 3-frame levels proscribe not only what we future predict we will see and understand in our experience, they proscribe what we don't or can't see in the experience in the outside world. While knowing the future before it happens has many advantages, these various frames imprison us inside the closed information loops of our own making, the making of our group, and the making of the nation-state we belong to.

If we are not able to take in new information, we as a species will not be able to adapt—to climate change, for example—blocking our species' ability to survive, which is the primary directive. But there is a solution to the problem of the disconnect between us and the world caused by our frames. In Part III, we describe the solution.

Part III
The Framing Solution

Introduction to Part III

The exceptional ability of human framing of our experience in the world allows us to see the world, not reactively, but in a seeing-as-understanding process. We understand what our experience will be before the experience, allowing us to predict and control our trajectory through the world, so that we can ignore what is irrelevant to the objective or efficiency of our trajectory-purpose. To us as a species, this ability is advantageous; it makes us exceptional. There is a drawback to the ability, however.

In Part II, we described the framing drawback of our human consciousness. We tend to become too comfortable relying on our future predicting frames, to the point of avoiding new information from the outside world that might contradict the frames. This imprisons our experience in the world inside a closed information loop. We described, in the case of Nazi Germany, the potential disastrous effects of this closed information loop. And there are countless other examples throughout human history. But the problem starts with the individual's openness to recognizing and finding new information.

Part III describes a solution, a way out of the closed information loop, which is in fact built into human consciousness. However, before returning to the solution, in this Introduction we briefly set up our problem-solution structure for information search, specifically for the Google type of information search that has become ubiquitous in modern life. (For greater detail, we refer you to Cole 2012; Cole et al. 2017.)

Information Need and Information Search

Information need is the start state or motivation for conducting an information search. It provides the organizing principle and the driving force throughout the search until the information that will satisfy the need is found. It is an extremely complex and important "trigger" and "drive" mechanism that underlies information search (Savolainen 2017). The odd thing is that when we conduct a search using Google or some other search engine, we operate as if the information need is easy to define, and easily satisfied or fulfilled. We think, all we have to do is wrap up the need in the right keywords and type them into the engine's search box. The search engines' matching algorithms are so good now, so personalized to the individual searcher with its suggestions that it seems to know what we need before we know it ourselves. But have you ever noticed that when we need information that will produce new knowledge the results list the search engine presents to us at the end of our search matches the keywords we typed in, but the list does not satisfy our information need. Paradoxical isn't it! And this paradox, that we are imprisoned in a closed information loop in the midst of information plenty as we are perusing the results list, is how the framing problem described in Part II inserts itself in the practice of our everyday information searching.

The Problem of the Information Need Frame for Finding New Information

In Fig. 1, we diagram the typical search using a search engine. A searcher begins the search with his frames firmly in place, of which there are three levels: the nation-level frame, the group-level frame, and the individual-level frame. From these three frame levels, the searcher derives his information need for that particular search. The need in turn forms the basis from which the searcher derives his query to the search engine, what keywords he types into the Google search box; and it will form the basis of what he expects to see in the results list at the end of the search.

Let us call this frame the "Information Need Expectation Frame." The searcher's Information Need Expectation Frame determines what he expects to see in the results list; it is the frame through which he views the list. The searcher peruses the results list looking for a citation that will best satisfy his information need.

The Meno Paradox (Part II, Chap. 10) at this point comes into effect. The searcher sees in the results list only what he already knows, what is already in his Information Need Expectation Frame. He is in fact imprisoned inside his frame, inside a closed information loop. This imprisonment actually works well for many information

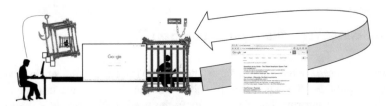

Fig. 1 The searcher imprisoned in his Information Need Expectation Frame, creating a closed information loop and preventing the searcher from seeing new information in the Google results list. (For Google search page and results page: © 2018 Google. Reprinted with Permission)

searches. But not all. There are in fact two different types of information searches: the command search and the questioning search (Taylor 1968). The command search is well taken care of by current search engines but the questioning type of search, whose objective is new knowledge production for the searcher, is not.

The Command Search

For many of our Google searches, we don't know the exact answer but we know the type of answer we will find in the Google results list. These are command-type searches. Many of these types of searches are for factual information:

- What are the flights to Paris next week and what do they cost?
- How tall is Milos Raonic?
- What is the capital of Poland?

For the command type of information search, the individual's Information Need Expectation Frame works well for both formulating the query from the information need and perusing the search engine's output for the citation in the results list that best satisfies the information need. The searcher knows exactly what he needs and exactly what he is looking for.

Current search engines answer these types of command searches beautifully. In fact, for famous people or common factual questions, they often provide the answer in a box at the top of the results list.

The Questioning Search

The second type of search is the questioning search where we have an information need but we don't know what information we need and we want the search engine to help us identify it. Most of our questions of this second type of information need are murky, involving multiple possible alternative answers and interpretation:

- Should I get a divorce?
- Why did the Roman Empire collapse?
- Was Julius Caesar good or bad for Rome?
- Why do some people believe in Climate Change and some people do not?

This is where Meno's Paradox applies. Confronted with the engine's search box, we must make a leap from what we know to what we don't know (but need to know) and somehow come up with a query that will bridge this gap (Dervin 1998; see also, Belkin et al. 1982). But it is in the results list that it gets really tough! We peruse the results list looking for our keywords. We see them there but paradoxically they don't satisfy our information need.

In these questioning search situations, our Information Need Expectation Frame is not adequate, and does not represent our real information need. It does not enable us to recognize the information we don't know we need in the results list, i.e., even if the information we really needed were there in the results list (despite our inadequate query), we would not recognize it because it is not expected. It is not in our Information Need Expectation Frame so we won't recognize it.

All the real information problems or needs we have in life, the ones that are important and that will change our lives, or at least make or lose us money, that will constitute our substantive contribution to the world, all these type of information needs are motivated by this complex, out-of-frame questioning information need.

Solution

Part III investigates a solution to the framing problem, the way out of the closed information loop we are imprisoned in by our Information Need Expectation Frame. We diagram this solution in Fig. 3.

First of all, we must recognize that the searcher's perusal of the results list during which he identifies his real information need is an episode of experience. In other words, the searcher escaping from his Information Need Expectation Frame when he identifies his real information need is an episode of experience with a beginning, middle, and end.

Let us attempt to diagram this beginning, middle, and end in Fig. 2. As we discussed in Part I, the perusing of the results list in an experience episode that ends

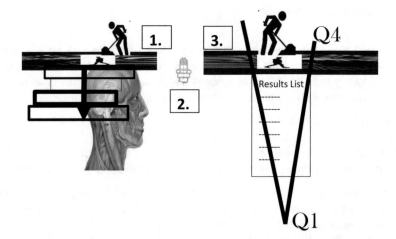

Fig. 2 Results list perusing is an experience episode: (1) Digging operation into consciousness to get at an understanding of real information need. The results page must provide (2) the sparkplug for this to occur, (3) facilitating the digging down from the comprised information need (Q4) into the real information need (Q1) represented as a "V"

with the searcher identifying his real information need is (1) a digging operation inside human consciousness. Shown in Fig. 2, the results list must provide (2) the "sparkplug" to initiate the digging operation. (3) We represent this digging into the information need via perusing the Google results list as a "V." At the top of the "V" is Q4, which represents the compromised information need searchers type into the search box when they don't know their real information need. The real information need, Q1, is at the bottom of the "V" (for the Q4-Q1 theory of information need, see Taylor 1968). The results list must be designed to provide this new digging feature for the searcher as he is questioning the new information provided to him in the results list by the search engine.

In Fig. 3, the searcher still has his frames, and formulates his search based on his Information Need Expectation Frame. This is his compromised information need (Q4). He types in his search terms based on his compromised information need in the Google search page based on this frame, and Google matches the search terms to websites/pages in its database. The Google results list, in this type of complex information search, must do more than give the searcher an answer he has commanded from the search engine, more than some factual answer. It must somehow change the levers of the searcher's Information Need Expectation Frame so that the searcher can actualize his real information need (Q4). So the results list must somehow do this, provide the spark plug for sparking the searcher's escape, "opening up" his closed information loop.

Search engines certainly do not do this now; they aren't designed to do this. They are designed for the simple information need previously described: the command information search. How do we redesign the search engine to "spark" the searcher

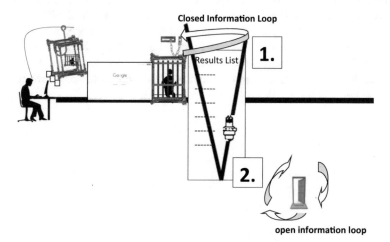

Fig. 3 (1) The searcher is imprisoned in the closed information loop controlled by his Information Need Expectation Frame. We insert a sparkplug into the Google results list, which (2) shifts the searcher's information loop open so that the searcher can see the new information in the results list that will satisfy his real information need (for Google search page: © 2018 Google. Reprinted with Permission)

opening herself up to new information, so that she can identify her real information need while she peruses the results list?

* * *

Part III is devoted to defining and describing the solution to the framing problem of our exceptional human consciousness. In Chap. 13, we give empirical archeological evidence for the solution to the problem of our frames described in Part II. The solution lies in our Mythic Mind layer of human consciousness, centered on the human belief system. We emphasize that "belief" here does not signify religious belief but rather the broader human concern for searching for meaning in our experience.

In Chap. 14, we differentiate belief from knowledge, and begin to model how our belief system opens the information loop between our frames and recognizing and experiencing new information in the outside world, thus begetting new knowledge production. In other words, belief-begets-knowledge. In Chap. 15, we model and describe what a belief-begets knowledge information search looks like in a case study.

In Chap. 16, we propose **The Consciousness' Drive Information Need-Search Model**, with an extensive case study of a student researching a history essay to illustrate the Model. We also illustrate a searching tool that facilitates the student searching Google and other search engines, called **The Real Information Need Finding Device**. The Model and Device conceptualize the book's title: The Consciousness' Drive: Information Need and the Search for Meaning.

The Conclusion (Chap. 17) to the book summarizes our view of the consciousness approach to information need and information search. We present a cautionary tale related to our exceptional framing ability, which can cut off new information by closing the information loop between humans and the world of new information. We compare this negative impact of our frames to AI-equipped robots, which have the potential to imitate human-like thinking based on the frame problem we described in Part II of the book. Our search for meaning intention, however, cannot be imitated, and it is this intention that draws us continuously back to the objective world in search of new knowledge.

Chapter 13
Solution: Opening the Information Loop: Constructing Information Channels

In this chapter, we present the archeological evidence for the solution to the frame problem of our consciousness. To open the information loop, humans literally constructed information channels to another realm. One of these in Carrowkeel, Ireland, from 5000 years ago, is shown in Fig. 13.1.

It seems as if our Paleolithic and Neolithic ancestors were interested in opening information channels to a parallel, hidden world, via tunnels in caves in the Paleolithic era, and later, in the Neolithic era, via carefully constructed tunnels inside artificial mounds.

We are focusing here on the pivotal Mythic Mind phase in Donald's (Donald 1991) four-phase theory of the evolution of human consciousness. Humans became interested in these new information channels beginning with the key evolutionary adaptation in human cognition roughly 40,000–60,000 years ago, which marked the transition from the Mimetic to the Mythic Mind phase (Donald 1991). The transition lasted until the start of the Theoretic Mind phase with the development of writing roughly 5000 years ago. But within this long period of time, there were incremental transitions in what motivated human thinking:

- From the early Mythic Mind phase (the Chauvet Cave painting)
- To the middle Mythic Mind phase (the Lascaux Cave painting), and finally
- To the late Mythic Mind phase (the Neolithic ruins at Göbekli Tepe, and later at Newgrange)

We analyze the archeological evidence in terms of this evolution in our species' motivation for building information channels in caves and mounds (the examples we use in this chapter are given in parenthesis in the just listed bulleted transitions). These intentions remain within our different layers of consciousness today, which we will come back to at the end of the chapter.

© Springer International Publishing AG, part of Springer Nature 2018
C. Cole, *The Consciousness' Drive*, https://doi.org/10.1007/978-3-319-92457-1_13

Fig. 13.1 Neolithic humans constructed their own tunnels in their search for meaning. Shown here, Carrowkeel, Ireland, from 5000 years ago (© 2014 Shane Finan. Creative Commons Attribution-Share Alike 4.0 International license)

From the Search for Understanding to the Quest for Meaning

The Chauvet Cave paintings painted roughly 32,000 years ago are very different from the Lascaux Cave paintings from roughly 15,000–20,000 years ago. Both represent some sort of spiritual dimension (Clottes and Lewis-Williams 1998; see also, Lewis-Williams 2002), but we can see the evolutionary transition that separates these two paintings, not only in terms of subject matter but also in terms of the artist's intention.

The older painting from the Chauvet Cave, shown in Fig. 13.2, is a section from a larger painting which also includes lions engaged in the hunt. We have already referred to the lions in Part I (Chap. 3, Fig. 3.9; Chap. 6, Fig. 6.3 and Chap. 7, Fig. 7.5). Here, Fig. 13.2 shows only the rhinoceroses part of the same hunting scene. Just as the artist(s) depicted a series of lions' heads in a line to give the feeling, like a film, of the quick advancement of one lion moving rapidly toward its prey, Fig. 13.2 shows a single rhinoceros, at different moments in time, rapidly moving his horn up and down. It is a tour-de-force in art.

The Chauvet artist(s) who painted this complex, multi-part hunting episode conveys the feeling and emotion he or she felt during the experiencing of the episode, which stays attached to the frame when they recalled it from memory to paint it on the wall. As a consequence, there is an intense and unique specificity to this individual's representation of their experience in the world. The representation

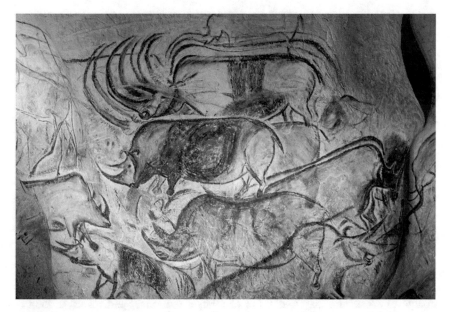

Fig. 13.2 Rhinoceros quickly moving his horn up and down, from Chauvet Cave, 32,000 years ago (© 2016 Claude Valette Creative Commons Attribution-Share Alike 4.0 International license)

contains the essence of the exceptionality of human consciousness as we defined it in Part I:

- The awareness that the episode happened in the past (Chronesthesia)
- The feeling of reexperiencing the episode when it is remembered, i.e., it has all the specifics of the actual experience, including the emotion of speed and excitement the artist felt at the time of the experience (Autonoesis)
- The realization that these are the artist's own memories, and his or hers alone, so the artist has absolute control of the memory (Self)

In the rhinoceros's horn rapidly moving up and down, to indicate speed and the emotion of excitement the artist felt at the time of the experience, we have evidence in this cave painting of the cognitively modern human form of episodic memory (Chronesthesia and Autonoesis). But there is something more. The artist gains self-recognition of her own identity by infusing the memory and the representation of it with her intention (Self).

What is this intention? In the case of the Chauvet Cave painting, the artist's intention is to understand what he/she experienced, the feeling of movement and the excitement he or she felt because of the rhinoceroses' rapid movement up and down of its horn.

Let us now move forward 15,000 years later to the Lascaux Cave painting, shown in Fig. 13.3, which we also previously discussed in Part I. In this cave painting, the episode of the hunt is juxtaposed with a man, possibly a shaman, lying next to a (dead) bison and a broken spear. There is also a symbol of a bird on top of a pole.

Even in the Paleolithic period, when humans were hunter-gatherers, they lived in shifting settlements of up to 150 people. A shaman was the person in the group in charge of connecting day-to-day life to a larger existence, perhaps some kind of parallel unseen world. The Lascaux Cave painting indicates an episode of the shaman's time-traveling out of his real life to this unseen world, represented by the symbol of a bird on a pole.

There is more than an episodic experience being depicted here; there is a complex paradigmatic intention of the artist indicating a theory or ideology that is not present in the Chauvet Cave painting of the rhinoceros. With the shaman and the bird on a pole, there is the artist's intention to represent a theory of human existence in the Lascaux Cave painting.

In contrast to the intention of the artist of the Chauvet Cave painting of the rhinoceros to understand the experienced episode and the world in which the episode occurred, the intention of the artist of the Lascaux Cave painting of the shaman and the bird on the pole is trying to understand the place of humans in the world. It is a different kind of search than the search for understanding intention of the Chauvet Cave painting. It is a search for meaning.

This incremental transition in intention within the Mythic Mind phase itself, from mainly a search in the Chauvet Cave for understanding of the world to a search for meaning on the Lascaux Cave wall is a key evolutionary transition. In fact, over thousands of years, the search for meaning became so intense, so important, that it crossed a threshold, causing the Neolithic Revolution.

The Neolithic Revolution

It is an interesting story, the genesis of the Neolithic Revolution, a story that we are still trying to unravel. We refer to an ongoing archeological expedition at Göbekli Tepe that has provided evidence for a new thesis (Lewis-Williams and Pearce 2005; Mithen 1996), one that brings into question long-held assumptions about the primary motivation that led to the Neolithic revolution (Mann 2011; and recently, Harari 2015).

The traditional thesis for the Neolithic Revolution—the shift from hunting-gathering to agriculture and permanent village settlement—was that global warming 12,000 years ago led to a population increase and the consequent need for an increase in food production, which only systematic agriculture practices could provide. Permanent villages ensued. According to this traditional climate-economic-based thesis, village life and the more complicated group dynamics that resulted from this sedentary lifestyle required a more organized religious framework for purposes of controlling the population (see, Geertz 1966). So the temple building followed.

Big transition! But a recent discovery of temple ruins has changed our thinking on what caused the Neolithic Revolution. It is now believed that the Neolithic Revolution occurred first in Turkey's Fertile Crescent, about 11,600 years ago, in a place called Göbekli Tepe, shown in Fig. 13.4 as it is today. We rely on Mann (2011) for our description of the intention motivating the construction of Göbekli Tepe that follows.

Fig. 13.4 Göbekli Tepe, Turkey, constructed 11,600 years ago (© 2011 Teomancimit. Creative Commons Attribution-Share Alike 3.0 Unported license)

Göbekli Tepe is a series of self-contained, open-air structures utilized for spiritual purposes. The structure is entered through a long tunnel, and in the center there is a circular labyrinth consisting of eight smaller pillars around two large pillars. The carved pillars are up to 18 feet in height and the largest of them weighs 16 tons. The pillars are oddly shaped, like a "T." It is hypothesized that the "T" was meant to represent a person with his or her arms held up to the spiritual world in the sky. To welcome this spiritual world, the builders carved animals on the pillars.

How this huge religious construction came about is mysterious and contentious. At a certain point, the belief system of the group of hunter-gatherers living in the forests around Göbekli Tepe pushed them to construct huge carved pillars grouped in a circle atop a hill. It is thought that the building of this circle required at least 500 workers, who had to be housed and fed over the many years it took to construct it.

It is plausible that, initially, wild wheat was transported from 18.6 miles away to feed the workers building Göbekli Tepe; then when seeds that had been accidentally dropped along the way sprang up the next year, it gave the gatherers the idea of domesticating wheat production. Steven Mithen (1996), in his book *The Prehistory of the Mind: The Cognitive Origins of Art, Religions and Science*, suggests this originating scenario as the genesis of agricultural production in the Neolithic era, again through accidental discovery, as a by-product of the temple building intention.

In addition to the workers who constructed Göbekli Tepe, after the temple was built, a village must have grown up around it to supply the needs of the keepers of the temple and the hordes of pilgrims that came to worship there, although there is no evidence of a village in the archeological remains. But housing must also have been provided for the Göbekli Tepe workers somewhere near Göbekli Tepe. Archeological digging is ongoing at Göbekli Tepe and perhaps evidence of these worker houses will eventually be found.

After a number of years, the original circle of pillars at Göbekli Tepe was deliberately buried. New pillars in a circle were then built. And they too were eventually buried. This successive building and then burying of circles of huge pillars went on for centuries. Thus far, there have been 20 such generations of circle temples discovered at Göbekli Tepe. And another odd thing: the quality of the pillar-making technology decreased as time went on.

Klaus Schmidt, the archeologist who discovered Göbekli Tepe in 1994, is still in the process of uncovering the pillar circles and other artifacts. But if he and the other archeologists are correct, this incredible discovery shows the power of the human Mythic Mind (using Donald's terminology), and its attendant evolving belief system, transitioned so far into the search for meaning intention that something else happened. As an offshoot of the search for meaning intention, some threshold was reached leading to a sudden spurt in new knowledge production to actually build and organize the temple building, in the fields of

- Engineering
- Labor organization systems
- Architecture

And as the most important side effect of the search for meaning intention, to the development of

- Agriculture practices: the domestication of wheat growing to feed the workers involved in constructing the temple. Which initiated systematic agricultural production;
- Villages: roads, water supply, sewage evacuation, etc. first for the construction workers, and later for the priest class and for the pilgrims who visited the site;
- Government; and
- To support a new class in the group (priests-pilgrims): commerce, leading to accounting, law courts, etc.

Scientific Knowledge Production

We know so little about Göbekli Tepe. But there are similar examples of knowledge production resulting from the search for meaning imperative from later Neolithic sites, which provide greater extant evidence of their function and therefore the intention behind their construction. We'll use as an illustrative example one of these, Newgrange, on the eastern coast of Ireland, constructed about 5200 years ago—long before the Egyptian pyramids. Figure 13.5 shows Newgrange as it appears today (after its restoration).

In Fig. 13.6, we take a closer look at the entrance to the tomb, after restoration, which emphasizes the peculiar design feature above the door. The restoration plucked white quartz stones found scattered on the ground around the entrance and attached them above the entrance. The granite stones were not local; they were quarried in the Wicklow Mountains about 38 miles away, so had to be transported there. The consensus is that the restoration was done correctly. But it is not the white quartz rocks above the entrance that is most interesting. The interesting feature is the box-like opening below the white stones and above the door, called the roof-box.

It is through the roof-box that the sun shines on December 21, at the winter solstice. Due to orbit shift, the sunlight now shines through the roof-box a little after sunrise on the solstice, shown in Fig. 13.7, but it has been calculated that it would have been spot on the sunrise when it was built 5200 years ago. The light lasts only 17 minutes, dramatically lighting up three spiral circles 12 inches in diameter on the back wall of the chamber. The triple or tri-spiral design is duplicated on the rock in front of the entrance, shown in Fig. 13.6.

It is believed that Newgrange served a religious purpose centered on the cult of the dead with a ceremony that venerated the dead. The Neolithic spiritual quest at Newgrange was episode oriented, centering around the ritual at the winter solstice. It appears that the participants in the ritual would enter the passage tomb on the winter solstice. The ritual would peak when the sun dramatically shone through the roof-box at precisely sunrise, lighting up the long chamber; and for 17 exhalant minutes,

Fig. 13.5 Newgrange tomb constructed 5200 years ago as it appears today (© 2016 Tjp finn. Creative Commons Attribution-Share Alike 4.0 International license)

dramatically illuminating the three spirals on the back wall of the chamber. It is believed the ritual participants then spoke to the spirits of the dead.

Lewis-Williams and Pearce (2005) believe these passage tombs duplicated the neurological structure of the human brain that a person has flashes of when in a trance. The original constructors of Newgrange perhaps had this inspiration for an information channel that would allow them to effectuate a complicated communication act with the dead, so that they could ask the dead what is on the other side; and any other information that could be given in their search for meaning. But again, the offshoot of this primary purpose was knowledge production: like the nearby cairns of Knowth, Dowth, and Lough Crew, Newgrange is an extraordinarily accurate calendar-astronomy-engineering device.

Belief Begat Knowledge

The archeological evidence from the recent discovery of the first Neolithic-era ruins at Göbekli Tepe indicates that the genesis of the shift of humans from hunting-gathering to sedentary agriculture and village life was our species' search for meaning. The concept of objective knowledge, i.e., knowledge of the laws

Fig. 13.6 Newgrange passage tomb entrance from after restoration in 1967–1974, exposing the roof-box above the entrance (© 2004 Kenia de Aguiar Ribeiro Creative Commons Attribution-Share Alike 3.0 Unported)

Fig. 13.7 Newgrange winter solstice, the sun shining through the roof-box, almost at sunrise, drenching the tomb passage in sunlight (© 2007 Quartz1. Creative Commons Attribution-ShareAlike 3.0 License)

underlying objective reality, was an offshoot of this primary intention. Göbekli Tepe, built 11,600 years ago near the end of the Mythic Mind phase of human consciousness, began the transition to the knowledge-based Theoretic Mind and the development of writing 5000 years ago.

The Mythic Mind paved the way for our present Theoretic Mind consciousness by opening up the information loop between the individual and the world, by creating:

- A much larger, and
- More powerful information channel to the world itself

By larger, in this book we mean paradigmatic—the paradigmatic frame through which the individual views his or her experience in the world. The paradigmatic frame created a much larger information channel than the linear frame of the Episodic and Mimetic Mind phases of our evolutionary development. By more powerful, we mean the new Mythic Mind consciousness equipped humans with a more powerful time-machine for mental time-traveling. Let's take these two notions, larger and powerful, one at a time.

The paradigmatic frame of the Mythic Mind consists of

- A system of symbols,
- Which acts to establish powerful, pervasive, and long-lasting moods and motivations in men by
- Formulating conceptions of a general order of existence (Geertz 1966).

These conceptions of the general order of existence require a network of interlocking concepts. These are very large, complicated frames for viewing the world. These frames, in turn, required factual or knowledge-based feature slots as part of support structure of the mythic-based story, leading to a surge in knowledge production on a scale never seen before. We give only two examples of such knowledge production features that are part of a Mythic frame, taken from Fig. 13.8:

(a) Scientific Features of the Frame

 1. Time
 2. Calendar
 3. Farming cycle

(b) Engineering Features of the Frame

 1. Lifting technology
 2. Carving technology
 3. Work systems
 4. Transportation technology

The addition of knowledge features in the frame, plus the need for interlocking concepts that make up the frame, required enlarging the size of the Mythic Mind information channel exponentially.

The Mythic Mind frame was also exponentially more powerful than the linear frame of the Episodic and Mimetic Mind evolutionary phases of human consciousness. The new intention of the search for meaning unhinged time from the linear, everyday episodes of life experiences of the individuals concerned. The individuals involved in Mythic Mind ritualistic ceremonies, like the winter solstice ritual we

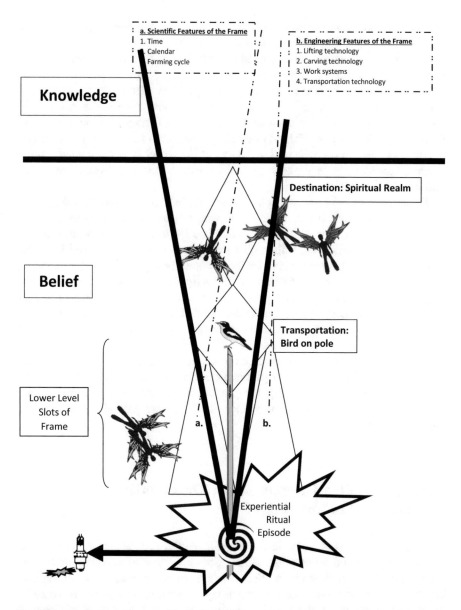

Fig. 13.8 Paradigmatic Frame for Neolithic Belief System. Sparkplug is the experiential episode in the cave or tunnel. The experiential ritual episode requires knowledge features that are physical laws of the objective world that are always true, in the upper part of the frame

know something about at Newgrange, used the ritual episode frame to time-travel beyond death in order to speak to the dead. Being able to create future predicted frames for these meeting-the-dead experiences, and constructing channels to another realm of existence where the dead existed, which was beyond the surface appearance of things, created a more powerful time-machine, with the commensurately more powerful fuel—the search for meaning intention.

But the time-machine could go farther still. It could enable the individual to mentally travel to the timeless world of objective reality, to what is timelessly true about reality—the constant physical laws underlying the seeming chaos of everyday existence. For example, the days shorten, and the winter solstice is always the shortest day of the year. The sun on that day is in a certain position, low to the horizon. This knowledge offshoot of building a tunnel to the dead with a roof-box that projects the sun onto the wall at the end of the tunnel is a very powerful time-machine indeed. Capable of piercing into the constant, timeless, physical laws of the real world in its objective form.

Think about it. The concept that the world you are walking through, which forces you to respond to stimuli it seems to be throwing at you in random sequence, willy-nilly, actually has rhyme and reason behind it. First in the Mythic Mind phase of human consciousness, you believe this rhyme and reason is supplied by some spiritual force, located somewhere up there where the birds fly to before a storm, to the unseen place that controls the world. But then, after thousands and thousands of years of mimicking the birds flying up into the sky, another human gets the winter solstice right, and builds a tunnel to the dead so that she can catch the solstice inside the tunnel for a 17 minute ritual. Then you come to know there are physical laws underlying the way the world works.

The opening up of the information loop between the individual and the world of the Mythic Mind, begat a new, larger and more powerful information channel to the objective world itself, unleashing the production of scientific, engineering, and societal system knowledge of the science-dominated civilization we are now in: the Theoretic Mind.

The Origins of the Theoretic Mind: The Creation of the Concept of Knowledge

We are now at a vital point in our modeling of a consciousness approach to information need and information search. The importance of intention attached to each layer of our consciousness. Each layer is an evolutionary phase in human development, but the four phases remain as layers in our present-day consciousness. Let us briefly summarize the intention feature of this evolution in terms of Donald's 4-phase/3-transition theory of the evolution of human cognition, thinking, and consciousness:

1. Episodic Mind: the consciousness' intention is framing human experience, storing it in memory, and recalling the memory at will
2. Mimetic Mind: the intention is the search for understanding the experience

3. Mythic Mind: the intention is the search for meaning,

- which required dramatically increasing the size and power of the information channel between the individual human and the world, leading to

4. Theoretic Mind: the intention is the search for understanding the objective world, creating

- Knowledge

In this book, we are interested in information need and information search for the production of new knowledge. We are getting there!

The evolutionary transition to the paradigmatic frame of the Mythic Mind gave our species the ability, through the larger and more powerful information channel the Mythic Mind frame provided, to contemplate the presence of a different reality, a different higher realm than their everyday experience in the world. This ability is the unique feature of human consciousness among all other species. Shockingly, we are placing the Theoretic Mind as a subsidiary side effect of the Mythic Mind, that belief begets knowledge. In Fig. 13.8, we diagram this relationship in a frame structure, with the belief system in the lower part of the frame and the knowledge system in the upper part.

In Fig. 13.8, we incorporate the time-travel dimension imparted to the episodic experience of the specific ritual ceremonies at Chauvet and Lascaux, and later in the Neolithic era, at Göbekli Tepe and at Newgrange, by the paradigmatic frame of the human Mythic Mind, symbolized in the figure by the bird on top of a pole. The bird on a pole welcomes humans to contemplate a hidden, spiritual realm that controls the world. Our ancestor humans tried to transport themselves there where the birds go, to this secret place, in a ritual in front of a complex painting depicting running lions and a rhinoceros rapidly moving its horn up and down. Thousands of years later, our further evolved species tried again to reach this other realm, at Göbekli Tepe, and later still at Newgrange when our species constructed a tunnel passage to the dead. They constructed the tunnel so that it caught the winter solstice sun, illuminating the time-travel spiral symbols for 17 min. This gave them a chance to pose their questions to the dead about the meaning of existence. It created an experiential episode that served as a sparkplug for knowledge production.

Scientific and engineering knowledge production, in Fig. 13.8, is placed in the upper level of the Paradigmatic Neolithic Belief System frame, as an offshoot of the Neolithic Belief System. It is the thesis of this book that the human belief system, via the paradigmatic architecture of the Mythic Mind, begets knowledge production. In other words, the knowledge features produced in the service of the search for meaning intention of the Mythic Mind frame, led to the production of a new type of frame through the search-for-meaning's requirement for these features, which eventually led to a more evolved type of frame: the knowledge frame. In the next chapters, we place these concepts in a theoretical framework.

Chapter 14
Solution: Belief-Begets-Knowledge—Definitions

Based on the archeological evidence for our belief-begets-knowledge thesis in the previous chapter, in this chapter we develop a theoretical framework for this thesis.

Göbekli Tepe and Newgrange were constructed as information channels to a parallel, unseen world that appeared to control the world our Neolithic ancestors inhabited. These channels produced an experiential episodic ritual that enabled its participants to engage in communication with a higher universe in the sky, in the case of Göbekli Tepe, and in conversations with the dead about the afterlife in the case of Newgrange. The production of new scientific and engineering knowledge, and in the case of Göbekli Tepe, the start of the Neolithic revolution marking the seismic transition of the human species to sedentary agriculture and permanent village life, was only a by-product of these meaning-quest rituals.

The knowledge resulting as a side effect of the search for meaning at Newgrange in Ireland led to an elaborate (a) calendar-astronomy-engineering device, perhaps for purposes of aiding the subsistence farming in the region at that time. The construction of Göbekli Tepe in Turkey led to, as a side effect, the (b) engineering technology knowledge necessary for the construction and transportation of the 16-ton stone pillars that formed the architecture of the temple.

(a) **Scientific Features of the Frame**

1. Time
2. Calendar
3. Farming cycle

(b) **Engineering Features of the Frame**

1. Lifting technology
2. Carving technology
3. Work systems
4. Transportation technology

© Springer International Publishing AG, part of Springer Nature 2018
C. Cole, *The Consciousness' Drive*, https://doi.org/10.1007/978-3-319-92457-1_14

Fig. 14.1 Belief, in Lower Part of frame, begets Knowledge in Upper Part of the frame. We use as examples of knowledge production (a) the calendar-astronomy-engineering knowledge at Newgrange, and (b) the engineering technology knowledge at Göbekli Tepe in Turkey

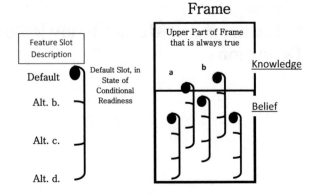

In Fig. 14.1, we begin modeling our belief-begets-knowledge thesis in terms of Minsky's frame theory. You'll remember that we extensively relied on Minsky's theory in Part II of this book to describe how humans frame their experiential intersections with the world, which are then stored in episodic memory. Prototype frames are based on these individual experiences. Each frame is made up of features of the experience. On the left-side of Fig. 14.1 is a generic feature. To cover all contingencies, and based on frequency, each feature has a set of possible alternative assignments; the most probable assignment is the default slot for that feature, the one automatically turned on to give the frame immediate "action" capability. The predictive frames enable us to see the world-as-understanding rather than being subject to stimuli thrown at us in real-time experience. We know in advance what is relevant and what is irrelevant, allowing us to control our experience in the world, and to get through the experience directed by our own goals.

The second aspect of the Fig. 14.1 belief-begets-knowledge frame is that it is divided into a belief system and a knowledge system. Features of the frame that are always true are in the knowledge Upper Part of the frame; features of the frame that have not been confirmed are in the belief Lower Part of the frame.

In this chapter and the next, we use the Minsky model, from Part II, Chap. 9, to develop our own model of knowledge production during information search. The model's central thesis is that knowledge starts and is constructed in the belief system Lower Part of the frame, and shifts into the knowledge system Upper Part of the frame when it is adequately supported by evidence collected from the outside world.

The objective of the rest of this chapter is to clarify the difference between belief and knowledge, but also how they are linked together. To do this, we must briefly leave information science for philosophy.

Some Preliminary Definitions of Belief and Knowledge

When we think of knowledge and belief, they seem very different. They are so different, in fact, that it seems like they come from completely different parts of our brain. We think knowledge is what is solid, what is true, while belief is something individuals construct from their experience in the world, what they guess or think the world is about, for parts of their experience that they do not or cannot know. Belief is almost a feeling, an intuitive impression about experience, which we represent in myths, folktales, and more substantially, in religion. In other words, we normally think of knowledge as objective, while belief, on the other hand, is subjective.

But Plato and the philosophers that to this day follow in his path link the concepts of belief and knowledge together. How could this be? Isn't knowledge what is real and belief indicates what we don't know about what is real, that we fill in with our own notions to make us feel more comfortable? Let's look at this linkage of the two concepts a bit more deeply.

In Plato's (2014) *Theaetetus*, Socrates discusses three possible definitions of knowledge:

1. Knowledge-is-perception (Theaetetus, 151d-e)
2. Knowledge-is-belief (Theaetetus, 187b)
3. Knowledge-is-justified true belief (Theaetetus, 201d-210a)

We will discuss each of these definitions in turn, emphasizing their linkage in a continuum.

Knowledge-Is-Perception

Knowledge-is-perception defines knowledge as that which is gained through our five senses. This definition of knowledge, on its surface, makes the most sense: we know what we are tasting, seeing, touching, smelling, and hearing. Empiricists would say that this direct interaction through our senses has "no cognitive content" (Chappell 2013). Sensory perception, therefore, is acquired *without* the intervention of human reasoning. In effect, because perception is direct human interaction with what is real, unfiltered, and unbiased by human thought, it is true knowledge.

There are various arguments against this. In Plato's account in the *Theaetetus*, at a very basic level, e.g., about whether a wind ascertained via sense perception is cold or warm, frequently two senses mutually come to the same conclusion about the sense perception. Therefore, this mutuality is evidence of the intervention of reasoning, which negates the notion that perception-is-knowledge (Theaetetus, 184–187). This is just one argument Socrates gives to refute this first definition, that knowledge-is-perception.

Let us look at this definition of knowledge-is-perception differently, within the framework of this book. In fact, this is where frames come in—Plato calls them "wax tablets in our mind." We automatically recall from memory a frame or wax tablet to see the incoming stimulus-as-understanding, so that we can form a belief or opinion about the incoming stimulus. We want to know: Is it dangerous? Is it safe? Because knowing this is an undeniable advantage in effectively acting in a hostile world.

But for the knowledge-is-perception definition of knowledge to be true, we have to go before frames are brought in, staying in this sort of no-man's land between the sensory perception of a stimulus and when we become aware of the stimulus. In a certain sense, this pre-awareness state of a stimulus that is perceived by our senses is part of what constitutes knowledge. Knowledge must have some basis in what we can feel and touch and see with our own eyes.

Do we "know" before being aware of the stimulus, or at least is this before-awareness a part of knowledge?

Our intersection with the world is so terribly acute when compared with other species, this pre-awareness of our sensory perception must be incorporated into our framing of our intersection with the world in real-time experience, and also in our cognitive record of experience in episodic memory.

In Part I (Chaps. 4-5) of this book, we have described the acuteness of our intersection with the world compared to other species in terms of Endel Tulving's (1972) three distinguishing aspects of human episodic memory: Chronesthesia, Autonoesis, and Self. Our memory of our experience of the world is so acute, combustible—we have described the intersection like dynamite going off—that it is almost as if there is a registry connected to the episodic frame that we were not aware of at the moment of experiencing it that leaves us with questions about our experience or intersection with the world.

In the chapter on Vermeer, we attempted to convey this search for understanding in our experience as a driving force of human consciousness. We relive an episode from our past and suddenly become aware of a detail for the first time, months, even years later, just by rethinking about it. In fact, detective stories, both in books and on TV, depend on this peculiar quality of human memory as a contrivance to drive the plot.

In Fig. 14.2, we diagram these pre-awareness questions attached to our memory of an experienced episode, using the book's Part I example of our prehistoric ancestor experiencing a solar eclipse while hunting a bison. The hunter does not see the eclipse because it is not in the framework of his existence. But there are question marks attached to his framed storage of the experience in episodic memory, below the state of awareness.

Is our pre-awareness perception part of knowledge, part of what knowledge is? Figure 14.3 models the pre-awareness state of the Fig. 14.2 question marks attached to the memory of the experience as it is framed in episodic memory. Being in the frame is being in some sort of awareness state for the individual. Being in a pre-awareness state means being out of the frame, but attached to it in some way as question marks. Even in Plato (Chappell 2013), there is some debate whether or not there has to be semantic properties (i.e., meaning-giving properties) attached to the sensory perception (Siegel 2006). These questions are in a state of pre-awareness and are, as shown in Fig. 14.3, stored in a pre-awareness registry attached as question marks to the frame.

For lack of a better solution, in Fig. 14.3 we give this pre-belief registration of the sensory perception low probability assignments, so they are below awareness but with the potential to be brought into the frame, to be brought into awareness. In other words, we assume there is some connection to the frame for it to be eligible to

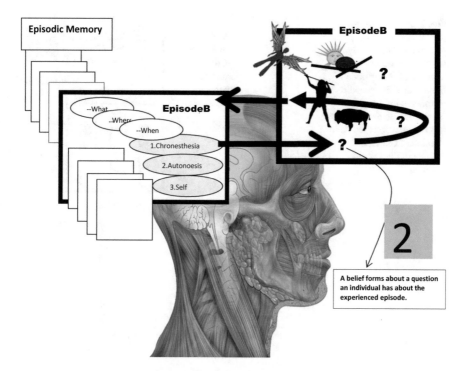

Fig. 14.2 Time-travel to the past to go over question marks, stored in episodic memory, that we were not aware of when we lived the experience. We use the example of an episode of our prehistoric ancestor out hunting a bison when a solar eclipse occurred. The large "2" refers the reader to the same number "2" in Fig. 14.5

continue through the process of the person becoming aware of it and eventually, in the future, bringing it into the frame.

Knowledge-Is-Belief

As a hypothetical, Socrates in the *Theaetetus* equates knowledge and belief, as in the phrase: "What is true is true for me." It almost puts knowledge in the category of being subjective. Socrates rejects this notion of knowledge because so many others may disagree with our belief about something. And our belief may be a false belief, he argues. A powerful demagogue can bring men and women to believe in a false belief without bringing them into a state of knowledge. Belief is not knowledge, Socrates concludes.

But what about true belief? True belief is a belief held by someone that actually is true, as in the example, I believe this is the road to Larissa and this belief is true. Is true belief, then, not the same as knowledge?

Fig. 14.3 Registry for pre-awareness sensory perception data is only vaguely connected to a memory of the episode frame stored in episodic memory. These registry pre-awareness data take the form of questions we have about the experienced episode in the Fig. 14.2 example

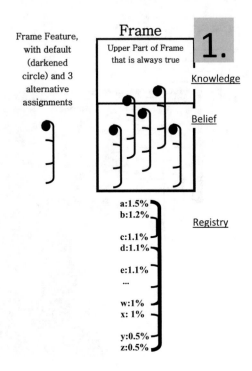

Pritchard and Turri (2014) analyze this possibility and say no. They take the example of this being the road to Larissa, and it is a true belief because it is actually the road to Larissa. What if, they ask, on coming upon a feature of the road that makes you question your true belief, for example, if you see a false sign saying you are on the road to Athens, you doubt your true belief? Pritchard and Turri conclude: If you knew it was the road to Larissa, you would not question your knowledge despite the false sign.

Let us go into true belief a little bit deeper: Plato's Ideal Forms as true belief.

We referred to "semantic properties" of sensory perception in the previous section. Let us say that these "semantic properties" trigger the individual going inward into his or her belief system to access Plato's Ideal Forms (Chappell 2013). The Ideal Forms constitute World 3 in Plato's 3-World conception of knowledge, illustrated in Fig. 14.4:

- World 1: The world of material objects. Material things have derivative or secondary existential status only.
- World 2: The world of psychological processes, where we gain awareness via remembering.
- World 3: The world of Ideal Forms, essences, ultimate realities.

Roger Penrose (1997, p. 125) lists the Platonic Ideal Forms as: mathematics, judgment, common sense, insight, aesthetic sensibility, compassion, morality, truth, and beauty. The Ideal Forms are innate to us, sitting there inside us waiting for us to

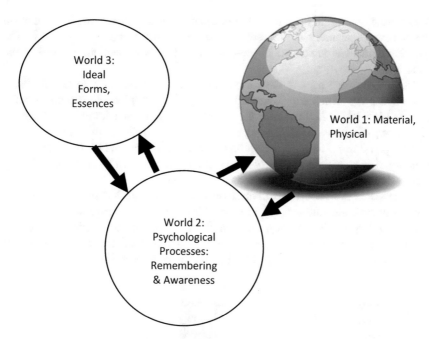

Fig. 14.4 Plato's 3-World theory of knowledge

recollect them. But we interact with World 3's Ideal Forms through World 2, the act of "remembering"—which is a mental or psychological process.

We illustrate how the Ideal Forms in World 3 are activated by returning to Plato's *Meno*. Socrates asks Meno, who is a rich man, to bring him one of his slaves, a supposedly ignorant man, whom Socrates will teach how to figure out the length of one side of a square that is double the area of a square whose sides are 2 feet long. The slave gives two answers that are wrong (4 feet then 3 feet long). Socrates then draws the diagonal of the original square, which is the answer. The slave immediately recognizes this as the right answer. Socrates claims the slave already knew it in himself, in the Ideal Forms, and had only to remember it. So all knowledge acquisition is recognizing something and remembering or recalling the Ideal Form from memory.

Leslie Brown (2005, p. xxiii) says in her introduction to the *Meno* that what Plato is demonstrating with the slave example is:

... the ability to extend one's knowledge from within oneself.

This "I know it when I see it" conception of knowledge, rings true with the big concepts like what is the good, what is a virtuous man, etc., which are hard to define but, ironically, these big notions are easy to recognize when we come across them. But let us return to the example previously described of our prehistoric ancestor who was hunting a bison when a solar eclipse occurred. He remembers a flock of birds taking flight at the moment the darkness occurred with the onset of the solar eclipse.

Many questions would arise in such a peculiar experience, attaching themselves to our ancestor's memory of this episode he had stored in episodic memory. The question marks were in a state of pre-awareness, but they made him go back to the memory.

He time-traveled back to the episode to examine the memory, to turn it upside down and every which way, over and over again in his mind. He remembered the flock of birds taking flight. And at the same time the idea came into his head that the birds were going into the sky to talk to the unseen controller of the universe.

In Fig. 14.5, we diagram going inward into one's true belief, or rather into a memory of an episode stored in episodic memory, in order to activate what is already there, which the slave already knew as a true belief.

Beliefs are our first answers to these question marks attached in a pre-awareness state to our memory frames. By time-traveling back via our representation of the episode in episodic memory, and thinking about it, the individual brings pre-awareness sensory data, stored in the Fig. 14.5 (1) Registry, into (2) the belief Lower Part of the frame. In Fig. 14.5 (2), on the right-hand side of the figure, we

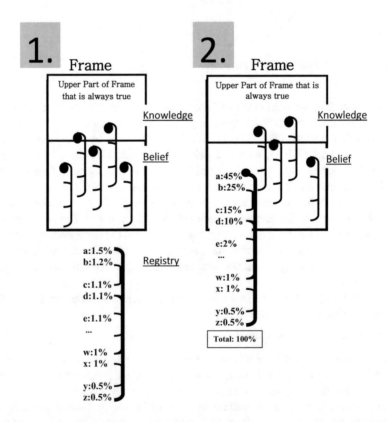

Fig. 14.5 (1) Sensory perception of incoming stimulus in Registry is outside of the Belief-Knowledge frame. (2) It is brought into the belief part of the frame

illustrate this entry of previously pre-awareness data or questions stored in a Registry, into the belief Lower Part of the frame.

Beliefs are a vehicle for bringing formerly incoherent data in a pre-awareness state stored in a sensory register, collected during an experienced episode, into the belief part of a frame, as Socrates did in the *Meno* dialogue when he got the slave to find the answer to a mathematical problem inside himself.

But Socrates also rejected this knowledge-is-true belief definition of knowledge.

Knowledge Is Justified True Belief

Plato's third definition of knowledge is the belief that something is true backed up by justification—by a reason, by a rational explanation, or by undoubted evidence—that supports the belief. Plato uses the word "shackle":

> ... the belief is not very good "until you shackle them by figuring out what makes them true .... And then, once they're shackled, they turn into knowledge, and become stable and fixed... and that's how knowledge differs from a correct [belief]: by a shackle. (Meno, 98a in Plato 2005, p. 130)

Belief is a state of mind, but in justifying the belief state via interaction with the outside world, the physical laws of nature become incorporated into the belief state, turning it into knowledge.

The definition of knowledge as justified true belief is considered the traditional definition of knowledge to this day (Gettier 1963; Stanford Encyclopedia of Philosophy 2014; Steup 2016). To illustrate justified true belief, we refer again to Karl Popper's (1967) Theory of 3-Worlds.

Popper's 3-Worlds theory explicitly dialogues with, but fundamentally revises, Plato's 3-Worlds, particularly with Plato's World 3 locating of knowledge in the individual's recollection of the Ideal Forms. As shown in Fig. 14.6, Popper eliminates Plato's World-3 Ideal Forms, substituting instead the world of objective scientific knowledge written down in books, articles, and other documents. World-3 contains both true and false theories, and open problems (Popper 1967, p. 74). Popper thus distinguishes between the outside objective state of knowledge in World 3 and the inward mental states of the individual in World 2.

World 2 "grasps" for understanding of human objective knowledge in World 3's written-down theories, models, etc., creating a succession of "states" of understanding. With the explicit objective of refuting the particular state of understanding the individual has at the time, the states of understanding are continuously checked against, confirmed, revised, or outright refuted by collecting evidence in World 1, the world of physical and material reality. Popper puts this "grasping," then checking back to evidence collected in the real world, into a formula of new knowledge creation called the "schema of conjectures and refutations" (Popper 1975, p. 168):

$$P_1 \gg TT \gg EE \gg P_2, \text{and so on}.$$

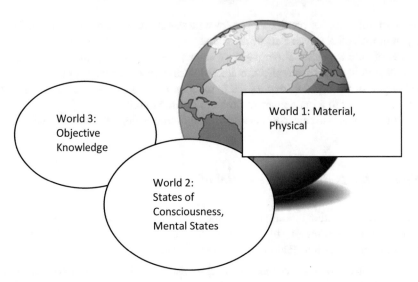

Fig. 14.6 Popper's version of 3-Worlds of human understanding and knowledge production

The individual begins with a first notion of the problem (P_1), and develops a tentative theory or tentative belief for its solution (TT). The individual then tests the tentative theory empirically in an error elimination phase (EE). This means taking the TT or belief outside into data collected in the physical world. At the end of this cycle, the individual's view of the problem, or problem state, is changed to P_2. This is repeated until the problem is either solved or abandoned (for greater detail, see Cole 1999). In Fig. 14.7, with the 3-Worlds circle symbol at the far right, we indicate this iterative cycle of positing theories then testing them for error elimination or outright refutation—TT_1 to TT_4—against empirical evidence gathered in the real world.

Popper's view of knowledge is probably what most people consider knowledge to be. We formulate a tentative theory or hypothesis about a problem, which is a belief about the solution to the problem. Then we test the belief in an objective fashion in an error elimination (EE) stage of problem solution. Thus, the concept of the null hypothesis in scientific research, where the scientist, instead of positing his or her belief as the predicted study outcome, deliberately biases the inquiry (in the null hypothesis) in the direction of refuting the theory-belief.

We diagram Popper's conception of justified true belief as the definition of knowledge in Fig. 14.8. It shows (2) Belief turning into (3) Knowledge via (2.1) Popper's schema of conjectures and refutations.

Popper describes the difference between his theory of knowledge and Plato's as nominalism versus essentialism respectively (Popper 1967, p. 75). Plato is an essentialist: the essences of concepts like the good, virtue, mathematics, etc. are located within us. Popper, like Plato's pupil Aristotle, is a nominalist, who shifts knowledge to the continuous creation and refutation of theories or beliefs that are, via rigorous scientific inquiry, tested against reality in the outside world. The

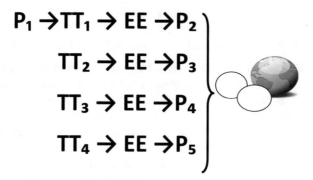

$$P_1 \rightarrow TT_1 \rightarrow EE \rightarrow P_2$$
$$TT_2 \rightarrow EE \rightarrow P_3$$
$$TT_3 \rightarrow EE \rightarrow P_4$$
$$TT_4 \rightarrow EE \rightarrow P_5$$

Fig. 14.7 Popper's schema of conjectures and refutations

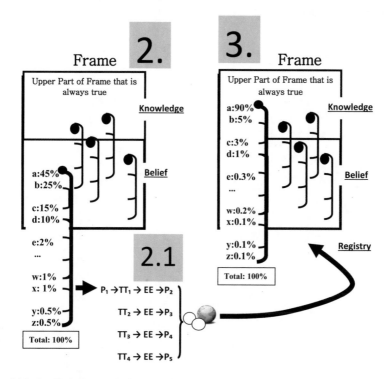

Fig. 14.8 Justified True Belief: (2) Belief becomes justified, via (2.1) Popper's schema of conjectures and refutations, and (3) turning into knowledge

objective here is the continuous quest for what is true by refuting what is believed (Popper 1967). As they are important distinctions in subsequent chapters of this book, we will emphasize here the difference between Plato and Popper, as Popper (1967) himself describes it:

- Plato: Knowledge is internal search for meaning (of the essences of life), accessed through the act of "remembering." (Popper 1967, p. 75)
- Popper: Knowledge is external quest in the outside world for objective truth.

The search for meaning in Plato requires internal examination of the human belief system, and the recollection or remembering of knowledge contained therein, while the search for truth in Popper's schema of conjectures and refutations is primarily the testing of beliefs—tentative theories and models—via the gathering of empirical evidence in the outside world; in other words, via an external examination of the world. They are two separate interests with two different focuses.

The corollary to this distinction between **meaning** and **truth** is that meaning may not be truthful (in the objective sense), or at least objective truth is not the main motivation of the seeker. This has huge implications for modeling information search and the design of information search systems like Google, which we will outline in the next chapter.

Chapter 15
Belief-Based Information Search

We have now come to the chapter where we outline the solution to the frame problem of information search described in Part II:

> How do we come to know that which we don't already know, that is not already in our frames? If we didn't know it before, we wouldn't be able to recognize it if we came across it. And if we do recognize it, we already knew it.

The solution to the frame problem can be summarized in two propositions and one conclusion, which we diagram in the chapter in three figures:

Figure 15.1: Knowledge production starts and takes place in the belief system.
Figure 15.7: Knowledge production is a side effect of the individual's search for meaning.
Figure 15.5: Therefore, information systems and search engines should be designed to ignite the knowledge production sparkplug in the searcher's belief system, by engaging the searcher's quest for meaning.

Knowledge Production Starts in the Belief System

Figure 15.1 describes the driving force behind the human consciousness approach—how we think and what we think about—to information search leading to knowledge production. Knowledge production is compared to a combustion engine fueled by the constant inflow of and search for new information from the outside world. The engine is divided into two systems, the knowledge system attached to the Upper Part of the engine frame and the belief system attached to the Lower Part of the engine frame. Attached to the belief system is a Registry. Because of the access it provides to pre-awareness data in the Registry, sparking the belief system emancipates the individual from imprisonment in the frame by opening a channel for new information from the outside world to get into the frame.

© Springer International Publishing AG, part of Springer Nature 2018   193
C. Cole, *The Consciousness' Drive*, https://doi.org/10.1007/978-3-319-92457-1_15

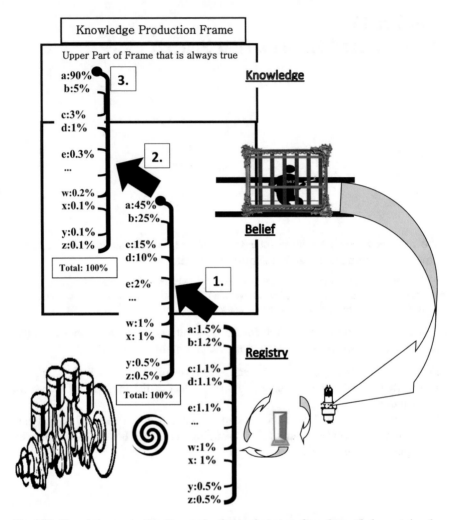

Fig. 15.1 Knowledge production (the combustion engine) starts from the sparkplug opening the information loop to new information entering the frame. Knowledge production cycle: (1) Pre-awareness data in the Registry, (2) shifts into belief part of the frame, then through testing of the belief via empirical evidence gathering, (3) belief shifts into the knowledge part of the frame

Each system is fueled by a different intention motivating the search for information:

- The knowledge system is fueled by the **search for understanding** of the objective truth intention, while
- the belief system is fueled by **the search for meaning** intention.

The knowledge system in the Upper Part of the Fig. 15.1 frame—these are features of the experience episode that are always true—is a closed information

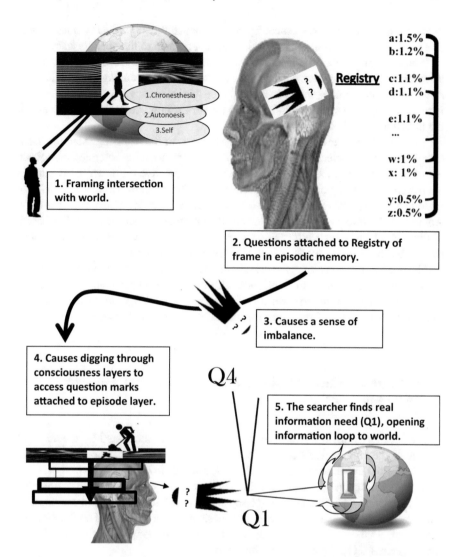

Fig. 15.2 Search for meaning: residue of unanswered questions in the framing of our intersection with the world, connected to the frame in the Registry. The unanswered questions drive the search, based on the searcher's real information need, which opens the information loop to new information in the world

loop, dependent on the framework of the scientific inquiry. The belief system in the Lower Part of the frame contains features of the object, topic, or episode that are not fixed or always true, but each feature contains a set of possible feature assignments with varying probabilities of being instantiated, allowing maximum flexibility. Some of the assignments in the set are in fact in a pre-awareness state, in the Registry.

These are data from an experienced episode of which the individual was not aware. The pre-awareness data are like question marks attached to the episode frame.

It is something about the question marks that provokes a feeling of unease and uncertainty about the experienced episode in the individual, causing the individual to recall the episode from memory to mentally reexperience it over and over again. The individual even seeks out new information by, for example, returning to the scene of the initiating episode for more information.

There are two levels of intention: the search for **understanding** intention associated with the knowledge system and the search for **meaning** intention associated with the belief system. The former is a search for objective truth, while the latter is the search for meaning or balance with the world. The residue coating attached to the episode memory frame causes a sense of imbalance in the episode in memory, requiring new information to re-balance it. Therefore, the cause for belief-based, Mythic Mind layer new information seeking behavior is the sense of imbalance created by the question mark residue attached to the memory frame.

The search for meaning is more about the individual's relationship with the world, the sense of being in imbalance with the world, rather than understanding the world. Understanding the world leading to new knowledge production is only a side effect or offshoot of resolving this initiating sense of imbalance.

Knowledge Production: Side Effect of Individual's Search for Meaning

Figure 15.2 diagrams the search for meaning intention, motivated by the sense of imbalance the searcher feels because of the residue coating of question marks on the memory of the experienced episode. We diagram this imbalance in five steps.

In Step 1, humans intersect with the world in an exceptional way. It is combustible intersection, resulting in a unique secondary consciousness system compared to other species that have a primary consciousness only. We have relied on the 3-aspect theory of Endel Tulving to get at this mysterious exceptionality of our consciousness-driven intersection with the world:

- The awareness that the episode happened in the past (Chronesthesia)
- The feeling of reexperiencing the episode when it is remembered, i.e., it has all the specifics of the actual experience, including the emotion of speed and excitement the artist felt at the time of the experience (Autonoesis)
- The realization that these are the individual's own memories, and his or hers alone, so the individual has absolute control of the memory (Self)

If our intersection with the world and our exceptional representation of it in episodic memory is ours alone, then our relationship with the world is also ours alone. It is an individual aloneness. But strangely, it is also a species' aloneness (separateness or alienation from the world). It creates a shared consciousness unlike any other species. We have the shared intention, based in our belief system, and the shared ability to try and find out, based in our knowledge system, to search individually and together for the meaning of the world and our place in the world.

In Step 2, our combustible intersection with the world creates an imbalance between the individual and the world, which leaves a residue coat of question marks on the representation of the experience episode we store in our episodic memory. What is the source of this imbalance residue that motivates us to constantly seek out further information in the world in a never-ending quest for the meaning of the world and our place in that world?

Our memory of the experience of our intersection with the world is so acute that it leaves a pre-awareness residue attached to our memory of the intersection, which is stored in episodic memory in a Registry. We are not aware of this residue at the moment of experiencing it, but it leaves us with nagging question marks about our experience intersection with the world. These questions are like an itch that we become obsessed with, driving us to time-travel back to the episode by recalling it from episodic memory, and reexperiencing the episode over and over again. It even leads us to seek out information by, for example, revisiting the scene of the initial episode.

In Step 3, the residue of questions marks causes *imbalance* between the individual and the outside world.

In Step 4 in Fig. 15.2, and enlarged in Fig. 15.3, humans dig into the frame of their intersection with the world afterward when they recall the episode from memory, investigating it and interpreting it in terms of the many layers of human

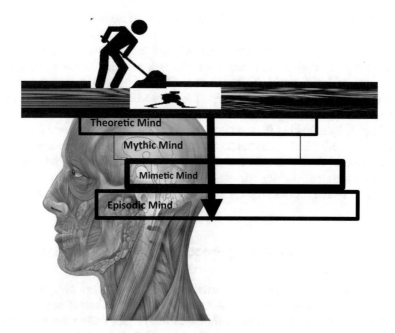

Fig. 15.3 Digging into the human framed intersection with and experience of the world through the four evolutionary layers of human consciousness

consciousness. Artists represent this digging effort either as Vermeer did on canvas in *The Little Street* 400 years ago, or the first recorded human artist did on the Chauvet Cave wall 32,000 years ago, but we all make this digging effort on a daily basis. The primary intention is the alienation-imbalance created by the residue of pre-awareness data attached to the memory episode frame; but the side effect of new knowledge production is frequently the vehicle for solving this imbalance.

The digging into the four evolutionary layers determines what and how we think about the world and our own specific place in the world. But they come with different motivations or intentions for seeking new information in the outside world. We briefly outline the central intention characteristic of each evolutionary phase:

- Episodic Mind

  - Framing our experience intersection with the world in a memory, with a residue of pre-awareness question marks attached to the frame

- Mimetic Mind

  - Searching for understanding by reexperiencing or mimicking the episode over and over again in our own mind, as well as to others in the group

- Mythic Mind

  - Searching for meaning of the episode intersection with the world

- Theoretic Mind

  - Searching for understanding of objective truth of the world

There is a difference between going out into the external world to seek the objective truth of reality and going inward to seek meaning of the world and our relationship with the world. They are two different intentions. But the outward intention starts and is constructed inside the human belief system, which is fueled by the search for meaning intention.

In Step 5, by accessing the search for meaning intention, we access our real Q1 information need, which immediately opens the information loop between ourselves and the world. Once the information loop is open, we can recognize the new information that will satisfy our real information need. As a side effect of the belief-based search for meaning intention is the production of new knowledge.

Belief-Begets-Knowledge Approach to Information Search

Current search engines design the search experience based on what the searcher already knows, that is already in the searcher's frame. Current search engines assume the searcher knows her real information need so she will be able to recognize information in the results lists that satisfies the need. In fact, current search engines assume the searcher knows in advance the general parameters of the answer. When she asks the search engine the height of tennis player Milos Raonic, she knows the answer is in feet/meters and inches/centimeters. As a result, the query to the system formulated by the searcher from their information need is transaction-based, as if the searcher was commanding information from the system (Cole 2012). Google performs this transactional search extremely well, so well in fact that for many of these type of searches, it confidently and correctly places the answer in a box at the top of the results list.

But what if the searcher is asking the search engine a question for which she does not know the outlines of the answer? These are the deeper questions, the why questions, the how questions; the kind of questions that form the basis of problem definition, problem solving, invention, creativity, and new discovery. The searcher requires the new information for the production of new knowledge.

In the rest of the chapter, we outline the underlying problem of information search as it stands now (Fig. 15.4), and the solution to the problem in the design of information search systems that purposely engage the human belief system and its search for meaning intention (Fig. 15.5).

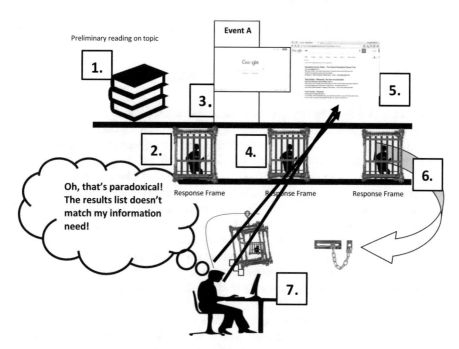

Fig. 15.4 The Meno Paradox problem of information search: the searcher doesn't know what he doesn't yet know so cannot formulate an effective query to the search engine. (1) The searcher reads on the topic before the search begins, (2) forming a topic frame. (3) Based on the topic frame, he types his query into Google's search box. (4) He is imprisoned in the same topic frame (5) for intersecting with (viewing) the results list. (6) The searcher is imprisoned in his topic frame, only seeing what he already knows. (7) The Paradox: The results list matches the searcher's query but not his real information need (Google search page and results page: © 2018 Google. Reprinted with Permission)

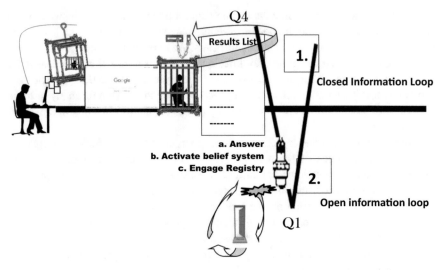

Fig. 15.5 *Sparking real information need*: Escaping imprisonment in (1) the closed information loop inside the searcher's frames by sparking the query from the frame controlled compromised need (Q4) into real information need (Q1). This is done in three steps: (a) answering query, (b) activating belief system, and (c) engaging Registry (Google search page: © 2018 Reprinted with Permission)

The Problem: Imprisoned in the Frames

Figure 15.4 indicates the problem of information search, which is the paradoxical notion that the searcher is confronted with the search engine's output in the results list that exactly matches his query to the system and yet the information in the results list does not satisfy his information need. How can this be?

Let us take a common example. The searcher is a student who comes to the search engine having read the Wikipedia article on his research topic. He has also read several subsidiary topic articles on Wikipedia that were hyperlinked to from the main article. In addition, he asked his teacher several questions after the teacher gave a 15 minute lecture on the topic in class. The student's topic frame as he sits down at the search engine is a result of all these information-seeking events.

The searcher recalls the topic frame from memory to guide his interaction with the search engine. Based on information stored in the topic frame, the searcher types in a query to the search engine, Google for example. Via a keyword index that is constantly updated, the search engine matches the concept terms in the searcher's query with the Internet websites/pages/documents in its database—literally billions and billions of separate items—then outputs the matches in the results list. The student reads through the list; he sees the key words he had typed into the search box, but nothing resonates; he only feels overwhelmed.

This is where Fig. 15.4's searcher exclaims:

Oh, that's paradoxical! The results list doesn't match my information need!

The problem is the student is imprisoned inside what he already knows, inside the topic frame he used when he typed in the query less than a minute before. This includes not only the topic frame based on his information gathering on the topic, but the other frames outlined in Part II of this book: the searcher's individual frame, his frame from the group he is a member of (his demographic group, for example); and finally, his nation frame. The nation frame gives each of us a different perspective on certain issues; the issue of power, for example, where an American would have a different perspective than a Scandinavian.

Our student searcher is imprisoned in a closed information loop extending from his frames to the query, then from the query to the search engine's matched output in the results page. The transactional approach does not acknowledge this problem while the human consciousness approach taken in this book meets the problem head-on and offers a solution.

The Solution: Escaping the Frames

For information searches where the searcher's goal is the production of new knowledge, the consciousness-based approach to information search shifts the focus of the search experience away from her knowledge system to the searcher's belief system. The levers of the searcher's brain must be activated (MacKay 1969) by accessing the pre-awareness data attached to the belief-part of the frame in the Sensory Registry, not by commanding the search engine for known-answer-type information. In other words, we investigate information search in terms of how humans think and what they think about in their interaction with the search engine.

The searcher must escape the imprisonment of her frames by accessing her real information need in her belief system. This is difficult because the searcher is comfortably guiding the search imprisoned inside her frames. Accessing the real information need is depicted in Fig. 15.5 as a "V," to indicate its verticality. The searcher starts at the top of the "V" using a compromised Q4-level of the need (Taylor 1968). To engage the searcher's **real information need,** shown at the base of the information need sign "V" as Q1, the system proposes three steps, Fig. 15.5a, b, and c. The purpose of the three steps is to "spark" open the information loop between the searcher and new information in the world, liberating the searcher from the prison of her frames and the Meno Paradox.

(a) Answering query: To begin tricking the Meno Paradox, the searcher must formulate the question or query to the search engine as the answer. This switches the searcher out of what she already knows to what the searcher needs to know—the answer to the question. This leads to the second step.

(b) Activating belief system: The second step is to push the searcher's query further into the belief system by starting the query with the words: "I believe the answer to my question is . . ." So instead of the usual formulation of the query starting from what the searcher already knows about the topic, we shift the mindset of the searcher into the belief system by using the words "I believe the answer to my question is …"

(c) Engaging Registry: Third, the search engine engages the Registry of the searcher, where pre-awareness data about the topic are connected to the frame. The searcher does this by stating four answers to her question, all beginning with the words: "I believe the answer to my question is … . **because** … ." By the third and certainly the fourth answer, the searcher runs out of snap answers, and begins to over-cognate, reaching outside of the frame to low probability feature assignments that were formerly in a pre-awareness state. The low probability assignments now snap into attention in the belief-part of the frame, and thus become part of the topic frame.

These three steps, listed in Fig. 15.5 as a, b, and c, result in this "spark" to the searcher's topic frame, switching him from being imprisoned in what he already knows to an open information loop ready for new knowledge production. (We have only outlined the belief-based search system here; we incorporate the three steps into a formal presentation of the system, illustrating it with a much more detailed case study, in Chap. 16.)

A Belief-Based Approach to Information Need and Information Search

Our human consciousness has an inexorable drive, a "need" that pushes us to seek out and recognize new information in the world, in a quest to attach meaning to our experience, a need that begins and is constructed in our belief system. What drives us back to the world with fresh eyes is the complexity of our representation of our intersection experience with the world. The human intersection with the world is so hard that it causes combustion, leaving a residue coating of question marks in the imprint of the intersection, a memory trace in a pre-awareness state that is stored in episodic memory. This memory trace is attached to the frame in a Registry. These question marks motivate us to understand the world as a side effect—they work together now in our present Theoretic Mind phase of our evolutionary development—because the residue coating of question marks creates an existential imbalance between our consciousness and the world and our place in the world. Our consciousness drives us to resolve the imbalance through the search for meaning. It is our search for meaning, in fact, that motivates us to produce knowledge in the service of our search for meaning, but this search for understanding of the world, leading to knowledge production, is a side effect for the deeper searching for meaning.

In many of our information searches, they are based in our knowledge system; we already know the type of answer we are looking for and we are "commanding" the search engine to deliver it to us. For this type of search, the current search engines work almost perfectly. But for searches whose objective is the production of new knowledge, the existential search for meaning to achieve a balance with the world and our place in it is our real information need in every information search episode we conduct using Google or any other search engine. We must design the search engine that shifts the searcher's query to the searcher's belief system to create an open information loop to new knowledge production.

We diagram this expression of the relationship between the consciousness' drive, information need, and the search for meaning, in the typical search situation using Google, in Fig. 15.6.

This is the most important part of the consciousness approach to information search and search engine design, the most important from the practical point of view. That is, by taking the consciousness approach, which shifts information search into the searcher's belief system, the searcher's information search, especially during the searcher's intersection with the results list, turns into an experience. In effect, because pre-awareness data stored in the Registry attached to the searcher's topic frame are now activated in the search, the closed loop becomes an open information loop based in the searcher's belief system. So it lets new information from the results list into the searcher's belief system, initiating the knowledge production engine, which can potentially lead to producing new knowledge for the searcher about his or search topic.

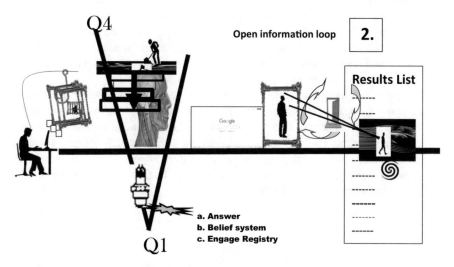

Fig. 15.6 A consciousness approach to information search and search engine design. The searcher starts the search utilizing his frames of knowledge. But the search engine intercedes when he types in the query, prompting: [(a) Answer; (b) Belief system; (c) Engage Registry], sparking him into his belief system (his real information need Q1), which actualizes an open information loop (the open door surrounded by arrows). The searcher is now freed from his imprisonment in his frame so he can intersect with the search engine's results list "open" to receive new information, leading to an experiential interaction (the spiral ball) and the production of new knowledge (see Fig. 15.7) (Google search page: © 2018 Reprinted with Permission)

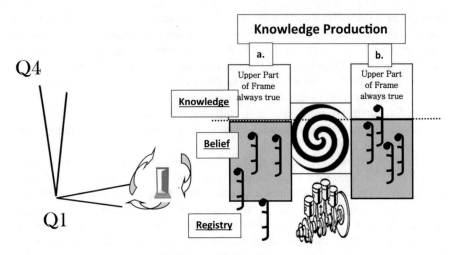

Fig. 15.7 The New Knowledge Production "engine" (a) before and (b) after engaging the searcher's belief system in information search via a consciousness approach to information system design (**shown in Fig. 15.6**). (a) Pre-awareness data in the Sensory Registry shift into (b) the searcher's belief system, and even her knowledge system

It is important to note that the consciousness approach views information search as an episode of experience rather than a transaction between the searcher commanding knowledge system-based, confirmatory information for which the searcher already knows the type of answer she needs from the search engine (see also the Conclusion chapters to Part I and Part II). The "engine" in the search engine is thus literally transferred inside the searcher's cognitive system, into the searcher's knowledge production system, as shown in Fig. 15.7.

The big idea underlying our model of knowledge production during information search is that human consciousness constructs new knowledge, not in the knowledge system—we only confirm or refute our theories in the knowledge system—but rather in our belief system. The process is fueled by the human search for meaning. We define the search for meaning as our human consciousness's drive or need, via information seeking, for an existential fit or balance, the feeling of being at one with the world and our place in that world.

Chapter 16
The Model of the Consciousness' Drive: Information Need and the Search for Meaning

We are now ready to model the consciousness approach to information need and information search in the **Consciousness' Drive Information Need-Search Model**, diagrammed in Fig. 16.1. The model is divided into five components. The aim of the model is to set out design parameters for harnessing the searcher's consciousness' drive by engaging the searcher's real information need in the search. In this chapter, we pay particular attention to the searcher finding her real information need, giving the finding process its own figure, Fig. 16.2's **Finding Real Information Need**.

We illustrate these two models with a case study example of a fictional student starting a school project with a compromised idea of her need, then interacting with topic information to find her real need.

At the heart of the Consciousness' Drive Information Need-Search Model is the notion that information need and information search should be thought of as an engine whose objective is the searcher's production of new knowledge. The engine is the topic frame created by the searcher-student to assemble the topic, to direct information searching, and to produce new knowledge. The topic frame is divided into three separate parts:

- Registry for topic data the student picks up in her information searching, which attaches to her topic frame in a pre-awareness state because she is not able to classify or label these data
- Belief system where new knowledge production starts and is substantially constructed
- Knowledge system where features of the topic shift into once the student has confirmed or refuted the tentative theories and hypotheses started and constructed in her belief system

Because new knowledge production takes place in the searcher-student's belief system, the real information need of the searcher-student is located in the belief part of the topic frame. New knowledge production must be "sparked" into functioning like a combustion engine, in the belief system. The fuel that sets the engine in motion is the search for meaning intention, which seeks information that will create a

© Springer International Publishing AG, part of Springer Nature 2018
C. Cole, *The Consciousness' Drive*, https://doi.org/10.1007/978-3-319-92457-1_16

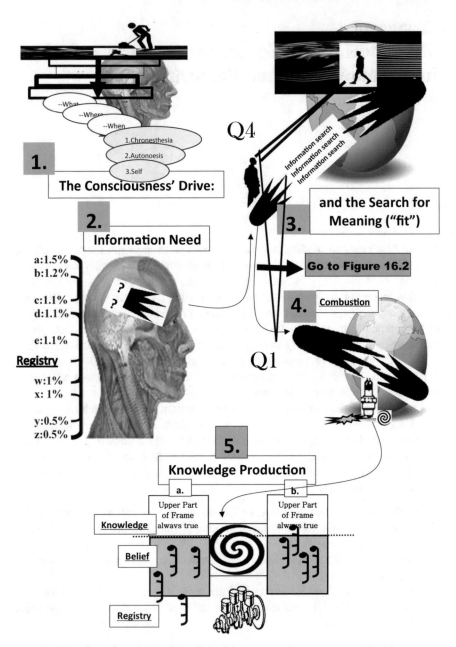

Fig. 16.1 The Consciousness' Drive Information Need-Search Model: (1) Consciousness Drive: (2) Information Need and (3) the Search for Meaning. (4) Finding meaningful information, creating "fit" with world, which sparks combustion of (5) the knowledge production engine (a–b)

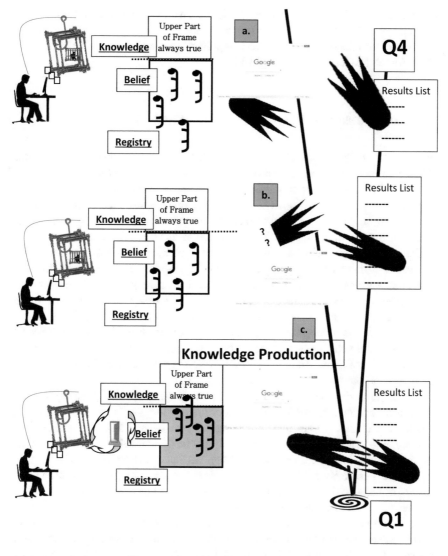

Fig. 16.2 Finding Real Information Need: (a) The searcher starts out with a compromised information need (Taylor's (1968) Q4-level of need). (b) The searcher engages in iterative information searching on the topic. (c) The searcher finds through information searching his real information need (Q1) (Google search page: © 2018 Google Reprinted with Permission)

balance or "fit" between the searcher's belief system and the outside world of information.

The chapter ends with the demonstration of an information system device, called the Real Information Need Finding Device, shown in Fig. 16.3. The finding device facilitates this shift of the searcher-student's attention to her belief system, by making her realize what her real information is.

We start with by outlining the five-component Consciousness' Drive Information Need-Search Model, shown in Fig. 16.1.

The Consciousness' Drive (Fig. 16.1, Image 1)

We start the outline of the Consciousness' Drive Information Need-Search Model with the human consciousness' drive, shown in "Image 1" at the top left-hand side of Fig. 16.1. We compare consciousness to a combustion engine requiring informational fuel in order to function. The fuel feeding this engine is the searcher's search for meaning, balance, or "fit" between her belief system and the outside world. At the heart of our exceptional species' consciousness is this drive for meaning or "fit."

Something happened to us along our human evolutionary path that fundamentally changed how and what we think; we feel and think about our experience differently than other species. We have argued in this book that the genesis of the difference began from the very beginning of our evolutionary journey, in the way we framed our intersection with the world in the unit of the episode. The episode unit of experience as it is represented in our episodic memory provides us with a unique and exceptional vehicle/channel, or frame as we call it in this book, through which humans need, seek, find, and use new information to construct new knowledge about the world and our place in the world.

Human episodic memory is different from all other species' memory of their experience, particularly our identification of the memory as (1) a past-event, (2) for which we feel that we are reexperiencing the past event when we recall it from memory, and that the experience is (3) uniquely the individual's alone. We are what we experience, and the more self-identity we have, the more we do with the experience—objectify it. We objectify our intersection with the world through the process of categorizing our experience in it, which includes the world itself.

These three things, causing our sense of being separate from the world and our sense of individuality because of the way we experience our intersection with the world, create the conditions for the individual feeling or sensing he or she is alienated from the world. This sense of being out of alignment with the world separates us from all other species. In this book, we have called this sense of being out of alignment being in a state of imbalance with the world.

Our unique existential feeling of being in a state of imbalance with the world drives us to achieve "fit" by seeking information that will "right us" with the world. But it is more than understanding our experience, or understanding the world that we seek, although the seeking understanding intention is part of it. The more important intention is our need to seek meaning for our experience. Seeking meaning is a more powerful fuel intention than seeking understanding.

We have argued in this book that the seeking-meaning intention is what marked us as truly distinct from other species, including our closest cousin species the

Neanderthals. The onset of the search for meaning intention with the onset of the Mythic Mind phase of our evolutionary development marks the point where we became cognitively modern humans, according to Donald (1991).

It is this exceptional human sense of being in a state of being "out-of-alignment" with the world, centered in the Mythic Mind layer of our consciousness, which creates the search for meaning intention underlying new knowledge production. Therefore, for searches whose goal is new knowledge production, our existential sense of imbalance with the world and our place in it, based in our belief system, is the source of the searcher's real information need.

Real Information Need Begins in a State of "Un-Fit" (Fig. 16.1, Image 2)

When the goal of our information search is new knowledge production, we are forced to start the search with a compromised form of our information need. We show this in Fig. 16.1, Image 2. We are in a state of imbalance or "un-fit" with the outside world of information due to the question marks residue attached in a Registry to our topic frame. Despite being in a pre-awareness state, these residue question marks drive the information search. They create a sense of being in a state of disequilibrium or "un-fit" with the outside world of information. The searcher doesn't know what information she is looking for, what her real information need is, so forced to make do with a compromised form of the need, the search is inefficient.

For example, the searcher quite logically starts seeking information by assembling facts about the problem they need to define or the facts to a problem they need to solve. A student who needs to write an essay will gather facts about the essay topic—the events that make up the topic, the date when the events occurred, the people involved, etc. But oddly, the searcher feels she is limping along, going this way and that through reams and reams of new information, never satisfying her real information need. The searcher may be gaining an understanding of her topic, but it is not through seeking an understanding of their new topic that searchers locate their real information need.

To get at the real information need, the searcher must go inward.

This seems odd, counterintuitive, but think about the number of times we do go inward for knowledge about right and wrong we already seem to know. In reaction to a photo of a Syrian child lying dead on a beach, or a Syrian child gasping for breath, knocked down by the chemicals used in the attack on the child's village, for example. We just know without proof this is unjust. Our certainty is not knowledge exactly. Because it is not proven by empirical evidence, it is really a belief that something is right or wrong. If asked, we would say we know something is subjectively true. We don't care about its objective truth. We belief it to be true so much that it almost seems like a deeper knowledge than scientifically proven knowledge. We'd bet our life on it. In fact, it is so much us, our inner core, that the belief is our identity; how we define our self.

We have highlighted Karl Popper's division of knowledge into knowledge-as-belief, defined by Plato's inner recollection theory where the individual goes inward to actualize belief-based knowledge, and Popper's own theory of objective knowledge, which requires the individual to go outward into the world to find objective truth about reality. We have located knowledge-as-belief in the belief system and the knowledge-as-objective knowledge in the knowledge system. These are two different but connected halves of the frame we humans use to objectify and individualize our own human experience in the world in our episodic memory. The difference in intention in the two notions of knowledge is as follows:

Belief System = search for meaning intention
Knowledge System = search for objective truth intention

It seems disturbing that the search for meaning and truth are not the same thing. It may help if we consider the search for meaning is the search for our subjective truth located in our belief system. The belief system is a holistic system where the searcher's entire life experience is melded into the essence of that individual's relationship with the world and his or her unique place in the world. It provides an anchor for the individual. Let us go a little bit further into this anchor to describe how we can be in a state of "un-fit" with the world.

We return to the photos we have all seen in the news of the Syrian children gasping for breath after a chemical attack, or of the 3-year-old boy lying dead on a beach, drowned when the boat he was fleeing Syria in capsized.

The components of these news photos caused us, the world viewing public, to crystallize our belief of "injustice" as a concept that is greater than the specific "facts" of the Syrian war. We would all agree that this sense of injustice is a form of knowledge, as in: "I know it when I see injustice." The photo crystallized rules and laws of thinking about the world and our place in it that are innate to our very nature as a species. It is not knowledge system-based, which we have defined in this book as being outside us in the objective reality of the world. Rather, it is something that we know from somewhere inside us. It is how we are wired—a wired reasoning system. This is in fact what Lesley Brown (2005) believes Plato was getting at with his Ideal Forms theory of knowledge-as-belief.

Plato explains knowledge-as-belief as the individual's recollection of the Ideal Forms, which we access by going inward and remembering "beliefs" (opinions) about any topic. Socrates uses Meno's slave as an example of a man who knew nothing about mathematics but is still able to recognize, from an inner source, the solution to a mathematical problem. (For Socrates' dialogue with Meno's slave, see Part III, Chap. 16 in this book). When the slave "recognizes" the solution to a mathematical problem, Socrates claims the slave already knew it in himself, in the Ideal Forms, and had only to recollect it. What Plato is demonstrating is the human ability "to extend one's knowledge from within oneself" (Brown 2005, p. xxiii). If we examine our own life experience, there is some validity to this Plato notion of belief-based inner knowledge.

How many times do we rely on an innate inner logic of the world and how the world works to transact with the world at work and in our daily lives? In a situation that we know nothing about, we say: "She wouldn't have done that. It doesn't make sense!" Then only after thinking or expressing such beliefs—tentative theories (TT) in Popper's jargon—do we go out into the world and search for evidence that justifies the belief or theory, or that refutes it. Confirmation shifts the belief up into the searcher's knowledge system. But this inner logic doesn't rely on objective knowledge from our knowledge system in the initial reaction.

Why? Because belief-based "knowledge" is from our "real" self-identified self. It cuts through the prejudices we have lodged in our individual, group, and national frames discussed in Part II of this book. In the German-nation frame 1933–1945, the Nazis deliberately targeted out of existence this individual sense of self, and they were largely successful in preventing the German population under their control from acting against the nationalistic frame. (Peter Hoffmann (2008) describes this battle of the authentic self against the Nazi-produced nation frame in the case of Claus von Stauffenberg, first in Stauffenberg's growing sense of being in a state of "un-fit" with the national frame created by the Nazi regime, and then in his drastic action to "re-fit" himself in his famous 1944 attempt on Hitler's life.)

The source of all our real information needs is the relational aspect of our belief system to the world around us, specifically the "fit" or "un-fit" between the outside world and our inner, innate, belief-based theory of self. Our real information need has to do with this identification of self in relation to the information outside us in the world, and our human goal of maintaining our equilibrium with the world.

The digging into our four-layers of consciousness, and finding the right new information that will enable the searcher doing this digging to find his real information need, is a little complicated to describe. We provide a Finding Real Information Need diagram, shown in Fig. 16.2. And in the next section, we illustrate this figure with a case study of a 14-year-old middle-school student using information to research a class history project.

Model of Finding Real Information Need (Fig. 16.2)

We switch from Fig. 16.1 to Fig. 16.2 to diagram how a searcher gets from her compromised information need to her real information need, illustrating the journey with a fictional middle-school student's process of researching a history essay. The student is an amalgam of real-life examples of students engaged in new knowledge production from a 4-year research study reported in Cole et al. (2015, 2017).

Our fictional student begins by selecting her topic "The Cause of the Fall of the Roman Empire." She selects this topic because her teacher has previously referred to it in a lecture, and she has seen the movie *Gladiator* on TV, which depicts one traditional historian-view of the start-point of the fall of Rome (when Marcus Aurelius died and his son Commodus became emperor). The student goes to the teacher to ask for advice.

The teacher knows that when a student first begins seeking information for a project, he or she begins with an angle on the topic of the search. This angle is based on the student's past experiences with information related to the topic. The teacher knows this, but she wants the student to think outside the box, to get out of her normal thinking patterns. The teacher also knows the student's parent is an executive in the mining industry, so she suggests:

> Why not investigate the hypothesis that the Roman Empire fell because the lead in Ancient Rome's water pipes caused the emperors to go insane. Caligula is often used as an example (for the lead pipe thesis of the Fall of the Roman Empire, see Nriagu 1983)

What our example student doesn't realize is that she has already picked up information about various features of her history topic, both factual information from the teacher's lecture on the topic, and vague notions she also stores in her developing topic frame. But there are also data on the topic she is not aware of reading or hearing that come into play, creating a three-level topic frame:

- The Upper Part of the frame, the knowledge part of the frame, which are features of the topic that are always true, so these are facts about the middle-school student's topic that the student is certain about
- The Lower Part of the frame, which are features of the topic she believes to be true but is not certain about
- The Registry, which is topic data she has picked up but is not aware of, meaning the student hasn't yet classified or labeled the data

Figure 16.2, Image a, shows the student's starting-position topic frame. She doesn't have much to go on. She goes to Google and types in search terms that she thinks stand out as the most important to her topic: "Fall of the Roman Empire" in quotation marks and the search term "insanity." This query does not represent the student's real information need; Taylor (1968) calls it the compromised Q-4 level form of the need (shown at the open-ended top of the "V" in Fig. 16.2). In response to the query, Google produces 364,000 citations to web pages/sites that are listed in the search engine's results list.

The student doesn't like what she sees. There is one citation to a website on the lead pipe thesis as the reason for the Fall of the Roman Empire. She clicks the hyperlink to this site but it is too complicated for her to really understand it. And there is one citation associating the insanity of Donald Trump, Ronald Reagan, and the Fall of the Roman Empire, which she doesn't click on because it seems strange. Most of the information she clicks on from the search engine results list is about the "decadence" of Rome being the reason for the Empire's fall, which she doesn't associate with "insanity." [If the student had typed in the search term "lead poisoning" instead of "insanity," she would have found a greater variety of evidence on the topic of lead poisoning being the cause of the Roman Empire's fall (evidence for the thesis, see Nriagu 1983, and evidence against, see Scarborough 1984).]

What struck the student the most was that during the Roman Empire, women used lead-infused makeup, risking skin disease. She read through the linked web page.

Apparently, the women knew the lead in the makeup would end badly for them, causing illness, but they used the makeup anyway.

The student could relate to these Roman women due to her eating problem. She ate alone in her room from a stash of food she collected over the course of the day. It was gone in an hour. Like the Roman Empire women, she knew it would in the long run be very bad for her. She was already a little overweight. But like the women in Rome, the student somehow didn't care. She called it, jokingly, her "dating-prevention death wish."

But on the whole, the student feels disappointed by the search. She thinks: "Everyone knows about this lead in the pipes anyway. I want to do something different, something outside the box!" As shown in Fig. 16.2, Image b, the search doesn't feel right to the student; the information doesn't "fit" her real information need. In fact, she feels more uncertain, more of a sense of "un-fit" about the topic than before the search.

The rise in uncertainty creates an even greater sense of being in a stage of "un-fit" with her topic, which in this book we attribute to the residue question marks attached to the topic frame in the Registry, shown in Fig. 16.2, Image b.

The Registry attached to the topic frame is composed of possible alternative assignments for a feature that is in the belief half of the frame. For example, when there is a controversy or debate in the world of information on the topic, the student picks up data on the controversy without understanding or realizing it, so she doesn't classify it with a particular feature to the point of awareness. Consequently, this particular datum in the Registry forms part of the residue of question marks creating her misalignment or "un-fit" with the topic. Her search for meaning intention is "behind the scenes" in control of her to search for topic information that will "fit" her with the topic.

This last part of the student finding her real information need is complex, so we return to Fig. 16.1, Image 3, which illustrates the search for meaning or "fit" component of our Consciousness' Drive Information Need-Search Model.

The Search for Meaning or "Fit" (Fig. 16.1, Image 3)

We have highlighted the difference between the search for understanding and the search for meaning as being two different intentions based in two different parts of the frame humans construct to mediate their intersection with the world. The development of the belief system in the Mythic Mind phase of the evolution of human cognitive development allowed us to guess at what we didn't understand, which is the beginning of the production of new knowledge. We have outlined this thesis and its archeological evidence for it from the Neolithic-era ruins at Göbekli Tepe (see Part III, Chap. 13).

Though our current era is dominated by the Theoretic Mind layer's understanding intention, and the tools and devices we have developed further this intention's scientific inquiry for understanding of the world, the real source of knowledge production remains the belief part of the frame humans create to define the world and their place in that world: i.e., the search for meaning or "fit" with the world and our place in it. For our illustrative example of the middle school student seeking information on the Fall of the Roman Empire, the student is in a position of imbalance or disequilibrium vis-à-vis her essay topic. She is in a state of "un-fit."

Because the "un-fit" is based in her belief system, her real information need requires "meaningful" information, not just information that will help her understand her topic. Only information that will fulfill this "meaningful" intention to establish her "fit" with the topic will fulfill her real information need.

In terms of information search, our student's real information need is the residue question marks attached to the belief part of the student's topic frame, in a Registry of topic data of which the student is unaware. The residue question marks cause the student's sense of "un-fit" with the world of information on her history topic.

Something or some type of "meaningful" information "spark" causes pre-awareness data to shift from the Registry into the belief part of the topic frame, allowing the student to gain awareness of these data as relevant to her topic.

The Spark (Fig. 16.1, Image 4)

To demonstrate how the spark works, we focus on one of these residue question marks attached to our student's topic frame in the Registry, the one linking Reagan and Trump together, which the student found strange and forgot about immediately. A few days after her initial search of Google, she participated in a dinner table conversation with her mother and father. It is important to see this dinner table conversation as an informal type of information search, one that can be just as effective as a search using a formal information channel such as Wikipedia and Google.

The family always eats dinner with the TV on turned to a major North American news cable channel, CNN. The pundits on CNN had been particularly critical of Trump that day. Her father says, "It doesn't matter what the TV and newspaper pundits say about him. In the end, the only thing that matters is if he gets his victories."

Her mother agrees, saying: "Yes, it's the same as Ronald Reagan . . ." She stops and looks across the table to see if her daughter knows who Reagan was. Our student nods. Her mother continues: "Good. Well Reagan was severely criticized by the pundits at the beginning of his term for being dumb, lazy, not knowing his briefs, for being almost a figurehead while the competent professionals worked behind the scenes really running the country. He was even criticized by Berliners when he was in Berlin giving his famous 'tear-down-this-wall speech.' But 2 years later, the Berlin Wall did come down, plus the U.S. economy performed well—and because of these victories, history considers him a successful president."

Her father raps it up. "As they say: History is written by the victors," he says, laughing.

Our student immediately thinks of something when her father says this. She suddenly links real-life events in the news—that is, the politics of Donald Trump in her family's real-life world—to her history topic:

- First, to the alleged insanity of Trump, linked by the citation in the results list of her first information search to the alleged insanity of Rome's emperors caused by lead pipes, which led to the Fall of the Roman Empire. Allegedly because "History is written by the victors" who have their own agendas.
- Second, that her historical event could actually be described by the same reasoning as today's news events.

The student has never thought of this second point before. This idea about the logic of the world, how the world works, came to her as if from nowhere, from somewhere deep within her, or as Plato would conceptualize it: (as if) it came from a previous life!

"Of course, it makes perfect sense," she says to herself. "It 'fits' perfectly."

We can describe the "fit" as two jagged-edged objects, one representing the student's topic frame and the other representing the world of outside information on the topic, suddenly coming together. We show this coming together or "fit" of two jagged-edged objects in both this chapter's diagrams, Fig. 16.1 (Image 4) and Fig. 16.2 (Image c). The "fit" produces a spark, a spark that sets off combustion of the new knowledge production engine. The student has now found her real Q1-level of information need (Fig. 16.2, Image c).

Let us examine this spark more closely. What is it?

The spark for our middle-school student is the Trump–Roman Empire association datum, of which she was unaware as it had been stored unclassified or unlabeled in the student's topic frame's Registry, suddenly shifting into her belief system, into full awareness. This movement to the awareness part of the topic frame is like an energy displacement. It zinged into the student's awareness from seemingly nowhere in an "a-ha" moment of recognition.

This is what often happens to us all the time. We say to ourselves: "That's it, that's the answer! I always knew it. Why didn't I think of that before?"

What we have done here in this book is model the trajectory of this thought displacement from unawareness into sudden awareness by describing it as data shift from the Registry part of the searcher's topic frame into the belief part of the topic frame. But there is a second level of this spark that is more important: the search for meaning intention being implicated in information search.

The belief system taps into a deeper part of the individual's consciousness, a more stable part than knowledge, because knowledge comes and goes as important or even relevant in an individual's life trajectory. The belief system, on the other hand, remains largely constant throughout one's life and self-identity.

To explain this nuance between knowledge and belief metaphorically: knowledge is how to use a dial phone. Or for the engineer working at one of the telephone companies: how to send a voice signal from the source/sender to the destination/receiver of the message. But this knowledge becomes irrelevant to the individual with changing phone technology, while the belief that one can talk to another person over large distances remains constant.

The two levels of the spark are essential. There is a testable, potential knowledge part of the spark that sets off knowledge production in our student's topic frame; and a level of the spark that is anchored in the student's belief system, that constitutes the student finding her real information need. It "fits" the student's own logic of the world, how the world works.

We can test the knowledge production part by collecting evidence for and against it in the outside information world, creating knowledge if the world confirms our belief-theory. The belief anchor part, on the other hand, is whether or not there is an existential "fit" between the essence of the student's belief about her relationship with the world around her and her place in it.

Our student's thesis statement for her history project came to her, or rather half a thesis statement because she only has the negative or negating half of her topic:

It is generally believed that the Fall of the Roman Empire was caused by the decadence and debauchery of its ruling class, signified by the insanity of its emperors brought on by lead in the water pipes, but this is because those who gained from the Fall of the Roman Empire, the victors, wrote the history, and it was in their interests to portray the Fall in this way.

The forward path to new knowledge production and her positive belief in what or who caused the Fall of the Roman Empire is now set for our student.

Resulting in New Knowledge Production (Fig. 16.1, Image 5)

We freeze our student's topic frame at this precise moment to bring in a device—we'll call it the Real Information Need Finding Device shown in Fig. 16.3—that is specifically designed to shift the student searcher's Q4-level compromised information need to her Q1-level real information need. It can be attached to Google or any other search engine for exploratory information searches whose objective is new knowledge production.

We will fill-in the Real Information Need Finding Device with our example middle-school student's situation at the precise moment when the student has half her thesis statement, that is, the negative part that rejects the hypothesis that the Fall of the Roman Empire was caused by lead in the pipes leading to the insanity of the Roman Emperors. She has knocked down this reason in her thesis statement. The student now has to come up with a positive cause for the Fall. The Device is filled-in in seven steps.

Step 1. The Device asks the student to come up with the question she wishes her information search to answer. There is room for four questions, but since the student fills it in quite late in her research, our student only puts down two questions.

Step 2. The Device asks the student to select the most probable question. She selects the second question: Who benefited from the Fall (of the Roman Empire)?

Step 3. The Device now asks the student to answer the question she selected in Step 2. This requires the student to dig down deep into her topic frame to,

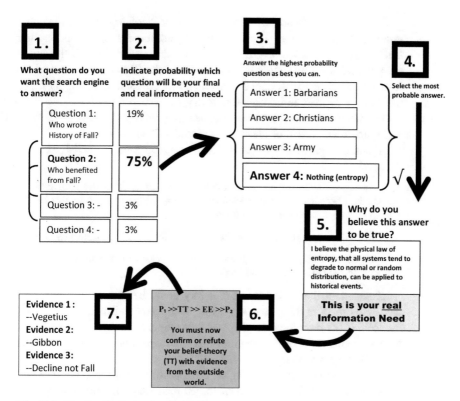

Fig. 16.3 The Real Information Need Finding Device: Your real information need is the reason why you belief in the answer to your information question, not your question to the information system (modified from Cole 2012)

in a sense, tap into data from the Registry part of her topic frame. She is able to come up with four answers to the question "Who benefited?": The Barbarians benefited. The Christians benefited. The Army benefited. And the final possibility she types in the word "Nothing." For some reason, she wrote "Nothing" instead of the more logical "No one," which would have been the more precise answer. Our student leaves the Device at this point, intending to come back the next day to fill in the rest.

The next day, the student looks at her answer "Nothing," and instead of seeing what she meant when she wrote it the day before (i.e., "No one"), the word "Nothing" makes her stop and think. Earlier that morning, her best friend had said to her: "There's nothing you can do about it." The "it" was her weight. For some unknown reason, this made her think of the previous search's citation about the Roman Empire ladies applying lead-infused makeup despite knowing it would kill them.

She thinks: What is it in our character, of being human, where we cede control because something else is operating here, some other, I don't know, law?

The word "law" suddenly caused the word "Nothing" to zing into her mind the Second Law of Thermodynamics and the concept of entropy her teacher had talked about in physics class two days before. This is the law in the physical sciences stating that the tendency for all systems is to degrade from organization to disorganization and normal or random distribution (for the entropy concept in information theory, see Weaver 1949).

The word "Nothing" accidently or wrongly written down in the Device had sparked an onrush of ideas into the student's topic frame.

Again, the spark had two parts. There was a potential-knowledge part of the spark:

Perhaps, she thought to herself, no one or nothing caused the Fall; it just degraded on its own; and others benefited from the vacuum left by the degrading organization that had previously held together Rome and its empire.

And there was a deep part of the spark anchored in her belief system:

We can transfer a method of analysis from the physical sciences to the analysis of her history topic on the Fall of the Roman Empire?

The student liked the idea that history could be governed by physical laws. No one or nothing caused the Fall of the Roman Empire; it degraded by itself. It felt right to her; like it was hers alone; it was a good "fit." It was an even better fit than her previous idea that someone benefited from the Fall: "History is written by the victors."

Step 4. The student selects "Nothing" as the most probable answer to her question of who benefited from the Fall of the Roman Empire, with "entropy" in parenthesis.

Step 5. The Device now asks the student why she believes this answer to be true. She writes: I believe my theory that no one or nothing caused the Fall of the Roman Empire to be true because entropy states that the organized state that was Rome inevitably had to degrade because all highly organized systems, be they physical or social systems like Imperial Rome, are destined to degrade to normal or random distribution. In other words, disorder.

Step 6. The Device states that the belief she expressed in Step 5 is her real information need and that she now must confirm or refute it by going to the world of information on her topic to test the tentative theory (TT in Popper's jargon) against real-world evidence.

The student goes back to her teacher. She tells her teacher about her thesis statement thus far. She then asks the teacher: "Could you tell me a historian who wrote about the fall of the Roman Empire so I can look him up on Google?" "Vegetius is your man," the teacher answers. The student goes back to Google and conducts a new search using the term Vegetius. Thanks to this search, she comes up with two pieces of evidence to confirm her belief-theory.

Step 7. The Device asks the student to write down her evidence confirming or refuting her belief that she indicated in Step 5. Our student writes down the following:

> Evidence 1: Vegetius, the Western Roman Empire historian writing in late fourth century AD, emphasized that soldiers in the late Roman Empire were no longer properly equipped with uniforms and armor. Indicating a decline of Roman institutional support for the army that was there to defend it against the influx of invading barbarians. So this supports the degradation of the Roman Empire from order to disorder, an inevitable law working in history as well as the physical sciences.

> Evidence 2a: Edward Gibbon (1776–1789), who wrote *The History of the Decline and Fall of the Roman Empire*, in six volumes, pinpointed the fall of the Roman Empire as September 4, 476 AD when Romulus Augustus, the last emperor of the Western Roman Empire, was deposed by Odoacer, a German chief. A major event of this decline occurred in 378 AD when Emperor Valens and 2/3 of his army (10,000 men) fell to Gothic migrants (Heather 2005). But Gibbon starts the decline at 98 AD.
>
> A third piece of evidence, which she joined on as a conclusion-addendum to Evidence 2, also came to the student's mind. Something she had seen in the results list in one of her previous Google searches that now bothered her. She had seen "Fall of the Roman Empire" but also "Decline of the Roman Empire" as well. The word "decline" indicated that there was a degradation of Roman institutions over time, allowing the vigorous barbarians to come in to fill the vacuum of the disorder of the Empire. The words "degradation" and "decline" now suddenly seemed qualitatively different than the word "Fall" in her topic, the Fall of the Roman Empire.

> Evidence 2b: Degradation/decline is slow and drawn out. While a fall is quick, with a definite and fast end point. Which was not the case here. The end point of the Fall of the Roman Empire was messy. A slow collapse. Gibbon's word is correct: decline.

Her eventual thesis statement turned out to be along these lines:

It is generally believed that the Fall of the Roman Empire was caused by the decadence and debauchery of its ruling class, but this is because those who gained from the Fall of the Roman Empire, the victors, wrote the history, and it was in their interests, the new adherents to the Christian religion, to portray the Fall in this way.

The real cause of the Fall of the Roman Empire was entropy: the inevitable and gradual decay and decline of Roman institutions over time, particularly the Roman Army, which allowed new forces, the barbarians and the Christians, to fill in the vacuum and take over.

Conclusion

In this chapter, we have illustrated the Consciousness' Drive Information Need-Search Model with the case study of a middle-school student researching a history essay on the Cause of the Fall of the Roman Empire. We have described how a device based on the model, called the Real Information Need Finding Device, can facilitate the student finding her real information need by shifting her search strategy away from what she already knows about her topic, that is already in her topic frame, to what she doesn't yet know but needs to know. The searcher's frames control what she sees in the world, creating a closed information loop. The model charts how the searcher can open the loop and escape from her frames, allowing the searcher to recognize the new information in the outside world that has the potential to produce new knowledge.

The outside world of information coming inside the searcher is a two-step process.

First, the searcher's previous intersections with the world of information, accessed either in conversations with others or via the Internet, leave residue question marks attached to the topic frame in a Registry. The residue is in a pre-awareness state. It can be thought of as a Trojan Horse. It creates a disequilibrium or sense of "un-fit" between the searcher and the topic information in the outside world that drives the information search.

Second, a "spark" causes the residue datum to shift into the belief part of the searcher's topic frame where the searcher becomes aware of it in terms of her topic. The "spark" breaks open the information loop between the searcher and outside information, allowing the searcher to recognize new information on her topic that is not in her frames.

The "spark" is caused by the sudden "fitting together" of the pre-awareness datum in the Registry and new information in the outside world. The "spark" suddenly shifts the pre-awareness datum from the Registry into the belief part of the topic frame where the searcher is aware of it and can begin using it to produce new knowledge.

We have described a spark with two levels:

- The potential knowledge top half of the spark, where data of which the searcher is unaware come into the searcher's awareness in her belief system. With enough testing and confirmation of the belief by testing it in empirical reality, this belief has the potential to become an objective truth that satisfies the searcher's search for understanding.
- The search for meaning bottom half of the spark is anchored in the searcher's belief system. This is a subjective truth that satisfies the searcher's search for meaning intention.

The spark opens up the information loop imprisoning the searcher inside her frames, allowing new information from the outside world to come inside the searcher, leading to the production of new knowledge if the belief or tentative theory (TT) is confirmed by empirical testing of the belief in the real world.

In the searcher's belief system, the searcher now feels a new "fit" with the world. The new knowledge acquisition is an act of self-recognition, a taking of a part of the searcher's experience with the world and possessing it as hers alone. The new knowledge thus strengthens the searcher's self-identity in the world.

We will return to this open information loop in the next chapter, the Conclusion of the book.

Chapter 17
Conclusion to Book: The Search for Meaning and the Open-Ended Question

We end the book where we began in Fig. 17.1, a human figure framing his experience of the world by entering a cave. What drove our cognitively modern human ancestors into caves, to crawl through the tiny passages they found there into hidden galleries, then to draw elaborate episodes from their experience on the walls and ceilings?

They had different intentions, or rather the intentions evolved, allowing our prehistoric ancestors to recognize and bring in new information from the outside world.

In this book, because of our interest in information need and information search, we have treated each one of these evolutionary-phases as having a different information need intention and a different channel of information flow between humans and the world. These channels were cognitively constructed by us. The intention fuel got increasingly more powerful as humans evolved through the phases of their cognitive development. The channels got larger, allowing greater information flow from the world into human consciousness.

In Table 17.1, we summarize the evolution of these intentions and information flow channels based on Donald's (1991) four-phase theory of the evolution of human consciousness.

1. The Episodic Mind phase: In this book, we have given precedence to the exceptional starting-point of our pre-(cognitively modern) human ancestors, in the initiating Episodic Mind phase of their cognitive development. These ancestors gained self-recognition in their intersection experience in the world, by framing their experience in the unit of the episode. The self-recognition intention is a process of separating or isolating oneself from everything else in the world. There are other animal species that have this ability to separate themselves from the flow of the ongoing world—the eight other species who today pass the mirror test (Part I, Chap. 2). But we assume our pre-(cognitively modern) human ancestors had the self-recognition intention in a stronger version than other species.

© Springer International Publishing AG, part of Springer Nature 2018
C. Cole, *The Consciousness' Drive*, https://doi.org/10.1007/978-3-319-92457-1_17

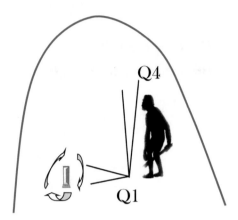

"We shall not cease from exploration, and the end of all our exploring will be to arrive where we started
and know the place for the first time." T. S. Eliot (1943, p.39)

Fig. 17.1 The human species enters the cave to find their real information need (Q1) so that they can open up the information loop and find the information that will satisfy that information need

Table 17.1 Summary of evolutionary phases of consciousness in terms of intention and channel

Evolutionary phase	Intention	Channel
Episodic mind	Search for self-recognition	Episode frame
Mimetic mind	Search for understanding of subjective experience	Internal and external representation of episode
Mythic mind	Search for meaning	Paradigmatic frame
Theoretic mind	Search for understanding of objective world	External memory, paradigmatic theories, technology devices

   If self-recognition was gained through their experience in the world, the more information they could glean from the experience the more self-recognition they would gain. Their episodes of experience gave them an ideal vehicle or channel to bring the information in the world outside inside themselves. They also needed special storage for these episodes in their memory system where they could glean more information out of the experience by mentally examining the experience. They needed a special memory system to do this: episodic memory. This end-part of the information flow channel became bigger and bigger.

2. The Mimetic Mind phase: The search for understanding intention of the Mimetic Mind phase of human cognitive development, was the "seed" that eventually motivated our prehuman ancestors into the caves. By mimicking their experiences mentally to themselves, and to others in the group, they could advance their understanding of their experience. The self-recognition intention of the Episodic Mind phase was still there as a layer of their consciousness, but the hand-stencils on the wall of the El Castillo Cave painted about 40,000 years ago, though they indicated an "I am here" self-recognition intention, have a strong search for

understanding intention as well, and their existential aspects also foreshadow or provide the seed for the next evolutionary phase.

Other animal species could do this mimicking too, but our human ancestors could do it differently, much more intensely. Human groups were larger than the Neanderthal groups, for instance. And it was at the end of this evolutionary phase that humans and the Neanderthals parted company, cognitively speaking. The Neanderthals did not evolve to the next evolutionary phase.

3. The Mythic Mind phase: The obsessive need for information to gain understanding of their experience morphed, in the Mythic Mind phase, into a different, much more powerful intention: the search for meaning intention. Due to the intense flow of information needed to satiate the self-recognition intention, the individual human was now out of balance, in a state of imbalance with the world. In this book, we have labeled this existential malaise as being in a sense of "un-fit" with the world. The search for meaning intention demanded more new information, thus a larger information flow channel. Paintings on the cave walls intensified, shifting their emphasis from understanding their experience of the hunt (the lions and bison in the Chauvet Cave), to a full-fledged search for meaning of their experience in the Lascaux Cave's shaman, broken spear, and the "bird on top of a pole" symbol. The search for meaning intention caused these early humans to go inward into their consciousness, dissecting their representations of their episode experiences, forcing or bursting the linear frame, changing it into a paradigmatic frame. This crossed threshold provided a much larger channel for information to flow from the outside world to these humans. They could now recognize so much more new information in the world flowing into their consciousness. They could liberate their experience in terms of time, leading to myths or storylines that occurred before and after the individual's death, which became a mythology or story giving meaning to the everyday experience of not only the individual but the group.

The search for meaning intention provided the fuel needed to power information flow in the larger paradigmatic channel of the Mythic Mind phase. The natural caves became too small, inefficient. The need for an ever-larger channel led our cognitively modern human ancestors to construct ritual temples beginning at Göbekli Tepe. Humans had become informavores. To facilitate their search for meaning, they needed technological devices to produce knowledge of the objective world.

4. The Theoretic Mind phase: The knowledge production needed to construct these larger information flow channels was a side effect or offshoot of the search for meaning intention. The search for meaning intention provided the seed that led us to the evolutionary phase we are in today, a search for understanding of the objective reality of our world. Our new information flow channels are technological devices: the camera obscura of Vermeer, the microscope lenses of Anton van Leeuwenhoek, and the CERN Large Hadron Collider (LHC), a particle physics tunnel 27 km long, built 100 meters underground.

We diagram the 4-phase evolution of human consciousness in Fig. 17.2.

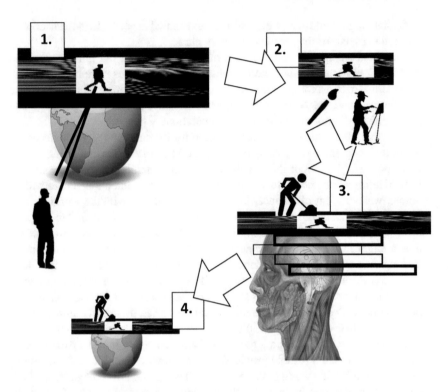

Fig. 17.2 The 4-phase evolution of human consciousness: (1) Episodic Mind: The framing of the individual's intersection and experiencing of the world in the unit of the episode. (2) Mimetic Mind: The search for understanding of experience through mimicking it to oneself and to others. (3) Mythic Mind: Digging into the layers of our experience frame in the search for meaning, constructing from our consciousness explanations that gave meaning to our experiences in the world. (4) Theoretic Mind: Digging into the natural world motivated by the search for understanding of objective reality

In this book, we have described these phases of evolution as human consciousness exploding through thresholds in its need for bigger information flow channels, fueled by more powerful information need intentions. But the major threshold was the development of a belief system. The two transitions that mark human secondary consciousness, which no other species has, started as a result of belief. Today, the notion of a parallel reality that we cannot see—a hidden, underlying force with an overarching story that explains our experience—is old hat. But how did the pivotal transition to the Mythic Mind phase and paradigmatic thinking behind this notion occur?

Our pre-cognitively modern human ancestors invented this hidden realm by digging into their consciousness, and inventing a belief system.

Or much later in the Theoretic Mind phase of human evolution, how did our ancestors light on the idea that the world is controlled by objective physical laws, which they could discover by digging into the world itself using technological devices? How did such revolutionary new ways of thinking about the world and our place in the world occur?

There must have been forces from the old way of thinking that fought against these new ways of thinking. But on a much more fundamental level, how did our pre-historic ancestors recognize new information in the world that was not already in the frame interfaces of their old way of thinking? How did they recognize the new information that caused them to see the world differently?

Imprisoned in Our Frames

We used Minsky's (1975) theory of the frames, which interface, control, and guide our intersection with the world, as the book's starting position for the central problem of information need and information search. Our frames guide and control what we will see, and prevent us from recognizing new information in the world that is not already in the frames, that we don't already know. These frames work on the individual, group, and nation levels.

There is a danger to us because of our frames' efficacy in anticipating and guiding our experience. The comfort and security they provide us if we restrict what we see to the anticipatory shadows they project on Plato's *Allegory of the Cave* wall, make us almost willing prisoners in the closed information loops they create. In Part II of this book, we recounted how living in this comfort zone, through the default setting of our frames, leads to closed information loops that can be potentially abused, either by the individual holding prejudicial stereotypes against outsider group members (outside the individual's own group), or by the nation-state in the case of the Nazi regime in Germany 1933–1945.

The Nazis' ideology-based frame system became a closed information loop. Information, instead of sparking new creativity, new inventions, etc., became a method of control, to correct behavioral errors and enforce the Nazi-frame ortho-doxy. The citizens became literally imprisoned inside the closed information loop of the Nazi frame, shown in Fig. 17.3.

The Allies had the power to bomb Dresden in 1945, ending Germany's citizens' belief in the Nazi frame. But with AI development in the next 10 years, there could be a more far-reaching problem with our frames.

Our current worry is AI-equipped robots going one better than the Nazis. AI algorithms and robots have the potential to outsmart totalitarian regimes like the Nazis by having more complete data for frame features, more exact probability calculations attached to all possible alternatives in the assignment set, and more complete frames networks with all possible features contained within them. The frame system would therefore operate more efficiently than the Nazis. If we built these superhuman AI-equipped robots, would they defeat us, control us, by imitating how we think but without human incompetence and laziness, by imitating and perfecting our framing system?

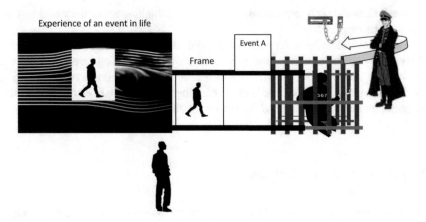

Fig. 17.3 Closed information loop imprisoning the information searcher or citizen behind a locked frame door, preventing the recognition of new information, and new information entering the individual's thinking system

The Universal Turing Machine

Alan Turing described as early as 1936 the interaction between artificial intelligence built into a machine and situations encountered by the machine, which was never built. It was this 1936 conception of such a mechanical computer, later called the universal Turing machine, which many believe began the computer age.

Turing asked these very questions: What is "thinking" and can it be imitated by artificial intelligence? Could humans develop a machine that would cross the line between mere calculation to thinking like humans? How does thinking differ from the mere calculation of machines? For Turing, there did not appear to be this dividing line between the "real" (human thought processes) and the imitation of these thought processes by a machine because there did not appear to be a difference between calculation and thinking, because the one involved the other. (See the Academy Award winning film of Turing's life, *The Imitation Game*, based on Andrew Hodges' (1983) biography of Turing, *Alan Turing: The Enigma*.)

The universal Turing machine models human "thinking" in terms of a machine that reads instructions from a tape and changes its state (response behavior) in consequence—a sort of stimulus–response mechanism. A response is defined as the change of state resulting from the stimulus. For example, when the hands of the clock reach the hour mark, this stimulus changes the response state of the clock's chime from off to on.

The perfectly conceived universal Turing machine is the nightmare scenario of Meno's Paradox because it reduces all human thinking to algorithms that distill human experience to what humans have experienced before, making possible a planned response that would mimic the human response to all possible event stimuli. We could theoretically create a program for every single human activity and put them all on the universal Turing machine's memory tape, an infinite tape capable of holding all (universal) planned-for contingencies.

We are not yet there. According to Penrose: "We may not know how to describe these things yet," but "if we knew the right kinds of computations to carry out, we would be able to describe all the mental things listed in Fig. 3.4" (Penrose 1997, pp. 98–99). Penrose's Fig. 3.4 lists emotion, aesthetics, creativity, inspiration, and art! The machine could even learn new things—which was considered by Lady Lovelace to be the ultimate criterion of human thinking—thus reducing learning to a "conditioned reflex," which we would be able to write into the machine's instructions like all the rest (Turing 1950, p. 450). Lady Lovelace objected to this, but Turing refuted Lovelace's objection (that such a machine "can never do anything really new" (Turing 1950, p. 450), as well as the "consciousness" argument against it:

> According to the most extreme form of this [consciousness] view the only way by which one could be sure that machine thinks is to be the machine and to feel oneself thinking. (Turing 1950, p. 446)

Turing believed such a machine could and would be built, on a limited scale by the end of the twentieth century, but eventually in its full conception, even if took a thousand years.

A Good Thing

The consciousness argument we make in this book against the possibility of a perfect AI-equipped robot being able to imitate the thinking of a real human being agrees with two arguments against the universal Turing machine Turing himself raised in his article in the journal Mind (Turing 1950). The first is Lady Lovelace's argument against Babbage's Analytical Engine, a much earlier machine with similar purpose to the universal Turing machine, who said that such a machine "can never do anything really new." And the second argument Turing raises is the consciousness argument against it: that one can't be sure such a machine thinks unless one is the machine and "feel[s] oneself thinking" (Turing 1950, p. 450, 446). Let's examine each of these two arguments in turn.

For Lady Lovelace's argument, it depends on the meaning of the word "new." An AI-equipped robot with a perfect and complete network of frames could do something "new" in the sense that it could be programmed to learn "new" things that had not been previously written into its instructions. AI is dependent on algorithm-derived neural networks, programmed into the machine, being able to gather data from the environment. The perfect AI-equipped robot would have to be able to collect all data in its environment, and perhaps all data beyond its physical position, from the whole world. This could be done with extremely sensitive sensory devices recording all the images, sounds, tastes, and smells in the world environment. AI-equipped robots would then have to "learn" new things from these collected data by detecting patterns in the data. This has already been done in limited settings. AI-equipped machines can be instructed to derive patterns in these limited settings, and with complete operating instructions, they can on their own learn new response behaviors (Metz 2017).

But detecting new patterns in environmental data is not, according to this book, how humans produce new knowledge. We define "new" differently. In this book, we define "new" as new information in the outside world that the individual human could not previously recognize. Humans have a way out of this closed information loop. They are able to break free of it because of our fundamental "un-fit" with the world due to our inflated self-recognition intention. Only our search for meaning intention, to right this existential imbalance, based in our belief system, can fundamentally change the game—change how we see the world.

The recognition of this type of "new" information begins in the human's belief system, and an AI-equipped does not have and can never have the same type of belief system. It can have a belief system in the sense of a guessing mechanism, as in "I believe or guess that the car's speed will have to be adjusted because there is a 60% probability there will be an avalanche on that road, given the weather condition data, and given the data "I" have (i.e., the machines has) on the condition of the snow on the mountain as defined by x, y, z features." An AI-equipped robot could do this sort of belief-based guessing much more efficiently than a real human. But real new knowledge production, which causes dramatic shifts in thinking of the kind that changed the evolutionary course of humankind, the new knowledge resulting from such a shift cannot be produced by an AI-equipped robot. These fundamental changes in thinking result from the human belief system, fueled by our search for meaning intention. Machines can never be able to make such changes in their thinking because they don't have the belief system of the type that is fueled by the search for meaning intention.

For the consciousness argument against the universal Turing machine Turing himself raises, it depends on the meaning of the word "feel" in his phrase "feeling ones thinking." An AI-equipped robot cannot "feel" its own thinking as humans do. In this book, we have outlined how a real human "feels" his or her own thinking. We divide this thinking into two parts.

First, when a real human's consciousness drives an individual, as part of its search for meaning intention, to seek out new information, and to seek out a certain kind of information, i.e., the kind that produces new knowledge, the human consciousness must "combust" with the world in the episode event of intersection with it. The combustion leaves a residue of question marks on the frame of the experience they store in their episodic memory, which is the genesis of the "un-fit" we feel with the world, and the search for meaning intention. This has partly to do with humans gaining self-recognition in their intersection experience with the world, which is uniquely human.

Second, when real humans "feel" newly found information entering their belief system in an "a-ha" moment, it immediately "hits" a datum in a frame's Registry, causing the datum to suddenly shift, to zing into the belief part of the frame. The human's sudden awareness of the datum creates a physical reaction in the belief system part of the frame, "sparking" the start of new knowledge production.

Because of the ferocious human self-recognition intention, which is fueled by new information, AI cannot reproduce the "zing" intensity of the human search for meaning intention, and the "spark" it causes in human thinking. AI can understand the way the world works; it can be taught to learn this understanding process. But it cannot be taught the search for meaning intention's ability to open up the information loop between our human frames and the world of information outside, which it cannot see except with a change in belief (belief in its broadest sense, not the religious sense).

Warning! We Are Not a Universal Turing Machine

We have come to the end of the book, leaving it with a warning if we are to obey our promise as an exceptional species. If we are going to avoid becoming like a universal Turing machine, living only in our frames and avoiding new information that threatens the secure life we know we can find there, we as a species must constantly prioritize our search for meaning intention. Only the search for meaning intention has the power to open the information loop to recognizing new information, both in the world and in the universe, leading to new knowledge production.

In ages past, though the excuses of searching for gold and silver were invoked, exploring the oceans and the new and strange lands of our own earth was motivated by the search for meaning intention. Our ancestors were on the edge of their seats waiting for news of what these explorers in their tiny ships had seen and discovered. But we know the width and breadth of our own earth now, or practically all. We are only beginning to explore the bottom of the oceans.

Another area for continued exploration is, paradoxically, the caves underground that form the basis of so much of the evidence in this book. The 15,000- and 32,000-year-old cave paintings in the Chauvet and Lascaux Caves were discovered only in 1994 and 1940, respectively. Why is this so? The entrances to the caves fill up with stones and earth, hiding them. Or an avalanche occurs shifting the earth; or a river overflows its banks uncovering a cave entrance that had been buried for tens of thousands of years. And even once inside the cave, the prehistoric artists were tricky—they crawled through tiny spaces to hidden galleries. We are only now discovering these protected galleries. But surely the four French adolescents who "discovered" the prehistoric paintings in the Lascaux Cave weren't the first modern era humans to enter this cave. There must have been others. But recorded history remained silent about them. Maybe we are only now ready to understand their importance, their significance, because we have a new belief.

Humans have the ability to change their belief state, thus opening the information loop allowing us to recognize new information in the world that was right in front of us all along. It is our belief system and the search for meaning intention that have the power to open the information loop, the genesis of all truly new knowledge production. AI machines can never imitate this ferocious underlying intention or drive of human consciousness that allows us to change our belief state, to change our perspective. We change our belief state constantly, and for thousands of minor things: believing a wall is actually a secure doorway, or believing that a secure doorway is actually a tax raising mechanism (a toll booth). But it is the grand change of belief states that lead to avalanches of new knowledge production.

The great exploration frontier remains space. In 1961, President Kennedy famously committed America to a man on the moon by the end of the decade, and it happened. Other moon shots soon followed in quick succession. We were all glued to our TV sets. But then the moonshots stopped in 1972. Space exploration became a downgraded human objective. We seemed to be satisfied with unmanned flights to Mars and the maintenance of a space station orbiting just above the atmosphere.

In the last decades, our species' focus has drifted away from space exploration and shifted to other things: civil rights, the equality of the sexes, the elimination of poverty, the eradication of diseases such as polio. All of these issues are extremely important, bringing into play vast numbers of people who were formerly disenfranchised. These groups, particularly in China and India by their sheer numbers, are now enfranchised in the open system quest for existential meaning. That is absolutely essential. But that is not enough. The technology giants have recently become interested in space exploration. We must, however, expand this interest to all of society by, on a species-basis, turning our full attention to space exploration. Only space exploration is opened-ended, offering us a truly open door to new knowledge production, as shown in Fig. 17.4.

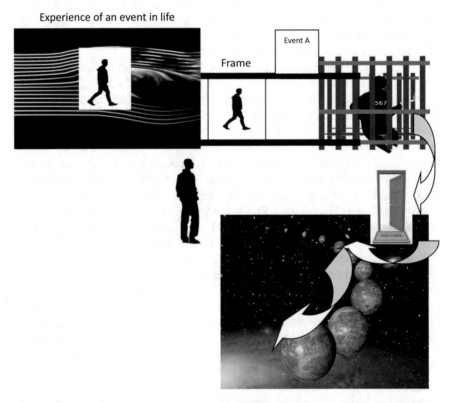

Fig. 17.4 The quest for meaning and knowledge in space exploration, opening the information loop to new knowledge production. Space Photo bottom right of figure (© 2015 NASA, ESA, and G. Bacon (STScI) Creative Commons Attribution 4.0 Unported license)

We thus end as we began. What makes us distinctly human and the exceptional species we are is our belief system and the search for meaning intention that fuels this system's outreach to the world and new knowledge production. It is the location of our real information need. As a society, a civilization, as a species, and as individuals conducting our own information searches, we are best served by focusing on linking belief and the search for meaning intention and new knowledge production together.

References

Abensour, M. (2007). Against the sovereignty of philosophy over politics: Arendt's reading of Plato's cave allegory. *Social Research, 74*(4), 955–982.

Alpers, S. (1983). *The art of describing: Dutch art in the seventeenth century.* Chicago: The University of Chicago Press.

Alpert, B. O. (2013). The meaning of the dots on the horses of Pech Merle. *Art, 2,* 476–490.

Arendt, H. (1963). *Eichmann in Jerusalem: A report on the banality of evil.* New York: Viking Press.

Arendt, H. (1990). Philosophy and politics. *Social Research, 57*(1), 73–103.

Bartlett, F. C. (1932). *Remembering: A study in experimental and social psychology.* Cambridge: Cambridge University Press.

Belkin, N. J., Oddy, R. N., & Brooks, H. M. (1982). ASK for information retrieval: Part I. Background and theory. *Journal of Documentation, 38*(2), 61–71.

Berti, A., & Frassinetti, F. (2000). When far becomes near: Remapping of space by tool use. *Journal of Cognitive Neuroscience, 12*(3), 415–420.

Bouricius, L. G. N. (1925). Anthony van Leeuwenhoek de Delftsche natuuronderzoeker (1632-1723). *De Fabrieksbode, 44*(10), Offprint 3pp.

Brookes, B. C. (1980). The foundations of information science. Part I. Philosophical aspects. *Journal of Information Science, 2,* 125–133.

Brown, L. (2005). *Introduction. In Plato. Protagoras and Meno* (pp. xi–xxiv). London: Penguin Books.

Bruner, J. (1986). *Actual minds, possible worlds.* Cambridge: Harvard University Press.

Cesarani, D. (2016). *Final solution: The fate of Jews 1933–1945.* New York: St. Martin's Press.

Chappell, S. G. (2013). Plato on knowledge in the *Theaetetus.* In: E. N. Zalta (Ed.). *The Stanford Encyclopedia of philosophy* (Winter 2013 Edition). Retrieved August 11, 2017, from https://plato.stanford.edu/archives/win2013/entries/plato-theaetetus/

Chatman, E. A. (1990). Alienation theory: Application of a conceptual framework to a study of information among janitors. *Research Quarterly, 29*(3), 355–368.

Chatman, E. A. (1996). The impoverished life-world of outsiders. *Journal of the American Society for Information Science, 47*(3), 193–206.

Chatman, E. A. (1999). A theory of life in the round. *Journal of the American Society for Information Science, 50*(3), 207–217.

Chatman, E. A. (2000). Framing social life in theory and research. *The New Review of Information Behaviour Research, 1,* 3–17.

Clayton, N. S., Bussey, T. J., & Dickinson, A. (2003). Can animals recall the past and plan for the future? *Nature Reviews Neuroscience, 4*(8), 685–691.

Clayton, N. S., & Dickinson, A. (1998). Episodic-like memory during cache recovery by scrub jays. *Nature, 395*(6699), 272–274.

Clottes, J., & Lewis-Williams, J. D. (1998). *The shamans of prehistory: Trance and magic in the painted caves*. New York: Harry N. Abrams.

Cole, C. (1999). The activity of understanding a problem during interaction with an 'enabling' IR system. *Journal of the American Society for Information Science, 50*(6), 544–552.

Cole, C. (2012). *Information need: A theory connecting information search to knowledge formation*. Medford: Information Today.

Cole, C., Beheshti, J., & Abuhimed, D. (2017). A relevance model for middle school students seeking information for an inquiry-based class history project. *Information Processing and Management, 53*(2), 530–546.

Cole, C., Beheshti, J., Abuhimed, D., & Lamoureux, I. (2015). The end game in Kuhlthau's ISP model: Knowledge construction for grade eight students researching an inquiry-based history project. *Journal of the Association for Information Science and Technology, 66*(11), 2249–2266.

Commins, B., & Lockwood, J. (1979). The effects of status differences, favored treatment, and equity on intergroup comparisons. *European Journal Social Psychology, 9*, 281–289.

Coolidge, F. L., & Wynn, T. (2009). *The rise of Homo sapiens: The evolution of modern thinking*. Chichester: Wiley-Blackwell.

de Kort, S. R., Dickinson, A., & Clayton, N. S. (2005). Retrospective cognition by food-caching western scrub-jays. *Learning and Motivation, 36*(2), 159–176.

Dervin, B. (1998). Sense-making theory and practice: An overview of user interests in knowledge seeking and use. *Journal of Knowledge Management, 2*(2), 36–46.

Dervin, B., & Nilan, M. (1986). Information needs and uses. *Annual Review of Information Science and Technology, 21*, 3–33.

Dobell, C. (1958). *Antony van Leeuwenhoek and his little animals*. New York: Russell & Russell.

Donald, M. (1991). *Origins of the modern mind: Three stages in the evolution of culture and cognition*. Cambridge: Harvard University Press.

Donald, M. (1998). Hominid enculturation and cognitive evolution. In C. Renfrew & C. Scarre (Eds.), *Cognition and material culture: The archaeology of symbolic storage* (pp. 7–17). Cambridge: The McDonald Institute for Archaeological Research.

Edelman, G. M. (1989). *The remembered present: A biological theory of consciousness*. New York: Basic Books.

Eliot, T. S. (1943). Little Gidding. In *Four quartets* (pp. 31–39). New York: Harcourt Brace.

Ford, B. J. (1991). *The Leeuwenhoek legacy*. Bristol: Biopress.

Gallup, G. G., Jr. (1970). Chimpanzees: Self-recognition. *Science, 167*(33914), 86–87.

Geertz, C. (1966). Religion as a culture system. In M. Banton (Ed.), *Anthropological approaches to the study of religion* (pp. 1–46). London: Tavistock.

Gettier, E. (1963). Is justified true belief knowledge? *Analysis, 23*, 121–123.

Gibbon, E. (1776–1789). *The history of the decline and fall of the Roman Empire* (6 Vols). London: Strahan and Cadel.

Harari, Y. N. (2015). *Sapiens: A brief history of humankind*. New York: Harper Collins.

Harari, Y. N. (2016). *Homo dues: A brief history of tomorrow*. Toronto: Signal.

Harnad, S. (1987a). Category induction and representation. In S. Harnad (Ed.), *Categorical perception: The groundwork of cognition* (pp. 535–565). Cambridge: Cambridge University Press.

Harnad, S. (1987b). Psychophysical and cognitive aspects of categorical perception: A critical overview. In S. Harnad (Ed.), *Categorical perception: The groundwork of cognition* (pp. 1–25). Cambridge: Cambridge University Press.

Heather, P. (2005). *The fall of the Roman Empire: A new history*. London: MacMillan.

Heidegger, M., & Sadler, T. (2002). *The essence of human truth: On Plato's cave allegory* (T. Sadler, Trans.). London: Continuum.

Hjorland, B. (2017). Theory development in the information sciences. Review of the book by D. H. Sonnenwald. *Journal of the Association for Information Science and Technology, 68*(7), 1796–1801.

Hodges, A. (1983). *Alan Turing: The enigma*. New York: Simon and Shuster.

Hoffmann, P. (2008). *Stauffenberg: A family history, 1950–1944*. Montreal: McGill-Queen's University Press.

Huerta, R. D. (2003). *Giants of delft: Johannes Vermeer and the natural philosophers: The parallel search for knowledge during the age of discovery*. Lewisburg: Bucknell University Press.

Jonas, E., Greenberg, J., & Frey, D. (2003). Connecting terror management and dissonance theory: Evidence that mortality salience increases the preference for supporting information after decisions. *Personality and Social Psychology Bulletin, 29*, 1181–1189.

Kuhn, T. (1962). *The structure of scientific revolutions*. Chicago: University of Chicago Press.

Lewis-Williams, D. (2002). *The mind in the cave: Consciousness and the origins of art*. New York: Thames and Hudson.

Lewis-Williams, D., & Pearce, D. (2005). *Inside the Neolithic mind: Consciousness, cosmos and the realm of the gods*. New York: Thames & Hudson.

Lohr, S. (2017, December 1). A.I. Today ay underwhelm, but before long it may overtake expectations. *The New York Times*, B3.

MacKay, D. M. (1969). *Information, mechanism and meaning*. Boston: MIT Press.

Malafouris, L. (2009). Between brains, bodies and things: Tectonoetic awareness and the extended self. In C. Renfrew, C. Frith, & L. Malafouris (Eds.), *The sapient mind: Archaeology meets neuroscience* (pp. 89–104). Oxford: Oxford University Press.

Mann, C. C. (2011). The birth of religion. *National Geographic, 219*(6), 34–59. Retrieved December 2, 2015, from http://ngm.nationalgeographic.com/2011/06/gobekli-tepe/mann-text

McLeish, K. (1996). Editor's introduction. In R. Graves (Au.), *The Greek myths* (pp. 11–20). London: The Folio Society.

Metz, C. (2017, December 1). In Toronto, developing a new way for machines to see. *The New York Times*, B3.

Minsky, M. (1975). A framework for representing knowledge. In P. H. Winston (Ed.), *The psychology of computer vision* (pp. 211–277). New York: McGraw-Hill.

Minsky, M. (1986). *The society of mind*. New York: Simon & Schuster.

Mithen, S. (1996). *The prehistory of the mind: The cognitive origins of art, religions and science*. London: Thames and Hudson.

Montias, J. M. (1989). *Vermeer and his milieu: A web of social history*. Princeton: Princeton University Press.

Nriagu, J. O. (1983). *Lead and lead poisoning in antiquity*. New York: Wiley.

Orwell, G. (1961). 1984. New York: New American Library.

Oxford Dictionary of Current English. (1985). (R. E. Allen, Ed.). Oxford: Oxford University Press.

Pasher, Y. (2014). *Holocaust versus Wehrmacht: How Hitler's 'final solution' undermined the German war effort*. Lawrence: University Press of Kansas.

Penrose, R. (1997). *The large, the small and the human mind. With A. Shimony, N. Cartwright, & S. Hawking*. M. Longair (Ed.). Cambridge: Cambridge University Press.

Plato. (2005). *Protagoras and Meno* (A. Beresford, Trans.). London: Penguin Books.

Plato. (2014). *Theaetetus* (J. McDowell, Trans.). Oxford: Oxford University Press.

Popper, K. (1967). Knowledge: Subjective versus objective. In D. Miller (Ed.), *Popper selections* (pp. 58–77). Princeton: Princeton University Press.

Popper, K. (1975). *Objective knowledge: An evolutionary approach*. Oxford: Clarendon Press.

Pritchard, D., & Turri, J. (2014). The value of knowledge. In Edward N. Zalta (ed.), *The Stanford encyclopedia of philosophy* (Spring 2014 Edition). Retrieved August 16, 2017, from https://plato.stanford.edu/archives/spr2014/entries/knowledge-value/

Rochat, P. (2003). Five levels of self-awareness as they unfold early in life. *Consciousness and Cognition, 12*(4), 717–731.

Rosch, E. (1973). On the internal structure of perceptual and semantic categories. In T. E. Moore (Ed.), *Cognitive development and the acquisition of language* (pp. 111–144). New York: Academic.

Savolainen, R. (2017). Information need as trigger and driver of information seeking: A conceptual analysis. *Aslib Journal of Information Management, 69*(1), 2–21.

Scarborough, J. (1984). The myth of lead poisoning among the romans: An essay review. *Journal of the History of Medicine and Allied Sciences, 39*(4), 469–475.

Schacter, D., & Addis, D. (2007). The cognitive neuroscience of constructive memory: Remembering the past and imagining the future. *Philosophical Transactions of the Royal Society of London Series B, 362*(1481), 773–786.

Schacter, D. L., Benoit, R. G., & Szpunar, K. K. (2017). Episodic future thinking: Mechanisms and functions. *Current Opinion in Behavioral Sciences, 17*, 41–50.

Sherif, M. (1966). *In common predicament: Social psychology of intergroup conflict and cooperation*. New York: Houghton Mifflin.

Shreeve, J. (2015). Mystery man. *National Geographic, 228*(4), 30–57.

Siegel, S. (2006). Which properties are represented in perception? In T. Gendler & J. Hawthorne (Eds.), *Perceptual experience* (pp. 481–503). New York: Oxford University Press.

Smith, S. M., Fabrigar, L. R., & Norris, M. E. (2008). Reflecting on six decades of selective exposure research: Progress, challenges, and opportunities. *Social and Personality Psychology Compass, 2*, 464–493.

Squire, C. (1905). *The mythology of the British Islands*. London: Blackie and Son.

Squire, L. R. (1992). Memory and the hippocampus: A synthesis from findings with rats, monkeys, and humans. *Psychological Review, 99*(2), 195–231.

St. Jacques, P. L., Szpunar, K. K., & Schacter, D. L. (2017). Shifting visual perspective during retrieval shapes autobiographical memories. *NeuroImage, 148*(1), 103–114.

Stanford Encyclopedia of Philosophy. (2014). *Epistemology*. Los Angeles: The Metaphysics Research Lab, Center for the Study of Language and Information (CSLI), Stanford University. Retrieved December 8, 2015, from http://plato.stanford.edu/entries/epistemology/

Steadman, P. (2001). *Vermeer's camera: Uncovering the truth behind the masterpieces*. Oxford: Oxford University Press.

Steadman, P. (2017). Vermeer's the little street: A more credible detective story. *Essential Vermeer Newsletter*, no. 35, December 2015. Retrieved March 9, 2018, from http://www.essentialvermeer.com/delft/little-street-steadman/little-street-steadman.html#.WqLsLUxFw2x

Steup, M. (2016). Epistemology. In E. N. Zalta (Ed.), *The Stanford encyclopedia of philosophy* (Fall 2016 Edition). Retrieved June 5, 2017, from https://plato.stanford.edu/archives/fall2016/entries/epistemology/

Suddendorf, T., & Corballis, M. C. (2007). The evolution of foresight: What is mental time-travel, and is it unique to humans? *Behavioral and Brain Sciences, 30*(3), 299–351.

Sweeny, K., Melnyk, D., Miller, W., & Shepperd, J. A. (2010). Information avoidance: Who, what, when, and why. *Review of General Psychology, 14*(4), 340–353.

Swillens, P. T. A. (1950). *Johannes Vermeer: Painter of Delft, 1632–1675* (C. M. Breuning-Williamson, Trans.). Utrecht: Uitgeveri Het Spectrum.

Tajfel, H. (1981). *Human groups and social categories: Studies in social psychology*. Cambridge: Cambridge University Press.

Tajfel, H. (1982). Social psychology of intergroup relations. *Annual Review of Psychology, 33*, 1–39.

Tajfel, H., & Turner, J. C. (1979). An integrative theory of intergroup conflict. In W. G. Austin & S. Worchel (Eds.), *The social psychology of intergroup relations* (pp. 33–47). Pacific Grove: Brooks/Cole Publishing Company.

Taylor, R. S. (1968). Question-negotiation and information seeking in libraries. *College & Research Libraries, 29*(3), 178–194.

Taylor, C. (1989). *Sources of the self*. Cambridge: Cambridge University Press.

Tulving, E. (1972). Episodic and semantic memory. In E. Tulving & W. Donaldson (Eds.), *Organization of memory* (pp. 381–403). London: Academic.

Tulving, E. (2002a). Chronesthesia: Conscious awareness of subjective time. In D. T. Stuss & R. C. Knight (Eds.), *Principles of frontal lobe function* (pp. 311–325). Cary: Oxford University Press.

Tulving, E. (2002b). Episodic memory: From mind to brain. *Annual Review of Psychology, 53*, 1–25.

Turing, A. M. (1936–1937). On computable numbers, with an application to the Entscheidungsproblem. *Proceedings of the London Mathematical Society, Series 2*, 42(2144), 230–265.

Turing, A. M. (1950). Computing machinery and intelligence. *Mind: A Quarterly Review of Philosophy, 59*(236), 433–460.

Weaver, W. (1949). Recent contributions to the mathematical theory of communication. In C. E. Shannon & W. Weaver (Eds.), *The mathematical theory of communication* (pp. 94–117). Urbana: The University of Illinois Press.

Wynn, T., & Coolidge, F. L. (2004). The expert Neandertal mind. *Journal of Human Evolution, 46* (4), 467–487.

Proper Names Index

© Springer International Publishing AG, part of Springer Nature 2018
C. Cole, *The Consciousness' Drive*, https://doi.org/10.1007/978-3-319-92457-1

Subject Index

© Springer International Publishing AG, part of Springer Nature 2018

C. Cole, *The Consciousness' Drive*, https://doi.org/10.1007/978-3-319-92457-1

Printed in the United States
By Bookmasters